Palgrave European Film and Media Studies

Series Editors
Ib Bondebjerg
University of Copenhagen
Copenhagen, Denmark

Andrew Higson
University of York
York, UK

Mette Hjort
Hong Kong Baptist University
Hong Kong, Hong Kong

Palgrave European Film and Media Studies is dedicated to historical and contemporary studies of film and media in a European context and to the study of the role of film and media in European societies and cultures. The series invite research done in both humanities and social sciences and invite scholars working with the role of film and other media in relation to the development of a European society, culture and identity. Books in the series can deal with both media content and media genres, with national and transnational aspects of film and media policy, with the sociology of media as institutions and with audiences and reception, and the impact of film and media on everyday life, culture and society. The series encourage books working with European integration or themes cutting across nation states in Europe and books working with Europe in a more global perspective. The series especially invite publications with a comparative, European perspective based on research outside a traditional nation state perspective. In an era of increased European integration and globalization there is a need to move away from the single nation study focus and the single discipline study of Europe.

Advisory Board
Tim Bergfelder, University of Southampton, UK
Milly Buonanno, University of Rome, Italy
Carmina Crusafon, Autonomous University of Barcelona, Spain
Peter Golding, Northumbria University, UK
Petra Hanakova, Charles University, Czech Republic
Sonja de Leeuw, University of Utrecht, Netherlands
Tomasz Goban-Klas, University of Krakow, Poland
Jostein Gripsrud, University of Bergen, Norway
Michelle Hilmes, University of Wisconsin-Madison, USA
Amanda Lotz, University of Michigan, USA
Ewa Mazierska, University of Central Lancashire, UK
Michael Meyen, University of Munich, Germany
Stylianos Papathanassopoulos, National and Kapodistrian University of Athens, Greece
Katharine Sarikakis, University of Vienna, Austria
Monica Sassatelli, Goldsmiths University of London, UK
Paul Statham, University of Sussex, UK
Isabelle Veyrat-Masson, Laboratoire Communication et Politique Paris (LCP-CNRS), France
Patrick Vonderau, University of Stockholm, Sweden
William Uricchio, MIT, USA

More information about this series at
http://www.palgrave.com/gp/series/14704

Aidan Power

Contemporary European Science Fiction Cinemas

palgrave
macmillan

Aidan Power
University College Cork
Cork, Ireland

Palgrave European Film and Media Studies
ISBN 978-3-319-89826-1   ISBN 978-3-319-89827-8 (eBook)
https://doi.org/10.1007/978-3-319-89827-8

Library of Congress Control Number: 2018949923

© The Editor(s) (if applicable) and The Author(s) 2018
This work is subject to copyright. All rights are solely and exclusively licensed by the Publisher, whether the whole or part of the material is concerned, specifically the rights of translation, reprinting, reuse of illustrations, recitation, broadcasting, reproduction on microfilms or in any other physical way, and transmission or information storage and retrieval, electronic adaptation, computer software, or by similar or dissimilar methodology now known or hereafter developed.
The use of general descriptive names, registered names, trademarks, service marks, etc. in this publication does not imply, even in the absence of a specific statement, that such names are exempt from the relevant protective laws and regulations and therefore free for general use.
The publisher, the authors and the editors are safe to assume that the advice and information in this book are believed to be true and accurate at the date of publication. Neither the publisher nor the authors or the editors give a warranty, express or implied, with respect to the material contained herein or for any errors or omissions that may have been made. The publisher remains neutral with regard to jurisdictional claims in published maps and institutional affiliations.

Cover illustration: YAY Media AS / Alamy Stock Photo
Cover Design: Laura de Grasse

This Palgrave Macmillan imprint is published by the registered company Springer Nature Switzerland AG
The registered company address is: Gewerbestrasse 11, 6330 Cham, Switzerland

Prologue: The Overlords Have Landed

As with many such endeavours, the ideas behind this book stem in part from a personal experience, one that crystallised for me both the inherently scary reality that Europe had found itself in and the strangely science fictional nature of the Eurozone crisis, or at any rate much of the optics surrounding it. It was late November 2010 and I sat alone anxiously watching the news in the small sitting room of a Cork house I shared with two other students. On screen, a handful of satchel-carrying men in overcoats walked along a Dublin quayside, en route to Ireland's Central Bank in Temple Bar. Rumours had been swirling for months that the Brian Cowen-led coalition government was on the cusp of formally applying for an economic bailout; indeed, that year's budget was the government's third in 18 months, as sure a sign as any that the nation's parlous financial situation had slipped finally and irrevocably beyond its control. Some €4 billion had been taken out of the state's coffers in that latest and last attempt to stem the tide of global financial chaos, with social welfare, public expenditure, and civil service wages severely cut (Magee, 'Few Surprises in Much-Leaked Budget'). Cowen, whose Fianna Fáil ('Soldiers of Destiny') party had from 1997 to 2011 presided as the main governmental coalition party during the unheralded prosperity of the 'Celtic Tiger' boom times, had been exposed as a hopeless bit player in the larger saga that was unfolding. On screen, instead, the true power brokers were emerging into the light: amidst much fanfare and yet somehow unexpected suddenness, the Troika had landed. With uncanny prescience, I had elected to commence my doctoral studies two years previously, and so, just as the country found itself in the teeth of the greatest financial crisis in its modern history, I found myself midway through a PhD with little money and fewer prospects. In the face of large-scale unemployment and the resumption of mass outward migration—a timeworn Irish solution to a nation's inability to cater for its populace—pursuing my research into transnational mechanisms in European cinema appeared frivolous, not least when there was a strong likelihood that my funding would soon evaporate. Many of my peers had already left, to the point that the small town in which I grew up seemed eerily bereft of adults under the age of 30, an increasingly common occurrence across the country. Historically there was nothing especially new in this—the phenomenon of mass Irish migration was explored by Karl Marx in Volume I of *Das Kapital* after all,[1] while many of my parents' contemporaries were faced with a similar predicament in the economically stagnant 1980s. Nevertheless, the collapse of Ireland's Celtic Tiger economy—which as early as 1997 was being heralded as 'Europe's shining light'[2]—was rapid, becoming 'one of the most dramatic and largest reversals in economic fortune ever experienced by an industrial country' (Donovan and Murphy, *The Fall of the Celtic Tiger* 2). With such thoughts in my head, I found myself gazing forlornly at the screen in front of me, struck by the appearance of the grey-suited Troika men (and they all seemed to be men) as they strode purposefully towards the Central Bank. Faceless technocrats all, yet it was clear that they—and not the familiar roll call of Irish government ministers—now called the shots and held the key to whatever version of Ireland would emerge into the future. They seemed almost alien in their austere uniformity (for one thing they appeared intent on walking to the bank instead of being ferried via publicly funded Mercedes in the Irish political fashion), and for some reason, I recalled an episode of *The Simpsons*, where newscaster Kent Brockman mistakes some ants that crawl across a camera on a space shuttle for human-sized hymenoptera, before swiftly proclaiming that 'I for one welcome our new insect overlords.' The quote was lifted from the 1977 film adaptation of H.G. Wells' short story *Empire of the Ants*, and though I did not recognise the source of the reference, what did stay with me was the oddly science fictional nature of it all. Empowered as they were to alter the course of history in a feckless nation neutered by the enforced surrender of its economic sovereignty, the Troika officials may just as well have been alien overlords, for their diagnosis would have a profound influence on the lives of hundreds of thousands of Irish men and women, a great majority of whom were far worse off than I was about to become. The date was 8 November 2010, and Vivian Sobchack's dictum that science fiction imagery 'may cause anxiety because it hits us—literally—where we live, close to home' (*Screening Space* 108–109), seemed bewildering apt. An existential, almost hyperreal sense of dread inched closer to home, and it was abundantly clear that nobody, least of all the government, had the slightest clue of how to respond.

A little over two years later, I found myself in Germany, having procured a postdoctoral post at the University of Bremen. The ideas that had struck me first on that winter night had matured enough that I had succeeded in producing a reasonably coherent research proposal centred on the theme of the science fictional nature of the various crises that had befallen the EU and how, if at all, these crises had in turn informed European science fiction (sf) cinema. I occasionally found myself explaining as best I could Irish responses to the financial crisis in the Eurozone to perplexed Germans, all the time noting the changing landscape back home and my own personal relationship to both my homeland and Europe at large. The emergence and popularity of esoterica such as a 'Generation Emigration' section in the online edition of the *Irish Times* or the podcast 'An Irishman Abroad' did not pass me by, and I followed both avidly. Ireland was still in dire straits, yet by comparison with other afflicted nations, it seemed reasonably well placed to recover in the medium term. Greece was another story, however, and apocalyptic newspaper headlines abounded in even the saner news outlets, amongst them 'Acropolis Now' in the *Economist*, 'Akropolis Adieu!' in *Der Spiegel*, or simply '$1,000,000,000,000' in the *Guardian*, which was accompanied by a picture of the Parthenon and the subheading: 'Governments prepare for worst as massive cost of Greek euro exit emerges.' Underpinning all such coverage was a deeper layer of post-apocalyptic hysteria still, as a new lexicon emerged, one that can most profitably be encapsulated by the blanket term 'contagion'. The financial crisis it seemed was contagious, with Greece the most afflicted patient of all. A casual observer, if such a creature still existed in Europe by this time, could have been forgiven for thinking that Greece was less a nation, than a fatal virus one might catch. We had been here before it seemed, or at least on screen, as a central narrative tenet of sf cinema, that of contagion, played out in real time. The Eurozone we were led to believe was laid low by the Euro and the Greeks, both maladies that were highly contagious and potentially fatal. Such thinking would have far-reaching repercussions. The very inclusive, collectivist nature of the European project, once trumpeted to the world as an example of how to unite in the face of adversity, now seemed a liability as national and supranational governments appeared helpless in the face of the coming darkness.

Notes

1. Irish immigration, Marx wrote, was a historical response to national turmoil as was a resultant reliance upon the national diaspora. In an analysis of the mass upheaval during and after the Great Famine (1845–1852), Marx engaged with a phenomenon that exists to this day and would later be referred to as chain migration: 'The exiles transplanted to the United States, send home sums of money every year as travelling expenses for those left behind. Every troop that emigrates one year, draws another after it the next. Thus, instead of costing Ireland anything, emigration forms one of the most lucrative branches of its export trade' (*Capital: A Critique of Political Economy. Volume I: The Economist* 486).
2. John Peet, the then European editor of the *Economist*, summarised Ireland's rapid elevation thusly: 'Surely no other country in the rich world has seen its image change so fast. Fifteen years ago Ireland was deemed an economic failure, a country that after years of mismanagement was suffering from an awful cocktail of high unemployment, slow growth, high inflation, heavy taxation and towering public debts. Yet within a few years it had become the "Celtic Tiger", a rare example of a developed country with a growth record to match East Asia's, as well as enviably low unemployment and inflation, a low tax burden and a tiny public debt' ('The Luck of the Irish').

Acknowledgements

This book would not have been possible without the kind help and support of several people and institutions. It began life in 2013, as a research project funded by the University of Bremen's Excellence Initiative. I will always be grateful both to the university and to the terrific colleagues I encountered there, chief amongst them Delia González de Reufels, Stefano Odorico, Mattias Frey, Rasmus Greiner, Christine Rüffert, and above all, Winfried Pauleit, who has been a wonderful mentor.

I have, in turn, been fortunate to receive financial backing from the Irish Research Council, which, since 2016, has supported my work via a Government of Ireland Fellowship. Since then I have continued my research at University College Cork, where I have long benefited from the expert guidance of my postdoctoral mentor and former PhD supervisor Laura Rascaroli, as well as her cohead of Film and Screen Media, Gwenda Young.

At Palgrave Macmillan, Lina Aboujieb and Ellie Freedman have been especially patient with me, as was Chris Penfold, who first expressed interest in turning my research into a book. I would like to thank them as well as the publisher's anonymous peer reviewers who generously provided me with highly valuable critical feedback.

Chapters 2 and 8 revise and update my articles 'Awakening from the European Dream: Eurimages and the Funding of Dystopia' and 'Panic on the Streets of London: Tourism and British Dystopian Cinema' which were published in *Film Studies* and *Science Fiction Film and Television* respectively. They are included here with the kind permission of the editors of the journals.

I have presented segments of this monograph in locations as disparate as Cork, Los Angeles, Berlin, Milan, Seattle, Dublin, Bremen, and Lund, all the while gaining insightful input from peers who, in many instances, have forgotten more about science fiction than I will ever know. I am grateful to each one of them for taking an interest in my work.

Many thanks to MJ and Lou for helping me to make sense of it all, as well as to the many engaged and enthusiastic students that I have been fortunate enough to teach over the years. Finally, and most importantly, I would like to thank Alessia and my parents Anthony and Maria for their endless love, support, and patience. In lieu of a more fitting tribute, I dedicate this book to them.

Contents

Part I Where Is Europe? National and European Science
        Fiction   1

1 Introduction: A Dream Called Rome   3

2 Shaping a European Narrative: Eurimages, SF, and
   the Auteur   29

3 SF in the EU's Newest Member States   53

Part II Contagion! Responding to the Financial Crisis   91

4 PIIGS to the Slaughter   93

5 PIIGS to the Slaughter II   139

Part III Shut the Gates! Scorched Earth, Fortress Continent   161

6 Climate Change, the Anthropocene, and European SF   163

7 Multiculturalism and the Changing Face of Europe   191

Part IV Another Planet: Hollywood SF Production in Europe   219

8 European SF and Hollywood   221

Part V Beyond Europe?   249

9 Conclusions and Roads Ahead   251

Index   261

LIST OF FIGURES

Fig. 2.1	'The Laurents'	38
Fig. 2.2	'The "Intruders"'	38
Fig. 3.1	'The Uncanny'	78
Fig. 4.1	'Champalimaud Centre for the Unknown'	108
Fig. 6.1	'Hell'	183
Fig. 7.1	'Banlieue 13: Ultimatum'	204
Fig. 8.1	'Welcome to London'	238
Fig. 8.2	'Rear Window'	239
Fig. 8.3	'28 Weeks Later'	239
Fig. 8.4	'Roman Holiday'	240

PART I

Where Is Europe? National and European Science Fiction

CHAPTER 1

Introduction: A Dream Called Rome

On the face of it, beginning with a prominent British Conservative leader's thoughts about European integration and the uncertain future that lies in store for Europeans may appear incongruous. After all, since David Cameron bowed to internal pressures and called a referendum on continued British European Union membership in May 2015, we have been assailed by the views of a host of Tory politicians, the most voluble of whom seem to have concluded that Europe, as we know it, is over: a view that a democratic majority of Britons ultimately endorsed. Yet, it wasn't always so. Speaking at the University of Zurich in 1946 during the immediate aftermath of the Second World War, Winston Churchill pondered the plight of Europe, noting that while 'some of the smaller states have indeed made a good recovery [...] over wide areas are a vast, quivering mass of tormented, hungry, careworn and bewildered human beings, who wait in the ruins of their cities and homes and scan the dark horizons for the approach of some new form of tyranny or terror,' adding apocalyptically that the 'Dark Ages could have returned in all their cruelty and squalor,' before allowing that they 'they may still return' (Greenwood, *Britain and European Integration Since the Second World War* 25). Having just concluded the 60th anniversary year of the signing of the Treaty of Rome, the dream of European integration is becoming ever more precarious, with the UK's future withdrawal from the European Union (EU) and manifold spikes in nationalist sentiment across the continent threatening to shatter an institution that, for all its lofty aims, has in recent years been successfully painted as remote and technocratic by its detractors, often with not inconsiderable justification. Further afield, 2017's candidature for *annus horribilis* status was well under way by mid-January when Donald Trump was sworn in as the 45th US president. His subsequent dealings with minorities, women, and international affairs, his repudiation of climate change, not to mention his deliberate blurring of fact and fiction under the rubric of 'fake news', have flattened distinctions between politics and science fiction (sf), with more than one commentator drawing parallels with Charles Lindbergh's unlikely rise to the presidency in Philip Roth's 2004 novel *The Plot Against America*.[1]

Sf will take centre stage in this book and will be a lens through which I will seek to engage some of the most pressing issues to assail Europe since the turn of the millennium. A genre that in Claudia Springer's words has 'been instrumental in visualizing and narrativizing the qualities associated with postmodernism: disorientation, powerlessness, fragmentation, disintegration, loss of boundaries, and hybridization' ('Psycho-Cybernetics in Films of the 1990s' 205), sf film is uniquely positioned to shed light on, critique, and offer alternatives to the paths followed by modern-day Europe; *ergo*, we should not be surprised that the genre has undergone a major resurgence across the EU since the year 2000. It is this phenomenon that I wish to track, for, although sf has existed on European screens since before Georges Méliès' *A Trip to the Moon/Le voyage dans la lune* in 1902,[2] it has all too frequently been overlooked, particularly as a Europe-wide entity. This study's novelty stems firstly from such an absence and, secondly, from a desire to analyse not just sf films but also the industries that sustain them, more of which anon. To begin with, some perspective is called for, and we would do well to remember that, bleak as things may seem in twenty-first-century Europe, the continent has endured worse, as the spectre of Winston Churchill reminds us. By the time of his Zurich address, Churchill was no longer Prime Minister, having seen the Conservatives roundly defeated by the Clement Attlee-led Labour Party in the 1945 General Election. Free from the day-to-day responsibilities of power, he felt suitably liberated to push for greater European integration and, in particular, the need for a rapprochement between Germany and France. In a notable departure from the rhetoric of his modern contemporaries in the Tory Party, Churchill stressed the need to 're-create the European family' and to build 'a kind of United States of Europe', a term he had first used in an article for the American *Saturday Evening Post* in

1930 (Morrissey, *Churchill and de Gaulle: The Geopolitics of Liberty* 96). The need to do *something* was urgent. As the sheer scale of the barbarism of National Socialism began to fully sink in, and with Europe's major cities in ruins, new ideas were clearly required, especially with the Soviet Union intent on drawing the Iron Curtain down across the continent's Eastern flank. Within five years, the first major steps towards post-war European integration were taken, with the Schuman Declaration calling for closer ties between the French and German coal and steel industries in 1950, followed by the signing of the Treaty of Paris in 1951 by Belgium, France, Italy, Luxembourg, the Netherlands, and West Germany, which created the European Coal and Steel Community (ECSC). In 1957, the same six nations signed the Treaty of Rome (or the treaty establishing the European Economic Community (EEC), to give it its full name) and in so doing brought the EU's forebear, the EEC, into being. In broad terms, the treaty sought to foster economic integration, paving the way for a single European market for capital and labour. This, in turn, it was hoped, would further sustain the economic revival of post-war Europe, a concerted process fuelled in part by the calculated largesse of the Marshall Plan. From political and security standpoints, instead, the establishment of the EEC was both vital and indelibly linked to the fallout from the Second World War. The clue here is in the Treaty of Rome's initial signatories: former Axis Partners West Germany and Italy; France, which was first occupied by the Nazis and was later the staging post for the D-Day Landings; and the geographically prone Benelux nations, all three of which were occupied by the Nazis following a simultaneous Wehrmacht invasion on 10 May 1940.[3] In providing a supranational body, the edicts of which would be tempered by consensus, the EEC was a huge fillip to beleaguered nation states; yet at the same time, it was carefully calibrated to curb nationalistic excess. In his speech, Churchill had pushed for a 'third way' that would allow for the plotting of a course between the Soviets and the United States and, while time-worn colonialist hubris coloured his vision of the role he saw Britain playing in this new Europe,[4] at a minimum closer integration offered the possibility of safety in numbers for individually vulnerable nations. Concerns over internal balances remain to this day, playing a large part in the narratives surrounding Brexit, for example; yet in broad terms, the EU has generally succeeded in providing a united security front that, for all the fudges and compromises required, provides assurance to its member states. Sixty years of relative peace bears this out and has been perhaps the crowning achievement of the European project, a core legacy worthy of celebration in and of itself, if we pause to consider the geopolitical landscape of Europe only four years prior to Churchill's Zurich address.[5] By September 1942, at the apex of the Nazi advancement, the Third Reich's sphere of influence stretched from French Morocco to the south-west of Europe to the continent's outermost northern edges where the tip of Norway meets the Barents Sea. Westward, the Nazi empire extended to the French island of Ouessant off the Brittany coast, while to the East it encompassed the puppet states of Bulgaria and Romania, as well as Belarus and large tracts of Ukraine. Although precise figures are contested, the eminent British historian Ian Kershaw estimates that at least 50 million people died during the war[6]: while the Nazis' 'treatment of the people of the newly conquered territory was unprecedented, its modern forms of barbarism evoking, though in even more terrible fashion, the worst barbaric subjugations of bygone centuries' (*Hitler* 1,070). When contemplating the post-war drive for European integration, then, we do so in the knowledge that the EEC and latterly the EU's aims were shaped indelibly by the dystopian horrors of the Second World War.

A Pragmatic Utopia

When first sketching the contours of this project in Bremen in 2013, I was struck not just by the science fictional nature of the financial crisis in the EU but also by the seemingly utopian ideals at the heart of European integration, ideals that were geared towards fostering cross-border collaboration in place of animus. To be cynical, one could posit that, at a minimum, the pursuance of closer ties recalibrated the contours of national self-interest sufficiently, so that finding mutually beneficial solutions to adversity would in time appear more efficacious to nation states. This in turn necessitated a rethinking of the outright primacy of the nation state, a requirement that a weary post-war Europe was suitably malleable to. In a development that was not without irony, extreme nationalism ultimately begat the conditions necessary for a flowering of transnational constellations to occur in opposition. As Richard Collins writes:

> Just as the mass slaughter of the First World War stimulated a reconstruction of Europe on the nationalist lines prescribed by the Sèvres and Versailles Treaties, so the mass slaughter of the Second World War, perceived to have grown from the poisoned soil of the nationalist vision of Versailles stimulated European reconstruction: this time on transnational, pan-European lines. (*Satellite to Single Market* 174)

Allowing that 'utopian proposals for European union may be found as far back as the seventeenth century (and perhaps earlier)',[7] Collins emphasises that 'it was the disaster of the Second World War which stimulated many Europeans to take practical steps to realise what had hitherto been only a fantasy' (*Satellite* 174). The lingering nightmare of totalitarianism expedited this process, with the Allies' victory serving, in Jürgen Habermas' words, to undermine 'the foundations of all forms of political legitimation that did not—at least verbally, at least in words— subscribe to the universalist spirit of political enlightenment' (*Postnational Constellation* 46). These practical steps included the establishment of a unique supranational body that could overcome centuries of rivalry and would instead be bound by consensus. European integrationists therefore strove to form a community bound in concrete terms by industry (initially coal and steel through the guise of the European Coal and Steel Community) and in looser aspirational terms by common understanding. In envisioning a new mode of politics, the signatories of the Treaty of Rome took a leap into the unknown to provide a platform for a brighter collective future. From the outset, however, a union of European nations was both the expression of a dream and a clinical exercise in pragmatism, as its utopian ideals were a direct response to the scarcely conceivable dystopian horrors of the first half of the twentieth century. It is moreover highly debatable whether the move towards European integration was in fact a utopian project at its inception: for one thing, it served the purpose of rehabilitating West Germany sufficiently in the eyes of the French to allow for the former's rearmament. This in turn endorsed the key American strategic imperative of creating a bulwark against westward expansion by the Soviet Union. A strong and unified Europe was certainly in America's interest, the value of which could be gauged in real terms via the $13 billion that underpinned the Marshall Plan, which, in addition to stimulating national economies, would, as Noam Chomsky has consistently argued, perpetuate American imperialism and in time lay the groundwork for 'establishing the basis for modern transnational corporations' (*Rogue States* 126).[8] And so, whilst the French diplomat and 'Father of Europe' Jean Monnet would unequivocally declare that 'to create Europe is to create peace', a certain paradox was in play whereby peace needed to be reinforced by rearmament and a tangible capacity for violence, the details of which remain contentious to this day as the controversy surrounding PESCO reminds us.[9] Utopian or not, what *is* beyond question is that the horrors perpetuated by the Nazis in their pursuit of the final solution sprung from the darkest recesses of dystopia: horrors to which the formation of the EEC/EU is at least in part a direct response.

WHICH EUROPE?

Weary of the legacy that European colonialism has inflicted upon much of the planet, Zygmunt Bauman suggests in *Europe: An Unfinished Adventure* that the very discrepancy between Europe's ideals and its actions may in fact be the single element that affords it utopian potential. For Bauman, 'perhaps the sole steady element that made of European history a consistent and in the end cohesive story was the utopian spirit endemic to its identity, a forever not-yet-attained identity, vexingly elusive and always at odds with the realities of the day' (*Europe: An Unfinished Adventure* 36). The title of Bauman's study points to a fundamental issue that must be tackled when questions about the EU arise, namely what exactly do we mean by Europe? Bauman points to this quandary in the book's introduction:

> Whenever we hear the word 'Europe' spoken, it is not immediately clear to us whether it refers to the confined territorial reality, tied to the ground, within the borders fixed and meticulously drawn by as yet unrevoked political treaties and legal documents, or to the free-floating essence that knows no bounds and defies all spatial bonds and limits. And it is this difficulty, nay impossibility of speaking of Europe while separating clearly and neatly the issue of the essence and the facts of reality that sets the talk of Europe apart from most ordinary talk about entities with geographic references. (*Europe* 6)

The EU and Europe are by no means synonymous, and just as Iceland, Norway, and Switzerland are European nations outside of the EU, Brexit will not cause Britain to float off into the Atlantic. Nevertheless, I should acknowledge that my focus upon filmic case studies from EU member states in this book (with the exception of Chap. 8, which engages with US productions) is born partly of necessity: spatial limitations, for instance, mitigate against detailed analysis of contemporary Russian sf films—of which there are numerous examples[10]—and similarly make consideration of sf from all of the Balkan countries, former Soviet Republics and the EFTA nations across Europe, an impossible task within one study. That said, my choice is also a calculated one insofar as it allows for deeper engagement with the EU at arguably the most turbulent period in its history. Whatever one makes of the political motivations behind the signing of the Treaty of Rome, it and closer European integration at large at the least represented an attempt to imagine a better future. A final difficulty, however, with viewing this process in utopian terms is terminological and relates to an understandable European skittishness about utopia itself. The Third Reich, after all, was imagined by Hitler as a utopian empire[11] illustrating neatly the precarious relationship between utopias and dystopia. Such can be seen in the foundational text of utopian literature, Thomas More's 1516 satirical work of fiction *Utopia*, which depicts a traveller's journey to the idyllic, eponymous island of Utopia where, as Mark Bould notes, religious tolerance is practised and where 'private property and unemployment (but not slavery) have been abolished' ('Between the Sleep and the Dream of Reason' 43). Utopia for some, in other words, and not for all. Similarly, the concept suffered in a European context from its association with the failed policies of the Soviet Union, with Fredric Jameson observing that 'during the Cold War (and in Eastern Europe immediately after its end), Utopia had become a synonym for Stalinism and had come to designate a program which neglected human frailty and original sin, and betrayed a will to uniformity and the ideal purity of a perfect system that always had to be imposed by force on its imperfect and reluctant subjects' (*Archaeologies of the Future* xi).

With the dissolution of the Soviet Empire, Western Europe lost its most obvious adversary and, perhaps with it, a significant portion of its *raison d'être*. EU expansions into the heart of former communist Europe in 2004 and 2007 seemed to copper-fasten the collective's security ambit and even herald its imminent, if incomplete, triumph over authoritarianism. Economically, things appeared just as bright, and whilst internal divisions remained, the financial attractiveness of joining the common market was obvious. By 2004, the year of its first major eastward expansion, the EU's economy when taken as a whole had become the largest on earth, accounting for 31.4 per cent of the world's GDP ('The EU in the World: Economy and Finance'). Within a year of the 2007 accession of Romania and Bulgaria, however, a cloud appeared on the horizon with the collapse of Lehman Brothers amongst the first prominent eruptions of the greatest financial crisis to afflict Europe since the cessation of the Second World War, one that would threaten to cripple the European banking sector and bring down the Euro itself. Suddenly, the great EU narrative of unassailable progress appeared a little less convincing. Fears began to emerge about the economic viability of the EU's 'peripheries', with particular suspicion falling upon the five so-called PIIGS: Portugal, Ireland, Italy, Greece, and Spain. The word 'contagion' entered the popular lexicon, quietly at first but soon building into a crescendo that would echo around the old continent. Anxiety that the collapse of one member state's economy could lead to the toppling of the Eurozone became pervasive. The EU responded by offering economic bailouts to stricken nations via the so-called Troika of European Commission, European Central Bank, and International Monetary Fund, while simultaneously demanding the implementation of severe austerity measures upon whole populations in return. Elsewhere the fallout from the Civil War in Syria ensured that European solidarity was further tested by the impact of large-scale migration into the EU and of late, clear splits have appeared between the European Commission and the EU's class of 2004 over how best to address the crisis. Elsewhere, while the decline of the USSR denied Europe a tangible other, newer, more slippery anxieties have crept into the zeitgeist, chief amongst them, perhaps, financial ruin but also a terrorist threat elevated by the activities of ISIS, which, even in decline, continues to present a decentred, amorphous, yet ever-present danger. In reality, the collapse of the USSR did not result in 'the end of history', to invoke Francis Fukuyama's oft-repeated description of the perceived triumph of Western capitalistic democracy, wherein he predicted 'the universalization of Western liberal democracy as the final form of human government' (*The End of History* 16). Instead, whilst neoliberal doctrines exacerbate inequality within European societies and extend in perpetuity historical imbalances between Europe and the Global South, existential threats to European democracy have become at once ever more diffuse and grimly familiar. Fear of the Muslim other, most saliently, has stoked a resurgence of violence by white supremacists, newly emboldened by the electoral successes of hard-right parties across the EU. A resurgence in extremism, sustained economic decline, and a complacent, floundering political class seemingly incapable of dealing with either occurrence have led some commentators with an eye on the 1930s to remark that, far from being at the end of history, we may in fact be at risk of repeating it.[12] Suffice to say that as we move deeper into the twenty-first century, the European dream has stalled, with the EU struggling to respond to major issues and, critically, no longer able to imagine a better future. Again, this steady atrophying of

INTRODUCTION: A DREAM CALLED ROME   11

utopia is a very science fictional theme, a conclusion shared by Harald Köpping Athanasopoulos in one of the few academic articles to link the genre to the EU:

> The EU has been unable to create a compelling narrative for itself following the demise of the post-World War II generation. While the early European integration process was driven by the need to build a lasting system of peace and prosperity, the renaissance of nationalism as well as the increasing Eurosceptic sentiment among large parts of Europe's population imply that this narrative is no longer regarded as universally convincing. Alternative narratives, such as the EU as a way to protect Europe from the negative fallout of globalisation, have failed to resonate. The supremacy of national over European identity is unchallenged in every member state of the European Union. ('Where no European Has Gone Before' 4)

Brexit is but the most obvious manifestation of this trend, yet fears that an economic crisis redolent of the 1930s would see a return to the political extremism of that decade were heightened during the 2017 French elections, until the unheralded centrist Emmanuel Macron emerged to stave off the challenge of Marine le Pen's far-right Front National. Becoming the youngest French leader since Napoleon, Macron's triumph at least ensured that the Treaty of Rome's 60th anniversary did not coincide with the ascension of a fascist to the highest office in the Republic. Alternative futures indeed. Not unpredictably, there has, in fact, been a voluble clamour for a reclaiming of national sovereignty across the continent, with populist anti-EU parties making gains in, amongst other countries, Austria, Britain, the Czech Republic, France, Poland, Hungary, and the Netherlands. The rhetoric of the far-right has accordingly grown in influence, and even in instances where such parties have been unable to secure major electoral gains, they have nonetheless succeeded in recalibrating the normalcies of political discourse, as leftists struggled for adequate responses and centrist and conservative parties veered rightward to offset losses to their electoral bases. Record levels of joblessness served only to further intensify public discord, and damningly for establishment parties across Europe, unemployment in the Eurozone had risen to an all-time high of 16.9 million people by March 2012, a figure that in turn would be topped the following October, when Eurostat, the European Commission's statistics branch, reported a figure of 18.49 million ('Unemployment Statistics').

And so, amidst the gloom, is there a way forward for the EU? To begin with, it's worth pointing out that the modern-day EU is an organic entity, one whose composition is constantly shifting. While narratives about Brexit have naturally taken up most of the headlines, we should recall that since 1957 the collective has continued to grow, with Croatia becoming the EU's 28th member state in 2013. In other words, prior to the spectre of Brexit, the EU has known nothing but expansion. Access to the open market as well as the security that comes with membership remains a draw, and both were key considerations in the accession of a host of former Eastern Bloc nations in 2004 and 2007. Furthermore, sub-nationalist movements in Scotland and Catalonia have both stressed a strong desire to retain EU membership in the event of their gaining independence from Britain and Spain, respectively.[13] In both cases, a certain paradox emerges where potential EU membership is seen not as a threat to national sovereignty, but rather as an institutional endorsement of it. Moreover, recent general election results in Britain and France defy predictions that the rise of populist, nativist politics in Europe is a *fait accompli*. So perhaps there is yet hope. The EU at any rate was never the utopian dream that it was cracked up to be, yet it at least sought to imagine something new, to forge a brighter future from the ashes of a tragic past. Its founders thought big. The question that now remains, however, is if it is still capable of doing so.

Why Science Fiction?

Thus far, I have endeavoured to provide the backdrop to this book on European sf cinema without making much mention of sf itself, an imbalance I will now seek to redress. Sf, a genre that exists in the interstices between utopia and dystopia, has long asked questions of society by creating worlds that closely mirror those they purport to represent, yet are sufficiently removed to lend an air of unreality to onscreen spaces. Fredric Jameson memorably observed that the genre 'enacts and enables a structurally unique "method" for apprehending the present as history, and this is so irrespective of the "pessimism" or "optimism" of the imaginary future world which is the pretext for that defamiliarization' (*Archaeologies* 288). Utopian sf film is unsurprisingly rare then; for mirroring a malaise evident in the real world, the genre is increasingly churning out dystopian visions of the future. Constance Penley synopsises Jameson's analysis thusly: 'our love affair with apocalypse and Armageddon, according to Jameson, results from the atrophy of utopian imagination, in other words, our cultural incapacity to imagine the future' ('Time Travel, Primal Scene, and the Critical Dystopia' 126). We will encounter abundant examples of bleak futures/alternate realities in contemporary European sf in the pages ahead, and even if such films cannot escape the paralysis of the moment, they can challenge its inevitability through what Tom Moylan describes as sf's unique 'ability to generate cognitively substantial yet estranged alternative worlds' (*Scraps of the Untainted Sky* 5). And that, perhaps above all, is the point: sf is important because it makes something new out of the familiar; it retains vitality, because in Isaac Asimov's wondrous formulation, it 'fights the natural notion that there's something permanent about things the way they are right now' (Freedman, *Conversations with Isaac Asimov* 135). Unsurprisingly then, sf cinema is currently enjoying a particularly fecund moment in popular and cultural discourses. Despite being historically viewed as something of an outsider genre, one that 'has always had sympathies with the marginal and the different' (Roberts, *Science Fiction* 29), a slew of recent sf films have attained extraordinary success. The most obvious recent example of this trend is *Avatar* (James Cameron 2009), which is the most lucrative film production ever made, while more recently, films such as *Star Wars: The Force Awakens* (J.J. Abrams 2015) and *Jurassic World* (Colin Trevorrow 2015) have entered the top ten highest grossing films of all time—a list that currently contains six sf-related films.[14] Sf's importance can be further gleaned from a facility for allegory that allows filmmakers' critical room in which to manoeuvre, a vital outlet in politically oppressive environments for, as Annette Kuhn has written, 'under the cloak of fantasy, issues of actuality may be addressed all the more directly' (*Alien Zone* 16). This state of being is to be welcomed when one considers that the most damning allegorical renderings often arise from particularly bleak moments in history. Yet, while the genre has historically thrived in the United States, in Europe it has often struggled for relevance. This struggle is due in part to a privileging of modernist filmmaking in post-war European cinema movements, yet nevertheless, as the world around us grows ever more science fictional, the genre itself has undergone a concurrent rejuvenation. Sf's suitability for the contemporary moment is elegantly captured by Lars Schmeink who writes that: 'in this world, we feel, that sf has become not just a literary genre but a mode of response, almost an epistemological category' (*Biopunk Dystopias* 18–19). Since sf cinema so frequently profits from societal anxieties, perhaps it should not surprise us to note that the genre in Europe has undergone a major revival since the turn of the millennium.

Historically, native sf cinema has struggled for relevance in a European context, a state of affairs that is not due to an absence of quality films.

After all, many of Europe's greatest directors have made sf films, including amongst others, Fritz Lang, Jean-Luc Godard, François Truffaut, Andrei Tarkovsky, Chris Marker, Alain Resnais, and Rainer Werner Fassbinder. In more recent years, high-profile directors such as Michael Haneke, Lars von Trier, and Yorgos Lanthimos have also turned to the genre as we shall see in due course. A difficulty, however, is that the shadow cast by national film movements in Italy, France, the UK, Czechoslovakia, and Germany, concurrent with the prominence of auteur theory, tends to mitigate against sustained investigations into European sf. Take the French Nouvelle Vague (NV) as an example: Jean-Luc Godard (*Alphaville/Alphaville: une étrange aventure de Lemmy Caution* 1965) and François Truffaut (*Fahrenheit 451* 1966) both turned to sf after the NV's initial exhilaration subsided, while Chris Marker and Alain Resnais of the affiliated Rive Gauche (Left Bank) group of filmmakers also made sf films in the respective shapes of *The Jetty/La Jetée* (1962) and *I Love You, I Love You/Je t'aime, je t'aime* (1968). Such examples provide us with a discernible intersection between the high art of European modernist cinema and the more institutionalised mores of genre cinema.[15] Yet, on the face of it, these films do not sit easily amongst wider sf canons, for in adhering to existing NV practices such as the use of on-location shooting, natural light, improvised dialogue, and self-reflexive editing techniques, the sf of Godard, Truffaut, Marker, and Resnais, though far from uniform in scope and execution, has tended to be seen more as an extension of their respective reflections on the evolution of cinema than as evidence of a concerted French turn to sf per se. For NV auteurs, moreover, playing with genre expectations was nothing new: Godard, most obviously, had previously experimented with the musical format in, for example, *A Woman Is a Woman/Une femme est une femme* (France, 1961). Broadly speaking, they privileged the manner of how a film's narrative unfurled over the actual story itself, meaning that genres were treated like 'expressive vocabularies rather than simply as constraints imposed by the film industry' (Flint, 'Genre' 31). Keith M. Johnston, who credits the NV sf films with reinvigorating the genre in late 1960s' Hollywood, sums things up thusly:

> the depiction of European cinema as artistic and critically acclaimed (particularly in contrast to American commercialism) stems from postwar cinema movements such as Italian neorealism and the French New Wave: films produced by film critics and writers who wanted to challenge the dominant film culture in their own countries and the outside influence of America. (*Science Fiction Film* 81)

We should also not underestimate the legacy of the Second World War. While a recent spate of European sf films would seemingly support the theory that the genre feeds off societal anxieties, this has not always been the case in Europe. Although the years following the First World War were notable for the otherworldly marvels of German Expressionism, the appeal of the fantastical was minimal in the aftermath of the second. In fact, sf's reliance upon the past and present for allegory may explain, in part, why the golden age of sf in Hollywood largely passed Europe by. For, while Hollywood was churning out a slew of alien invasion and monster pictures to widespread popular appeal in the early 1950s, even the most fantastic of imagined terrors ran the risk of indifference in a continent still reeling from first-hand experience of the Holocaust. Humanist responses, nowhere more salient than in the Italian Neorealismo, seemed more in keeping with the moment. Cesare Zavattini's call for audiences to 'think about reality precisely as it is' ('A Thesis on Neo-Realism' 68) typifies the approach of the neo-realists and perhaps encapsulates why, during the 1940s and 1950s, sf in Europe struggled for any sort of prominence at all, a fate shared by other genres of the era. Indeed, it was arguably not until the French auteurs turned their attentions to sf in the mid-1960s that the genre re-emerged in the popular consciousness: even if they wilfully stretched the boundaries of formal genre classification, an approach that was not uncommon in Europe at the time.[16] Therefore, serious analysis of the sf output of such auteurs tends to be considered in light of the overall body of work that they have undertaken and not within a canon of European sf, a trend that endures to this day as we shall see in Chap. 2 of this monograph.

DEFINITIONS AND OTHER LIKELY BONES OF CONTENTION

Before providing an overview of sf cinema in Europe and then concluding with a chapter synopsis, I should first offer some brief clarifications of both my understanding of sf as a concept and my reasons for choosing the films that I have. To begin with, this book concerns itself with film for reasons of brevity (one could just as easily devote a whole book to European sf literature or television) and methodological pragmatism (unlike many dedicated sf specialists, my training has been primarily that of a film scholar[17]). A key aim, however, is that in addition to providing a survey of twenty-first-century European sf films, I wish to contextualise such films within wider industrial frameworks and, in so doing, illustrate how, in some instances, their very production dovetails with processes of European integration. On the issue of taxonomy, instead, scholars remain divided as to what constitutes a viable definition of sf cinema, just as disagreement reigns over the precise contours of the genre at large. Arthur C. Clarke neatly summed up such confusion, when writing that 'attempting to define science fiction is an undertaking almost as difficult, though not so popular, as trying to define pornography... In both pornography and SF, the problem lies in knowing exactly where to draw the line' (*Greetings, Carbon-Based Bipeds! Collected Essays, 1934–1998*). Taking our cue from literary studies, we may note a formative definition by Isaac Asimov for whom sf is 'that branch of literature that deals with the human response to changes in the level of science and technology—it being understood that the changes involved would be rational ones in keeping with what was known about science, technology and people' (*Asimov on Science Fiction* 10). Darko Suvin provides a deeper conceptualisation still, positing that: 'Science Fiction is distinguished by the narrative dominance or hegemony of a fictional 'novum' (novelty, innovation) validated by cognitive logic' (*Metamorphoses of Science Fiction* 63). For Suvin, who borrows in turn from Viktor Shklovsky's concept of *ostranenie* and Bertolt Brecht's definition of *verfremdung*, the genre thrives on its capacity for 'cognitive estrangement' (*Metamorphoses* 63): a phenomenon described by Christine Cornea as a 'literature that defamiliarises reality and encourages the reader to contemplate upon the known world from a distanced perspective' (*Science Fiction Cinema* 3). Cornea, in teasing out her own formulation of the genre, draws upon Tzvetan Todorov's contestation that 'the best science fiction texts are organized analogously. The initial data are supernatural: robots, extraterrestrial beings, the whole interplanetary context. The narrative movement consists in obliging us to see how close these apparently marvellous elements are to us, to what degree they are present in our life' (*The Fantastic* 56). Cornea aptly deduces that 'science fiction has forged a relationship with realism that makes it a far more indeterminate genre' than others (*Science Fiction* 7). For Geoff King and Tanya Krzywinska, indeterminacy is central to the mechanisms of the genre itself, for 'it is precisely science fiction's diversity and flexibility, through its ability to absorb ideas from other domains, that has kept the genre alive for more than a century' (*From Outerspace to Cyberspace* 4). It is my own contention that reconciling oneself with such magpie tendencies is the most suitable approach for undertaking a study of the magnitude that I propose here. I am aware, for example, that including *28 Days*

Later (Danny Boyle 2002) as dystopian sf may be a provocation too far for some genre purists, yet I would argue conversely that the film's whole premise is predicated upon a science experiment that goes awry. Such ambiguities can be traced back to Mary Shelley's *Frankenstein* and are unlikely to be resolved here. At any rate, I have no wish to do so, choosing instead to see the possibility in hybridity, in keeping with Paul K. Alkon's contention that 'the polysemy of the term science fiction, reflected in the inability of critics to arrive at agreement on any one definition, is a measure of science fiction's complex significance for our times' (*Science Fiction Before 1900* 9). As such, I understand genres as being intrinsically unstable, ongoing sites of negotiation between contested canons and new interpretations, from which stem myriad imperceptible mutations over time. Accordingly, my choice of films is diverse and seeks to address as wide a cross-section of EU member states as possible while shifting from micro-budget to blockbuster films and taking in assorted art-house, commercial, and b-movie productions in the process. My analysis is in turn lent structure by themed chapters: a potential difficulty of such an approach being that one runs the risk of conducting an a priori reading of selected films or that, like Abraham Maslow's boy with a hammer, of eyeing every problem as a prospective nail. I hope that I have been at least partially successful in avoiding such pitfalls: for one thing, I have sought to place these films firmly within the contemporary contexts that unite them all. Nevertheless, some notable filmic omissions naturally remain, each of which I will seek to acknowledge as the occasion demands.

A Growing Body of Work

Until quite recently, most studies of sf cinema have unsurprisingly afforded prominence to American-based productions. Indeed, a central motivation behind the commissioning of this book is that the importance of sf's role in the shaping of European cinema is not adequately reflected in scholarly literature. Nationally based studies in a European context are gradually emerging, including Hunter (1999), Näripea (2010), Sardar and Cubitt (2002), Hochscherf and Leggott (2011), Rickels (2015), and Jones (2017). The emergence in 2008 of the Liverpool-based *Science Fiction Film and Television* has also been a welcome development, even if it has strong international inflections and, as its title suggests, is not focused solely on film. Comprehensive anthologies of European sf are also rare: recent exceptions are provided by Fritzsche (2014), whose edited collection features six dedicated chapters on mostly twentieth-century European sf; Bould (2012), who provides a valuable conceptual framework for understanding the genre in Europe; and Eleftheriotis (2001), who offers insight into 'Europeanness' and sf. My aim here, instead, is to blend industry-based and filmic analyses to engage the question of European sf while also filling a research gap by exclusively addressing twenty-first-century iterations of the genre in Europe. While impressive examinations of specific films do exist—amongst them Thomas Elsaesser's book on *Metropolis* (2000), Chris Darke's on *Alphaville* (2005), or Kim Newman's on *Quatermass and the Pit* (2014)—they tend to focus on canonical productions, whereas the absence highlighted here is the need to provide a comprehensive investigation of contemporary European sf films, many of which have escaped in-depth analysis. Fritzsche's work on East German films of the 1970s (2006), Merrill's analysis of Eastern European sf cinema (2014), and Torner's study of East German/Polish sf (2014), instead, are strong contextual resources yet, at the same time, regionally and temporally specific in scope.[18] Telotte (1999) does undertake a detailed investigation of sf within several national cinemas in Europe, yet his study is largely restricted to inter-war films. It is nevertheless an invaluable contextual resource, as are those by Rickman (2004), Roberts (2007), and Johnston (2011), which are especially strong on the origins of the genre in Europe. Baxter (1970), Johnson (1972), and Rottensteiner (1999) finally provide early commentary on European sf literature and film in Europe and, as such, are antecedents for this publication, yet their mention here also serves to underline the absence of contemporary books on European sf cinema. Such a study, I contend, is long overdue for, while an overarching transnational investigation of European sf has still to be undertaken, elsewhere, relatable and informative studies have been published, including cross-border studies on the European road movie (Mazierska and Rascaroli 2006; Eleftheriotis 2010; Loshitzky 2010), the European horror film (Allmer et al. 2012; Olney 2013), and the European Western (Broughton 2015). While not claiming to be definitive per se, this study can hopefully be viewed as a first step towards beginning a similar conversation about European sf cinema.

Five Parts, Nine Chapters

This book is divided into five distinct parts comprising nine chapters and merges aesthetic analysis of key films with industrial analysis of the industries that sustain them. Formative questions such as what it is to be

European, where is Europe, and how is Europe bound together cannot be satisfactorily answered without first addressing imbalances, both internal and external that threaten to undermine long-held assertions. To this end, the following chapter summary outlines how European sf engages with these very issues, providing at once both a counter history of contemporary events and a series of warnings about their possible consequences. Part I, 'Where Is Europe? National and European Science Fiction', is emblematic of this two-pronged approach and surveys both 'officially sanctioned' European sf—films financed by the premiere transnational European funding agency Eurimages—and sf from the newest EU member states that feature diverse production histories. Chapter 2 ('Shaping a European Narrative: Eurimages, SF, and the Auteur') investigates how European funding models have impacted upon sf in recent years and outlines how European cinema operates on an industrial level by taking in the work of two of European cinema's foremost contemporary auteurs in Michael Haneke and Lars von Trier, as well as the partly crowd-funded co-production *Iron Sky* (Timo Vuorensola 2012). Balancing an attention to Eurimages' macro-politics with the onscreen versions of Europe presented by each film, I illustrate how even the most dystopian visions of Europe ultimately play into the Council of Europe's institutional strategies. Chapter 3 ('SF in the EU's Newest Member States'), instead, surveys how European integration has impacted upon sf productions from four post-Nice Treaty EU states in Bulgaria, Croatia, Hungary, and Lithuania. Since the expansion of the EU in 2004, formerly national film studios are in some instances becoming fertile ground for cheap Hollywood location shooting, a trend I track with a study of sf films shot at the Nu Boyana Film Studios in Sofia since the turn of the century, before turning to something altogether different in the Croatian micro-budget media satire *The Show Must Go On* (Nevio Marasović 2010), a film in which EU accession ultimately results in the country's ruination. Frequently othered within European discourses, in recent years the former Eastern Bloc has become a region where tradition competes for ascendency with realpolitik and is increasingly turning into a testing ground for the continued viability of Europe's institutions. In this vein, I analyse how rising nationalist sentiment across the Visegrád Group manifests itself onscreen in *Jupiter's Moon/Jupiter holdja* (Kornél Mundruczó 2017), which through its depiction of a Syrian refugee with superpowers takes aim at the Hungarian government's pursuance of an illiberal political agenda. This chapter concludes with a close textual analysis of Kristina Buožytė's provocative *Vanishing Waves/Aurora* (2012), which self-consciously evokes a history of modernist cinema and is both the first-ever Lithuanian sf and the first Lithuanian production of any kind to be released in the United States.

Arguably, the greatest threat to Europe's institutions to have emerged since the turn of the millennium has been the financial crisis in the Eurozone, a topic that I turn to in Part II: 'Contagion! Responding to the Financial Crisis'. Owing to the sheer enormity of the crisis and in order to engage with films from the five most affected EU member states—the so-called PIIGS of Portugal, Italy, Ireland, Greece, and Spain—I have devoted both chapters of this section to the topic. Chapter 4 ('PIIGS to the Slaughter') takes in case studies on generational conflict in Portugal—as relayed through *Real Playing Game* (Tino Navarro and David Rebordão 2013) the only sf film to emerge from the country during the crisis—before turning to an industrial analysis of sf production in Ireland, the bulk of which curiously coincides with the advent of the economic crisis. In keeping with the continuing erosion of worker security across the EU in recent years, I conclude the chapter with a study of precarity and the commodification of social life in Gianni Pacinotti's *The Last Man on Earth/L'ultimo terrestre* (2011), a film that uses the trope of an impending alien invasion to shed light on latent inequalities across Italian society. Chapter 5 ('PIIGS to the Slaughter II') continues the investigation into the fallout from the Eurozone crisis by focusing upon key films from Greece and Spain. Starting with an analysis of Yorgos Lanthimos' *The Lobster* (2015), a film, it will be argued, that is both an industrial endorsement of European integration and an onscreen evisceration of the EU's austerity policies, the focus then shifts to Spain, where the same policies have further destabilised the relationship between the central Madrid administration and the semi-autonomous region of Catalonia. Through a case study of Àlex and David Pastor's *The Last Days/Los Últimos Días* (2013), a film that depicts a panic-stricken Barcelona where citizens have become terrified of venturing outside, this study concludes by exploring how austerity has inadvertently breathed new life into the Catalan independence movement and also exacerbated gender inequality in the Spanish workforce.

Part III ('Shut the Gates! Scorched Earth, Fortress Continent') extends the theme of crisis to take in what is ultimately the greatest existential threat to the EU and, indeed, to the world at large in climate change. Chapter 6 ('Climate Change, the Anthropocene, and European SF') argues that we cannot divorce climate change from its economic drivers, taking in analysis of two unconventional sf films in the process: Franny Armstrong's 'sf documentary' *The Age of Stupid* (2009) and Tarik Saleh's fully animated sf *Metropia* (2009), which imagines the consequences for the EU when corporations begin to subsume the social functions of states. Despite their formal differences, both films present systemic critiques of Europe's central role in forging the Anthropocene and envisage catastrophic futures of the kind depicted in the post-apocalyptic landscapes of *Hell* (Tim Fehlbaum 2011) and *The Quiet Hour* (Stéphanie Joalland 2014), analyses of which bookend the chapter. A primary consequence of climate change is that it is almost certain to increase migration into the EU in the decades ahead. Beginning with what the leaders of its three largest economies described in 2010/2011 as the 'failure of multiculturalism', Chap. 7 ('Multiculturalism and the Changing Face of Europe') explores issues of identity, race, and belonging in British and French sf, with case studies of urban dystopias in Paris and London, both European economic powerhouses in addition to being two of the most ethnically diverse cities in the EU.

Cognisant of the rise of European sf, I am also keenly aware that it exists firmly within the shadow of Hollywood. Part IV ('Another Planet: Hollywood SF Production in Europe') therefore traces the pre-eminence that American sf continues to enjoy within a European context, arguing that, counterintuitive though it may seem, no study of European sf cinema can hope to claim any sort of authority while ignoring what remains, by a colossal distance, the largest player in the European market. Blending industrial and filmic analysis, Chap. 8 ('European SF and Hollywood') seeks to quantify the extent of Hollywood sf dominance within EU cinemas, before analysing how *28 Weeks Later* (Juan Carlos Fresnadillo 2007) retools the mechanics of its predecessor to present a version of Britain that is shaped almost entirely by US cultural conceptions of Europe.

Part V ('Beyond Europe?') lastly considers the future for both the EU and European sf alike and is comprised of a concluding chapter ('Conclusions and Roads Ahead') that reflects upon the changes that Europe has gone through in the past five years and considers future possibilities for both the EU and the, for now, 28 member states that comprise it.

NOTES

1. In an interview with the *New Yorker*, Roth allowed that 'It is easier to comprehend the election of an imaginary President like Charles Lindbergh than an actual President like Donald Trump [for] Lindbergh, despite his Nazi sympathies and racist proclivities, was a great aviation hero who had

displayed tremendous physical courage and aeronautical genius in crossing the Atlantic in 1927' (Thurman, 'Philip Roth E-mails on Trump').

2. Although Méliès' film is often referred to as the first European sf film, Auguste and Louis Lumière's *The Mechanical Butcher/La Charcuterie mécanique* (1895) predates it by seven years. The Lumière brothers' film was, as Stephen Kern notes, the first film to depict time reversal techniques 'by running film backwards through the projector' (*The Culture of Time and Space, 1880–1918* 30).

3. Of the Treaty's security aims, Luisa Rivi writes: 'It is worth noting how the first signatories of the Treaty of Rome, "the Six"—France, Germany, Italy, Belgium, the Netherlands, and Luxembourg—were in fact geographically arranged around the western side of Germany: They could control Germany's military growth and constitute an outpost against Soviet Communism' (*European Cinema After 1989* 16–17).

4. As Quintin Peel puts it: 'As Churchill urged a Franco-German partnership to lead his vision of a new Europe, he declared that Great Britain and the British Commonwealth, along with the US and USSR, should be "friends and sponsors" of the project. He did not talk of the UK becoming a member itself [...] For Churchill, as for the overwhelming majority of the British establishment in those early postwar decades, the British empire (and the Commonwealth that succeeded it) and the "special relationship" with the US, were the nation's two most important strategic priorities' ('Historic Misunderstanding Underlies UK-EU Relationship on Churchill Anniversary').

5. Decades of political violence in Northern Ireland and the Basque country, to name but two prominent examples, illustrate that peace in Europe was by no means total.

6. Kershaw writes that 'Hitler was the main author of a war leaving over 50 million dead and millions more grieving their lost ones and trying to put their shattered lives together again. Hitler was the chief inspiration of a genocide the like of which the world had never known, rightly to be viewed in coming times as a defining episode of the twentieth century' (*Hitler* 5).

7. Collins writes: 'The genesis of the Council of Europe and the European Union are sometimes traced to utopian projects of European Government, notably to the Duc de Sully's "Grand Design for a Union of European Christendom" [...] and William Penn's "Essay towards the Present and Future Peace of Europe by the Establishment of a European Diet; Parliament or Estate" of 1693, but are usually dated from the foundation of the International Committee of the Movement for European Unity in 1947 (which was inspired by Winston Churchill's speech in Zurich a year before)' (*Satellite to Single Market* 182).

8. Chomsky's analysis gains further weight if we consider that aid was primarily received in the form of US-produced goods rather than money, even if, as Rhiannon Vickers notes, 'the goods that the ECA [US Economic Co-operation Administration] authorized for export as part of the European Recovery Programme (ERP) did not always tally with the goods that the European states had requested' (*Manipulating Hegemony: State Power, Labour and the Marshall Plan in Britain* 45).
9. In November 2017, 25 EU member states signed the PESCO ('Permanent Structured Cooperation') defence pact. The pact, which was first outlined in Article 46 of the Lisbon Treaty, proposes that participating members raise their annual defence budgets to 2 per cent of GDP and paves the way for closer European military integration. Critics contend that PESCO may in fact signal the first step towards a European army by stealth.
10. Prominent amongst a recent spate of Russian sf films are *Night Watch/ Nochnoy dozor* (Timur Bekmambetov 2004), *Day Watch/Dnevnoy dozor* (Timur Bekmambetov 2006), *Dark Planet/Obitaemyy ostrov* (Fyodor Bondarchuk 2009), *Hard to Be a God/Trudno byt bogom* (Aleksey German 2013), and *Attraction/Prityazhenie* (Fyodor Bondarchuk 2017).
11. As Kershaw notes of Hitler: 'His speeches were not simply negative, not just an attack on the existing system. He presented a vision, a utopia, an ideal: national liberation through strength and unity' (*Hitler* 459).
12. Dalibor Rohac sums up many such concerns, noting that 'much like in the 1930s, today's Europe has five distinct elements of a geopolitical disaster in the making': it endures 'a dysfunctional monetary system', faces 'a rising revisionist power' (Russia), suffers from 'a lack of leadership', exists amidst 'a crumbling system of international cooperation', and is in danger of 'losing the battle of ideas' ('Europe Returns to the 1930s').
13. The Scottish, for instance, voted overwhelmingly against Brexit, with 62 per cent of the electorate favouring remaining within the EU.
14. Other top ten sf-related films include *Star Wars: The Last Jedi* (Rian Johnson 2017) and the superhero movies: *The Avengers* (Joss Whedon 2012) and *Avengers: Age of Ultron* (Joss Whedon 2015). The list changes considerably when adjusted for inflation, in which case it would include only *Avatar* (James Cameron 2009), *Star Wars* (George Lucas 1977), and *E.T. The Extra-Terrestrial* (Steven Spielberg 1982).
15. I have written in some detail about the intersections between modernism and European sf elsewhere. See the chapter 'Modern Inclinations: Locating European Science Fiction Cinema of the 1960s and 1970s' (2017).
16. Outside of auteur sf, there existed a number of hybridised films that poked fun at genre codes for expressly comedic effect. Such parodies, according

to Tim Bergfelder, worked parasitically, often by 'drawing on the conventions of all the other major genres in circulation' ('The Nation Vanishes: European Co-productions and Popular Genre Formula in the 1950s and 1960s' 138).
17. This distinction became clear to me while attending the 2017 Science Fiction Research Association conference in Riverside, California. There, I listened to countless fascinating papers on sf literature that left me at once intrigued and in little doubt as to my own unsuitability for conducting a crossover study of European film and literature.
18. Again, the focus here is on film. For analysis of sf television in Europe, see, for example, Bignell and O'Day's *Terry Nation* (2004), Cook and Wright's *British Science Fiction Television: A Hitchhiker's Guide* (2005), Chapman's *Inside the Tardis: The Worlds of Doctor Who: A Cultural History* (2006), Geraghty's *Channeling the Future: Essays on Science Fiction and Fantasy Television* (2009), or Cornea's 'British Science Fiction Television in the Discursive Context of Second Wave Feminism' (2011).

Bibliography

Alkon, Paul K. 2002. *Science Fiction Before 1900: Imagination Discovers Technology.* New York: Routledge.
Allmer, Patricia, David Huxley, and Emily Brick, eds. 2012. *European Nightmares: Horror Cinema in Europe Since 1945.* New York: Wallflower.
Asimov, Isaac. 1982. *Asimov on Science Fiction.* New York: Avon.
Athanasopoulos, Harald Köpping. 2017. Where No European Has Gone Before: Representations of Europe (an Integration) in Science Fiction. *Space Policy* 41: 60–64.
Bauman, Zygmunt. 2004. *Europe: An Unfinished Adventure.* Cambridge: Polity.
Baxter, John. 1970. *Science Fiction in the Cinema.* New York: A.S. Barnes.
Bergfelder, Tim. 2005. The Nation Vanishes: European Co-productions and Popular Genre Formula in the 1950s and 1960s. In *Cinema and Nation*, ed. Mette Hjort and Scott Mackenzie, 139–152. London: Routledge.
Bignell, Jonathan, and Andrew O'Day. 2004. *Terry Nation.* Manchester: Manchester University Press.
Bould, Mark. 2012. *Science Fiction.* London: Routledge.
———. 2017. Between the Sleep and the Dream of Reason: Dystopian Science Fiction Cinema. In *Future Imperfect: Science Fiction Film*, ed. Rainer Rother and Annika Schaefer, 42–63. Berlin: Bertz/Fischer Verlag.
Brecht, Bertolt. 1961. On Chinese Acting. *The Tulane Drama Review.* Trans. Eric Bentley, 6 (1), 130–136.
Broughton, Lee. 2015. *The Euro-Western: Reframing Gender, Race and the Other in Film.* London: I.B. Tauris.

Chapman, James. 2006. *Inside the Tardis: The Worlds of Doctor Who*. London: I.B. Tauris.
Chomsky, Noah. 2000. *Rogue States: The Rule of Force in World Affairs*. London: Pluto Press.
Clarke, Arthur C. 2001. *Greetings, Carbon-Based Bipeds! Collected Essays, 1934–1998*. London: St Martin's Griffin.
Collins, Richard. 1998. *From Satellite to Single Market: New Communication Technology and European Public Service Television*. Abingdon: Routledge.
Cook, John R., and Peter Wright. 2005. *British Science Fiction Television: A Hitchhiker's Guide*. London: I.B. Tauris.
Cornea, Christine. 2007. *Science Fiction Cinema: Between Fantasy and Reality*. Edinburgh: Edinburgh University Press.
———. 2011. British Science Fiction Television in the Discursive Context of Second Wave Feminism. *Genders Journal* 54.
Darke, Chris. 2005. *Alphaville*. Urbana: University of Illinois.
Eleftheriotis, Dimitris. 2001. *Popular Cinemas of Europe: Studies of Texts, Contexts and Frameworks*. London/New York: Continuum.
———. 2010. *Cinematic Journeys: Film and Movement*. Edinburgh: Edinburgh University Press.
Elsaesser, Thomas. 2000. *Metropolis*. London: British Film Institute.
Flint, Sarah Berry. 1999. Genre. In *A Companion to Film Theory*, ed. Toby Miller and Robert Stam, 25–44. Malden: Blackwell.
Freedman, Carl. 2005. *Conversations with Isaac Asimov*. Oxford: University of Mississippi Press.
Fritzsche, Sonja, ed. 2006. East Germany's Werkstatt Zukunft: Futurology and the Science Fiction Films of Defa-futurum. *German Studies Review* 29 (2): 367–386.
—, ed. 2014. *The Liverpool Companion to World Science Fiction Film*. Liverpool: Liverpool University Press.
Fukuyama, Francis. 1992. *The End of History and The Last Man*. New York: Free Press.
Geraghty, Lincoln, ed. 2009. *Channeling the Future: Essays on Science Fiction and Fantasy Television*. Lanham: Scarecrow.
Greenwood, Sean, ed. 1996. *Britain and European Integration Since the Second World War*. Manchester: Manchester University Press.
Habermas, Jürgen. 2001. *The Postnational Constellation: Political Essays*. Trans. Max Pensky. Cambridge, MA: MIT Press.
Hochscherf, Tobias, and James Leggott, eds. 2011. *British Science Fiction Film and Television: Critical Essays*. Jefferson: McFarland.
Hunter, I.Q. 1999. *British Science Fiction Cinema*. Abingdon: Routledge.
Jameson, Fredric. 2005. *Archaeologies of the Future: A Desire Called Utopia and Other Science Fictions*. London/New York: Verso.

Johnson, William, ed. 1972. *Focus on the Science Fiction Film*. Englewood Cliffs: Prentice-Hall.
Johnston, Keith M. 2011. *Science Fiction Film: A Critical Introduction*. New York: Berg.
Jones, Matthew. 2017. *Science Fiction Cinema and 1950s Britain: Recontextualizing Cultural Anxiety*. London/New York: Bloomsbury.
Kern, Stephen. 1983. *The Culture of Time and Space, 1880–1918*. Cambridge, MA: Harvard University Press.
Kershaw, Ian. 2008. *Hitler: A Biography*. New York: W.W. Norton.
King, Geoff, and Tanya Krzywinska. 2000. *Science Fiction Cinema: From Outerspace to Cyberspace*. London: Wallflower.
Kuhn, Annette. 1990. *Alien Zone: Cultural Theory and Contemporary Science Fiction Cinema*. London/New York: Verso.
Loshitzky, Yosefa. 2010. *Screening Strangers: Migration and Diaspora in Contemporary European Cinema*. Bloomington/Indianapolis: Indiana University Press.
Mazierska, Ewa, and Laura Rascaroli. 2006. *Crossing New Europe: Postmodern Travel and the European Road Movie*. London: Wallflower.
Merrill, Jason. 2014. Gender and Apocalypse in Eastern European Cinema. In *The Liverpool Companion to World Science Fiction Film*, ed. Sonja Fritzsche, 104–117. Liverpool: Liverpool University Press.
Morrissey, Will. 2014. *Churchill and de Gaulle: The Geopolitics of Liberty*. London: Rowman & Littlefield.
Moylan, Tom. 2000. *Scraps of The Untainted Sky: Science Fiction, Utopia, Dystopia*. Boulder: Perseus.
Näripea, Eva. 2010. Aliens and Time Travellers: Recycling National Space in Estonian Science-Fiction Cinema. *Studies in Eastern European Cinema* 1 (2): 167–182.
Newman, Kim. 2014. *Quatermass and the Pit*. Houndmills: Palgrave Macmillan.
Olney, Ian. 2013. *Euro-horror: Classic European Horror Cinema in Contemporary American Culture*. Bloomington: Indiana University Press.
Peel, Quentin. 2016. Historic Misunderstanding Underlies UK-EU Relationship on Churchill Anniversary. *Financial Times*, September 19.
Penley, Constance. 1986. Time Travel, Primal Scene, and the Critical Dystopia. *Camera Obscura* 5 (3): 66–85.
Power, Aidan. 2017. Modern Inclinations: Locating European Science Fiction Cinema of the 1960s and 1970s. In *Future Imperfect: Science, Fiction, Film*, ed. Rainer Rother and Annika Schaefer, 29–41. Berlin: Bertz & Fischer.
Rickels, Laurence A. 2015. *Germany: A Science Fiction*. Germany: Anti-Oedipus Press.
Rickman, Gregg, ed. 2004. *The Science Fiction Film Reader*. New York: Limelight.
Rivi, Luisa. 2007. *European Cinema After 1989: Identity and Transnational Production*. New York: Palgrave Macmillan.

Roberts, Adam. 2000. *Science Fiction: The New Critical Idiom*. London/New York: Routledge.
———. 2007. *The History of Science Fiction*. London: Palgrave Macmillan.
Rohac, Dalibor. 2015. Europe Returns to the 1930s. *Politico*, September 9. www.politico.eu/article/europe-returns-to-the-1930s-revolt-leadeship-nazi/. Accessed 1 May 2018.
Roth, Philip. 2004. *The Plot Against America*. New York: Houghton Mifflin.
Rottensteiner, Franz. 1999. *View from Another Shore: European Science Fiction*. 2nd ed. Liverpool: Liverpool University Press.
Sardar, Ziauddin, and Sean Cubitt, eds. 2002. *Aliens R Us: The Other in Science Fiction Cinema*. London: Pluto.
Schmeink, Lars. 2016. *Biopunk Dystopias*. Liverpool: Liverpool University Press.
Shelley, Mary. 1818. *Frankenstein*. London: Lackington, Hughes, Harding, Mavor & Jones.
Shklovsky, Viktor. 2015. Art, as Device. *Poetics Today*. Trans. Alexandra Berlina, 36 (3), 151–174.
Springer, Claudia. 1999. Psycho-cybernetics in Films of the 1990s. In *Alien Zone II*, ed. Annette Kuhn, 203–220. London: Verso.
Suvin, Darko. 1979. *Metamorphoses of Science Fiction: On the Poetics and History of a Literary Genre*. New Haven: Yale University Press.
Telotte, J.P. 1999. *A Distant Technology: Science Fiction Film and the Machine Age*. Middletown: Wesleyan University Press.
The EU in the World: Economy and Finance. 2016. *Eurostat*, March. ec.europa.eu/eurostat/statistics-explained/index.php/The_EU_in_the_world__economy_and_finance. Accessed 1 May 2018.
Thurman, Judith. 2017. Phillip Roth E-mails on Trump. *The New Yorker*, January 30.
Todorov, Tzvetan. 1975. *The Fantastic: A Structural Approach to a Literary Genre*. Trans. Richard Howard. Ithaca: Cornell University Press.
Torner, Evan. 2014. Casting for a Socialist Earth: Multicultural Whiteness in the East German/Polish Science-Fiction Film Silent Star (1960). In *The Liverpool Companion to World Science Fiction Film*, ed. Sonja Fritzsche, 118–138. Liverpool: Liverpool University Press.
Unemployment Statistics. *Eurostat*. ec.europa.eu/eurostat/statistics-explained/index.php?title=Unemployment_statistics. Accessed 1 May 2018.
Vickers, Rhiannon. 2018. The Marshall Plan and Consumerism. *The Vienna Review*, June 1. www.viennareview.net/news/front-page/the-marshall-plan-and-consumerism. Accessed 1 May 2018.
Zavattini, Cesare. 1978. A Thesis on Neo-Realism. In *Springtime in Italy. A Reader on Neorealism*, ed. David Overbey, 67–78. London: Talisman.

CHAPTER 2

Shaping a European Narrative: Eurimages, SF, and the Auteur

After the signing of the Treaty of Rome in 1957, the EU's forebear, the European Economic Community (EEC), was established with the express intention of ensuring that the horrors of two world wars would never again be repeated on European soil. Nearly a decade previously, and some two years before the signing of the Treaty of Paris, which brought about the formation of the European Coal and Steel Community, the Council of Europe (CoE) was formed in London in 1949, following increasingly voluble calls for greater European integration. Though not enjoying the legislative powers of the separate EU, the CoE is a pivotal advocate for democracy in a European sphere and styles itself as an exemplar of transnational cooperation and exponent of European integrationist ideals (even if the presence of members such as Azerbaijan calls the distance between its aspirations and its actions into question). In its role as watchdog for human rights and democratic values, for example, the CoE has most notably overseen the establishment of the European Convention on Human Rights and is a leading proponent of cultural and artistic collaboration between member states. Salient within its cultural wing is Eurimages, a film-specific funding body that has sought to perpetuate the CoE's integrationist ideals in productive form ever since its founding in 1988, some four years before the launch of the EU's MEDIA (Mesures pour l'encouragement et le developpement de l'industrie audiovisuelle) funding programme. Described by Luisa Rivi as 'the mainstay of the new

© The Author(s) 2018
A. Power, *Contemporary European Science Fiction Cinemas*,
Palgrave European Film and Media Studies,
https://doi.org/10.1007/978-3-319-89827-8_2

29

Europeanism' (*European Cinema After 1989* 61), Eurimages is the original modern European film support programme, one that predates the EU itself, just as the CoE predated the EEC. More specifically, and in the body's own words, 'Eurimages supports full-length feature films and animation as well as documentaries of a minimum length of 70 minutes, intended for cinema release … and aims to promote European co-productions' ('Eurimages Support for Co-production: Feature-length Fiction, Animation and Documentary Films' 6). A practical illustration of this cooperative spirit can be gleaned from Eurimages' insistence that all film projects submitted for consideration must have at least two co-producers from different member states of the fund. Closely examining Eurimages-funded sf films from industrial, aesthetic, and socio-cultural standpoints, I aim to demonstrate here how the CoE in fact seeks to promote a utopian version of Europe, one free from the rancour of nationalistic sentiment and imbued instead with the vision of a progressive collective of equals all pulling in the same direction. Balancing an attention to Eurimages' macro-politics with the aesthetic choices of some of their funded sf filmmakers, I will seek to show how artistic decisions often resonate with, sometimes defy, but perhaps above all play into, the CoE's institutional strategies and, by proxy, the European project. More specifically still, I will do so with recourse to *Time of the Wolf/Le temps du loup* (Michael Haneke, 2003), *Melancholia* (Lars von Trier, 2011), and *Iron Sky* (Timo Vuorensola, 2012), three sf films that will also provide us with an insight into the oft-uneasy balance between auteurist cinema and sf in the Europeans sphere.

EURIMAGES: AN INTEGRATIONIST MODEL

The European project, as Mariana Liz reminds us in her recent monograph *Euro-Visions: Europe in Contemporary Cinema*, is driven by a desire for closer integration on three fronts, being 'aimed at the democratic and peaceful integration of different peoples, in economic, political and cultural terms' (2). A personal contention, one I will expand upon in detail in Part Two of this book, is that the former consideration, that of the economic, has overridden the latter two to the detriment of the EU itself, but for now it is important to gain a closer understanding of how all three coalesce within the European film industry. As we will see, culture plays a key role in the institutional perpetuation of European ideals, even if a precise definition of the term can be elusive with regard to Eurimages, a body that has historically tended to ignore sf while nevertheless (and paradoxically) supporting some of the key European examples of the genre in the twenty-first century. This qualified support makes Eurimages interesting from an sf perspective, particularly as little scholarly attention has been afforded to the link between the two. Additionally, although MEDIA is by a distance the larger fund,[1] its aims are far wider than Eurimages, which is principally concerned with film production. MEDIA instead largely focuses upon aspects prior to and after completion of production. Liz succinctly differentiates between the two bodies thusly:

> Apart from the sums invested, the main difference between MEDIA and Eurimages is that only the latter gives direct support to film production. Whereas MEDIA's budget has been allocated to pre-and post-production initiatives, over 90 per cent of Eurimages' funding is attributed to co-productions. Conversely, in the last phase of MEDIA, 55 per cent of the budget was devoted to film distribution, whereas only 3 per cent of Eurimages' support was given to that area. (*Euro-Visions* 37)

Nonetheless, in sharing a devotion to closer cultural union, both bodies endorse a distinctly European aim, one that Randall Halle argues separates the EU from other globalist projects. Citing multiple free-trade agreements as well as the League of Nations, the United Arab Republic, and the United Nations as examples, Halle observes that while economic and political integration is common globally, 'the quest for cultural union marks the European project as distinctive' (*Europeanization of Cinema* 12). Closer cultural integration is in many ways logical from economic and political standpoints for it serves to remove barriers to both, yet Eurimages has grown cagier in its promotion of European identity and is careful to specify that such a goal is compatible with regional and national distinctions. This is hardly surprising given the growth of Eurosceptic sentiment in recent years, yet there are sound historical reasons for moderation too, given the cultural obliteration inflicted upon much of the continent by totalitarian regimes. We will get to such issues in due course, but firstly it may be efficacious to examine with more precision how Eurimages works on an elemental level.

Simply put, Eurimages aims to support integration within the European film industry and does so by providing interest-free loans to film productions which are repaid if and when they turn a profit. To this end, the body requires that to be considered for funding, all submitted projects must have at least two co-producers from different member states of the fund.[2] As such, Eurimages requires of its contributors a base level of transnational cooperation, even if this is not guaranteed to result in a pluralist European final product. Such cooperation is embedded in the fund from the outset given that it is paid for by member states who contribute annual membership rates. With a current annual budget of €25 million, however, Eurimages must be selective in the films it chooses to finance, and to this end, the appeal of proven and distinguished players, such as Michael Haneke and Lars von Trier, should be obvious. Yet this same reliance can also create several difficulties, whether falling back on English and French as a lingua franca[3] or on an entrenched auteur system that has tended to override considerations of genre in a European context, including studies on European sf. The former trend is evident in all three films that are treated here in depth, with both *Iron Sky* and *Melancholia* shot in English and *Time of the Wolf* in French, and while the cheerfully trashy *Iron Sky* hints that a bias toward auteur cinema is far from total, it remains something of an exception to wider rules as we will soon see. At any rate, Thomas Elsaesser, for one, has suggested that EU funding bodies are less concerned with onscreen realities than with creating an economic illusion of an integrated European cinema, stressing that 'without their content being necessarily multicultural or trans-national, these national-international films help to make cinema part of the process of European Union integration' (*European Cinema: Face to Face with Hollywood* 506). In this vein, one can easily draw parallels between, on the one hand, idealistic calls for European integration and the regular bureaucratic fudges that the pursuit of such ideals entail and, on the other, the struggle to reconcile a desire for a European cinema with the nationally and regionally specific tensions such a process ignites. As Karen Diehl has noted, 'European policy representatives uniformly claim film to be an expression of cultural identity, but more often than not it is left to national or regional support programmes to consider such matters', while Europe-wide funding bodies instead base their support primarily upon 'financial criteria and on the requirement that these films be multinational collaborations' ('A Conflicted Passion' 243). This ambiguity is not aided by Eurimages, which, though described by Elsaesser as an EU body, is in fact independent of the organisation, despite the two sharing a common flag.

Selecting films on the basis of artistic and production criteria,[4] Eurimages issues four calls for projects each year, with ultimate funding decisions falling on the Eurimages board of management once projects are first deemed to be eligible by its secretariat. The board, which consists of representatives from each member state of the fund and is currently under the stewardship of Catherine Trautmann, a former French government minister and MEP, avails of the services of independent professional script readers in coming to their final decision ('Financial Regulations'). While its productive aims are plain enough, Eurimages' cultural purpose remains ambiguous: it has, for instance, seemingly backed away from a previous (and somewhat problematic) mission statement that it 'endeavours to support works which reflect the multiple facets of a European society whose common roots are evidence of a single culture' ('Financial Regulations'). Perhaps mindful of the loaded question of how one defines a single culture, Eurimages has since toned down its language and now claims simply to promote 'the European audiovisual industry by providing financial support to feature films, animations and documentaries produced in Europe [...] in doing so, it encourages co-operation between professionals established in different European countries' ('Eurimages Support' 4). Here a further layer of ambiguity arises, however, one that highlights a fundamental difference between the CoE and the EU. Unlike the latter body, which is *currently* composed of 28 member states, the CoE counts 47 countries amongst its membership including nations such as Albania, Bosnia and Herzegovina, Georgia, and Turkey that for a myriad of reasons remain outside the EU. Furthermore, the CoE has a broad interpretation of Europe, stretching eastward to encompass Azerbaijan, Armenia, and the Russian Federation, for example, while its more aspirational mandate ensures that, unlike the EU, it needn't be curtailed by the latent fears, human rights issues, and abundant historical red herrings that help keep Europe west of the Bosporus. It is important to point out, however, that only 37 of these nations are members of Eurimages, with an inadvertent preview of things to come provided by the UK electing to cancel its membership in 1996. The recent addition of Canada as the 38th and first non-European member of the fund, moreover, reflects the impact of globalisation upon European film industries and shines a light on the ultimate fiscal pragmatism of this 'European' body.[5]

While it is not Eurimages' stated intention that every funded film must glowingly endorse European integration, it is also significant to highlight that the maximum outlay it will provide for any one film is €500,000[6] and that any 'financial support shall not exceed seventeen per cent of the total production cost of the film' ('Eurimages Support' 9). In other words, although it deploys a point system to verify how 'European' a production might be, there is no suggestion that Eurimages dictates that content must reflect its integrationist ethos. It does, however, as Rosalind Galt has noted, 'define the parameters within which production choices are made' ('Functionary of Mankind' 238) and expressly states in its regulations that 'projects of a blatantly pornographic nature or advocating violence or openly inciting to a violation of human rights are not eligible' ('Eurimages Support' 6) Yet in its avowal of a European cinema, Eurimages is complicit in sustaining a chimeric brand, an entity that in Elsaesser's words 'does not exist, except as a bureaucratic dream or a promotional tool for national producers and distributors of art house films' ('Postheroic Narrative' 703). It is thus, in many respects, a paradigm of European technocracy, one where conceptions of Europeanness itself are measurable by frequently arbitrary criteria. For feature-length projects, Eurimages assesses the 'European character' of films via a point system that awards points for the nationality and/or residence of key personnel. Employing an eligible director will earn a project three points, as will the presence of an eligible scriptwriter and lead actor. A suitable main supporting actor is worth two points meanwhile, while all other roles including cinematographer, editor, and art director are worth one point each ('Eurimages Support'). To be considered for funding, a production must secure at least 15 out of the 19 available points.

OFFICIALLY SANCTIONED EUROPEAN SF

Although Eurimages has not traditionally been a prolific backer of sf, it has of late been receptive to the genre and in addition to *Time of the Wolf*, *Melancholia*, and *Iron Sky* has part-funded films such as *Metropia* (Tarik Saleh 2009), *Mr. Nobody* (Jaco Van Dormael 2009), *Womb* (Benedek Fliegauf 2010), *Vanishing Waves* (Kristina Buožytė 2012), *The Lobster* (Yorgos Lanthimos 2015), and *Jupiter's Moon* (Kornél Mundruczó 2017). The latter three films are in many ways paradigmatic examples of auteurist European sf and will be examined in closer detail in Chaps. 3 and 5, while I will analyse *Metropia* in Chap. 6. It should be noted, however, that all these films were at least partially shot in English, and all, with the exceptions of *Iron Sky*, *Vanishing Waves*, and *Jupiter's Moon*, feature Hollywood stars, thus providing a level of insurance against the genre's struggle for commercial success in a European context. *Mr. Nobody* exemplifies this conservatism insofar as it was shot in English with Jared Leto in the lead role and benefited from a budget of some €33 million, making it the most expensive Belgian-directed film of all time. Its dismal performance at the box office[7] highlights how funding sf is not an actuarial science, yet to a degree this is beside the point, for although Eurimages presumably failed to recoup its outlay of €600,000, its institutional aspirations were met by the collaboration of film professionals and financiers from Belgium, Germany, France, and the UK, as well as Canada and the United States. Tarik Saleh's animated sf *Metropia* is also Anglophone despite having a Swedish director and production crew, while it features Hollywood actors Vincent Gallo and Juliette Lewis. The comparatively modest budget of 34 million SEK (around €3.75 million) meanwhile, ensured that the financial risks were never likely to be enormous, even with Eurimages' considerable €400,000 investment, figures that are near identical to those of *Womb* which features Eva Green and Matt Smith and was produced for an estimated €3,660,000, €440,000 of which was provided by Eurimages. In all cases, moreover, *Iron Sky* excepted, the above films can be classified as 'arthouse', sombre in tone, self-reflexive, and resistant to narrative expediency, and while their quality varies, they owe far more to a mode of filmmaking embodied by Godard and others than to the predominantly narrative-driven sf historically produced by major Hollywood studios. The chimeric brand that the CoE seeks to sustain is indeed one that taps into a long-standing tradition of auteur cinema, one that I outline in the introduction to this book. Elsaesser describes Michael Haneke and Lars von Trier as poster children for this European mode of funding, noting that 'it is not unusual, for instance, to find up to a dozen different funding bodies and production companies listed in the credits of a Michael Haneke or Lars von Trier film' ('Postheroic' 703). This assumption is strengthened further when one considers that every Haneke film from *Code Unknown/Code inconnu* (2000) onwards has enjoyed backing from Eurimages, while von Trier's *Dancer in the Dark* (2000), *Manderlay* (2005), and *Melancholia* have all been part-funded by the body (as an up-and-coming director whose work has frequently drawn comparison with Haneke, Yorgos Lanthimos was ideally placed to profit from these developments, and his move into English language films should be viewed at least partially within this context). When grappling with the thorny issue of defining a European cinema then, a definition that in and of itself runs the risk of eradicating difference, the CoE and Eurimages are selective, as explicitly acknowledged by their former Executive Secretary Jan Vandierendonck, who stated that 'We only deal with the creme de la creme of European productions. Receiving Eurimages monies also holds a certain prestige, and our support opens doors' (Hofmann, 'Eurimages Tries to Cut the Red Tape'). There are of course several practical reasons for this, even leaving aside the accountability of Eurimages as a publically funded body, chief amongst them being the public relations benefits that accrue from being associated with directors that enjoy pre-existing name recognition and prestige. Accordingly, when films such as Haneke's *The White Ribbon* and *Amour* win the Palme d'Or at Cannes, Eurimages and, with it, European integrationist strategies are implicitly and explicitly endorsed.

My rationale for choosing *Time of the Wolf*, *Melancholia*, and *Iron Sky* as case studies here is governed by several primary considerations, the first and most obvious being that Eurimages has not historically funded a raft of sf productions and certainly not those privy to wide-scale international release, a trend that thankfully seems to be slowly changing. Thematically, all three are concerned, at least in part, with the future of Europe, for which they each project an exceptionally bleak future. The gap between the release of Haneke's film and those of von Trier and Vuorensola furthermore allows for a broader focus so that more than contemporary anxieties about terrorism and the economy can be surveyed. More pressing still, Haneke has arguably been the most important and thought-provoking European director of the new millennium, someone whose films always attract investment from European funding agencies no matter that they frequently lampoon the disparity between the EU's purported ideals and its actual actions. Haneke himself is surely aware of this paradox, given that at the height of the Eurozone crisis, he wryly referred to himself in an interview with *Screen Daily* as being a 'poster boy for the success of the European financing system' (Hazelton 'Michael Haneke'). On a formal level moreover, *Time of the Wolf*'s ruminations on the war in the former Yugoslavia require that some of the bloodiest episodes of the twentieth century be engaged with in order to better understand the evolution of the EU in the twenty-first century. Lastly, all three films are paradigmatic of transnational production trends insofar as they are each funded by a wide coalition of international partners and thus perfectly embody the Eurimages model.

Time of the Wolf

Haneke's *Time of the Wolf*, to begin with, counts among its production companies Arte France Cinéma, France 3 Cinéma and Canal +, Bavaria Film from Germany, and the Austrian production company Wega Film, in addition to Eurimages. The film is voluble in its critique of modern-day Europe, albeit in a typically vague Hanekesque manner where location is abstracted and Europe is both everywhere and nowhere at once. As he later achieved with *The White Ribbon/Das weiße Band* (2009), Haneke places conceptualisations of nationhood and belonging at the centre of his narrative by conversely accentuating their absence.[8] To that extent, *Time of the Wolf* is by far the most vocal of the three films analysed here in its depiction of an alternate Europe, one where an unspecified disaster has led to widespread suffering and societal decay. It is post-apocalyptic in the same way that it is a critique, abstractly, and as such thwarts genre expectations while being of a piece with Haneke's wider oeuvre. Onscreen, Haneke's bleak mise en scène is pervasive, characterised by cinematographer Jürgen Jürges' shadowy long takes that work in tandem with the near unremitting darkness of the film's plot. Deliberately underlit, *Time of the Wolf* denudes the titillation often associated with a genre where the absence of societal rules and regulations can make even the most prosaic task an adventure. There are no fetishistic vistas of great cities aflame nor hedonistic grab-all-you-can sprees through empty supermarkets. Instead, we are deposited in a bleak landscape where the shock of the opening scene aside, violence is often threatened but seldom seen and never sensationalised. Where sf frequently works to make sure that 'the image is identifiable' and is careful to include 'culturally symbolic and discrete architectural features ... that makes its imminent destruction seem an immediate, contemporary event' (Sobchack, 'Cities on the Edge of Time: The Urban Science Fiction Film' 130), *Time of the Wolf* takes us far off the beaten track to a nameless state where cities and civilisation go unmentioned, save for a few brief snatches of dialogue that nevertheless refrain from referring to them by name.

Haneke is especially interesting because, as Galt has written, he is the closest individual imaginable to a pan-European auteur ('Functionary' 236), and as such his interpretation of dystopian sf filmmaking picks up on a tradition perpetuated by Godard and others, one whereby auteurs experiment with the genre and reconfigure its mechanics to suit their own ends. Unlike *Iron Sky*, which is campishly emphatic in its avowal of

Fig. 2.1 'The Laurents'

Fig. 2.2 'The "Intruders"'

sf tropes, or *Melancholia*, which internalises and perhaps even fetishises the end of the world, *Time of the Wolf* is dark, claustrophobic, and largely devoid of action, save for a brutal opening where the Laurent family (husband Georges [Daniel Duval], wife Anne [Isabelle Huppert], and their two children Ben [Lucas Biscombe] and Eva [Anaïs Demoustier]) are accosted in their rural home by a family of interlopers (see Figs. 2.1 and 2.2). Also comprising a father, mother, daughter, and son, the intruding family mirror the Laurents but are less white, less polished in their French, and are residing in the house illegally, at least as far as we can ascertain. Their patriarch shoots and kills Georges, thus setting the film's narrative in motion. The scene is highly provocative and projects ciphers onto its characters that are too obvious to be taken or indeed decoded at face value. Like, for example, Haneke's characterisation of Maria (Luminita Gheorghiu), the Romanian beggar in *Code Unknown*, the interloping family is almost stereotypically othered and stands in for any number of reductive right-wing fantasies centred on the theme of EU enlargement and the sanctity of national borders. In the Laurents, however, they encounter another parody, albeit a waspish middle-class one, a tabula rasa[9] whose heavy-handed coding as old-world, corduroy-clad bourgeoisie demarcates the interloping family and encodes them in opposition as other. This doubling strategy which pits the Laurents against uncanny doppelgangers is thus suggestive of the conflicts that Europeans routinely ignore, as well as the anxieties they wilfully suppress. The remaining Laurents are forced out into the wilderness to survive in a post-apocalyptic landscape where refugees gather listlessly at abandoned railway stations and physical and sexual violence against the most vulnerable is a regular occurrence.

The European terrain that the Laurents must navigate is a deliberate no man's land, notable only for its grey banality. We assume it is indeed continental because the characters speak French, but then we have been here before with Haneke; *The Piano Teacher/La pianiste* (2001), for example, was based in Vienna and on Elfriede Jelinek's German language novel *The Piano Teacher/Die Klavierspielerin* (1983), yet its protagonists speak French. This was no doubt due in part to Haneke's desire to cast Isabelle Huppert in the film's lead role, even if it's also worth noting that Eurimages' other official language, English, is one that Haneke seldom speaks publicly. As a production, *Time of the Wolf* is demonstrably European: it is filmed in Austria and funded by Austrian, French, and German backers, yet the irony is that the only European integration on display onscreen is one designed out of self-interest, one where a cabal of disparate characters bind together to survive at the expense of others. Context as ever is key here and if we wish to mine the film and the circumstances of its production for socio-political commentary in the grand tradition of sf, we might well conclude that *Time of the Wolf* ultimately takes aim at Europe itself and the failure of the European community to answer its neighbours' cries for help during the worst episodes of the Yugoslav Wars. *Time of the Wolf* was in fact first conceived of in 1993, at the height of the war in the former Yugoslavia, and as Evan

Torner has observed, 'the inability of the European Community to prevent the humanitarian crisis before it would escalate and assume genocidal features may have caused Haneke to consider how thoroughly unsafe for Europeans the present version of European civilization turned out to be' ('Civilization's Endless Shadow: Haneke's Time of the Wolf' 539). For Torner such paralysis is borne of bourgeois complacency as flagged from the outset by Georges' death, which signals 'the ineffectiveness of Enlightenment-style social negotiation and channels the macrocosmic violence of the off-screen apocalypse into the Laurent family's microcosm' ('Civilization's Endless Shadow' 535). Thinking he can placate the family (and that he understands both them and their motives), Georges calmly reasons with the armed man 'believing to the last that he is in control and can persuade him to accept a compromise' (Lykidis, 'Multi-cultural Encounters in Haneke's French Language Films' 460). That he is hopelessly misguided in his aims should not surprise us. Where turning a blind eye to struggles elsewhere is a luxury he could thus far afford, his adversaries call to mind a conflict where mass murder and rape camps were deployed as state-sanctioned measures.

By visually distancing his film from images of Europe as the EU or CoE would like to present it, Haneke lays bare the fallacy at the heart of European integration: namely, that integration only works in opposition to a concurrent process of exclusion. Official Europe's historic failure to come to its neighbours' aid during the Yugoslav Wars is evocative of a mob mentality in reverse, one where the herd provides sanctuary for those who wish to avoid action. Where the relinquishing of national sovereignty is ordinarily decried at moments of crisis (if in doubt, just look at the outcry that greeted the acceptance of Troika bailouts in EU member states at the height of the Eurozone crisis), Haneke's native Austria was able to point to its membership and adherence to the tenets of the UN (it did not join the EU until 1995) as sufficient grounds for ignoring genocide and mass rape on its very doorstep in neighbouring Yugoslavia. The chickens, it seems, have come home to roost, and while Alex Lykidis is correct in his assertion that *Time of the Wolf* channels 'the rhetoric of "invasion" and emphasis on residential spaces in recent anti-immigrant discourse' ('Multicultural Encounters' 459)—it was after all released a year before the largest EU expansion in history—Haneke's weary diagnosis of the failures of modern Europe also evinces a broader, historical sweep. In fact, Haneke transfers the Yugoslav conflict directly into the heart of the EU, a process he achieves by defamiliarising the landscape and in so doing gesturing towards the arbitrary nature of borders in a post-apocalyptic world. On a formal level, this empties out CoE rhetoric by exposing the crevice that exists between its aspirations and realities, a gap most recently exposed by the body's allegedly corrupt relationship with Azerbaijan.[10] In fact, *Time of the Wolf*'s European post-apocalypse is uncannily like stolid daily reality elsewhere (for a contemporary nightmarish equivalent one need look no further than Syria), and how we delineate 'European' becomes problematic in the extreme when it comes to turning our backs on the plight of others. Haneke traces this link to its gradual conclusion. He visually ties Europe's inaction towards atrocities in Kosovo and Srebrenica to the moral paralysis that enabled the Nazis to rise to power, by repeatedly cutting to shots of eerie ghost trains that rattle through the scorched earth of his post-apocalyptic world, much as death trains circumnavigated rural Poland en route to Auschwitz. These trains also put the question of Austria's culpability in historical context by calling to mind the Alpine Republic's post-war 'first victim' status, a dexterous sleight of hand that was tolerated at the time in the name of European integration. While some scholars have detected some hope in *Time of the Wolf*, Roy Grundmann, for instance, suggests that the myriad examples of ethnic and class conflict on display 'also implies the possibility of a utopia—if these parties were able to create a new, more democratic, and genuinely pluralistic society' ('Haneke's Anachronism' 33), Haneke, whose film is part-funded by a body that champions such laudable aims, seems to suggest that the time for utopia has passed and dystopia instead will be the new normal. The film ends with a static shot facing out from within one of the ghost trains, and while Haneke's intentions may be ambiguous, we should, based on all evidence, expect the worst. As an incredulous neighbour at one point exclaims to Anne Laurent: 'You really don't know what's going on? Or are you just acting stupid?'

Melancholia

Melancholia is in some ways just as abstruse as *Time of the Wolf* and has been analysed from a multitude of standpoints, in keeping with the oft-divisive effect that von Trier's work tends to have on critics. A Danish/Swedish/French/German co-production that features no fewer than 20 separate production companies among its credits, *Melancholia* (as with many of von Trier's releases) benefited hugely from transnational cooperation and the opening-up of European markets. Ostensibly the film is centred round the activities of sisters Justine (Kirsten Dunst) and Claire (Charlotte Gainsbourg) during a wedding feast that coincides with the advancement of a rogue planet (Melancholia) into the earth's orbit, setting in train a collision course that will likely wipe out both the earth and humankind. The feast in question is in honour of newlyweds Justine and Michael (Alexander Skarsgård) and is held on Claire and her husband John's (Kiefer Sutherland) vast country estate. As Robert Sinnerbrink has noted, 'what *Melancholia* shares with more arthouse "end of days" movies, however, is the manner in which the apocalypse [...] is reflected or refracted by a familial drama or melodrama', a trait he also observes in *Time of the Wolf* 'with its "biopolitical" focus on a mother and her two children reduced to "bare life"' ('Anatomy of Melancholia' 113). At the same time, the impending catastrophe is also strongly tied to Justine's acute depression, which leads her to behave increasingly erratically as the narrative unfolds. On a superficial level, the film has links to Nazism as a consequence of von Trier's provocations at the 2011 Cannes Film Festival, where he was declared 'persona non-grata' by the Cannes board of directors after he 'sympathised' with Hitler, praised Albert Speer, and referred to himself as a Nazi (Higgins, 'Lars von Trier Provokes Cannes with "I'm a Nazi" Comments'), and more spuriously in its devotion to German Romanticism and Richard Wagner, yet it does not call Europe's troubled past into question in the manner of Haneke's stark parable. Unlike *Manderlay* or *Dancer in the Dark*—von Trier's previous Eurimages-backed productions, which are nominally based in Alabama and Washington State, respectively—*Melancholia* is set in Sweden even if the film features a cohort of international actors and makes little play of national specificity. Keen to sidestep outward political statements, *Melancholia* instead juxtaposes the personal with the collective and in Sarah French and Zoë Shacklock's poetic description: 'works centrifugally, scattering Justine's battle with depression across the unfathomable scale of the universe' ('The Affective Sublime' 347). Beginning with a beguiling series of tableaux vivants set to Wagner's opera *Tristan and Isolde*, the film is in constant dialogue with European art history and culture, even if it is incapable of seeing a future for the arts, or humankind itself, beyond the impending apocalypse. In Sinnerbrink's terms, *Melancholia* is a fusion of 'Dogme-style melodrama, apocalyptic disaster movie, and mock-Wagnerian Gesamtkunstwerk' that combines 'Bergmanesque psychodrama and Tarkovskian melancholia, Schopenhauerian pessimism and German romanticism', an impressive list to which we might add

Resnais-like flattening of time and Kierkegaardian angst ('Anatomy of Melancholia' 111). Where the largely silent *Time of the Wolf* gives the briefest of nods to this same cultural heritage via the strains of Beethoven's 'Violin Sonata No. 5' overheard from a Walkman (an occurrence that Peter Brunette described as a 'rather obvious signifier ... of the threatened but defiantly inextinguishable voice of "civilization"' (*Michael Haneke* 110)), von Trier revels in creating an apocalypse that is as much cultural as it is anthropocentric. Therefore, where the sparse *Time of the Wolf* seeks to draw attention to such details by omission, *Melancholia* radiates with overt intertextual fullness, in its prologue at least, which references amongst others the works of Andrei Tarkovsky, Alain Resnais, Ingmar Bergman, William Shakespeare, John Everett Millais, and Pieter Bruegel the Elder, before giving way to more familiar Dogme aesthetics, including the use of improvised dialogue, natural lighting, and defiantly shaky hand-held cameras. Such intertextuality is not unusual for von Trier, who, ever since signing the Dogme 95 Manifesto (or 'vow of chastity') with Thomas Vinterberg in 1995, has sought to position himself both as a continuation of and as a response to modernist, auteur-centric European cinematic traditions.[11] The reversion to a minimalist and stripped-bare style after the extended prologue cannot redress the imbalance of a world tilting off its axis; far from gesturing towards any pretence at realism, it simply offers another statement in the film's ongoing dialogue with the history of European cinema.

Released at the height of the worst financial crisis to hit Europe since the end of the Second World War, the film wryly comments on the bloated fin de siècle decadence of late-capitalist Europe, albeit through a knowingly ironic hyper-aestheticisation that itself runs the risk of indulgent excess. The melancholic here can be traced to the hollowness of consumption, for even in the throes of what should nominally be one of life's high points, the conspicuous opulence of her surrounds (nineteenth-century castle, full-scale golf course, stables, etc.) does little to assuage Justine's growing sense of emptiness and dread. There is, in other words, no way of escaping the coming crisis, endorsing Sinnerbrink's contestation that *Melancholia* operates as 'an allegory of the unsustainable character of the globalised consumer capitalism, and of our inability to envisage a different world as our own confronts the threat of cascading ecological, economic, and geopolitical crises' ('Anatomy of Melancholia' 113). Indeed, a conspicuous degree of financial insouciance is foregrounded as a motif from the outset, when the newly married Justine and Michael's lavish stretch limousine proves too large to navigate the narrow road leading to their wedding reception. Despite its seeming innocuousness, the scene in question opens 'Part One' of the film (which is titled simply 'Justine') and lasts for a full three minutes as the limo driver tries in vain to extricate his comically oversized vehicle (darkness falls before Justine and Michael eventually arrive to the reception on foot). Alive to the absurdity, Michael teasingly asks the driver if he can hear him 'up there', before greeting the resultant silence with the terse observation that he must be 'in a different county'. The newlyweds' casual approach to timekeeping earns the opprobrium of the awaiting Claire and John who remind them that amongst other expenses, they have enlisted (and are thus wasting) the services of 'the most expensive wedding planner on the planet'.[12] A state of tension is thus immediately established, and despite the celebrations, a growing sense of unease becomes palpable.

Although *Melancholia* is seldom explicit about such things, at the time of its release, EU citizens had been besieged by doom-mongering and sensational media headlines predicting the end of the EU itself for well over three years. Greece lay teetering on the edge of an abyss, threatening to spread contagion across the Eurozone, a post-apocalyptic scenario playing out in real life and one that, as I have alluded to in the introduction to this book, was heavily coded with sf vernacular. A telling opinion piece in *The Guardian* published in the wake of the film's release indeed compares media coverage of the Eurozone's travails to *Melancholia*, noting that 'the Eurozone crisis has begun to resemble the giant planet in Lars von Trier's *Melancholia*' before presciently adding that 'one thing is certain, that its press is lurching towards an abyss of catastrophe metaphors' (Gerry Feehily 'European Press Reaction'). Sweden of course remains outside of the Eurozone, but like other EU members, it was still affected by rising unemployment figures (in 2010, 9.6 per cent of EU citizens were unemployed, while in Sweden the figure was at 8.6 per cent).[13] The gloom that descended over Europe re-enacted familiar political choreographies, chief among them a resurgence of the far-right (and here Sweden was no exception) and a general retrenchment into nationally specific concerns such as budget deficits, border control, and national sovereignty. Ironically, all such issues depended on wider fortunes within the EU, which after the Lisbon Treaty carried such economic clout that, together with the IMF and the European Central Bank, it largely rendered national parliaments redundant anyway. Here the film industry was no exception, with Eurimages' outlay in 2010 (the year that it contributed €600,000 to *Melancholia*) dwindling to just over €19 million, the lowest recorded rate since 2002 ('Co-Production Funding in 2010'). *Melancholia* then is not just concerned by the financial crisis, it was shaped by it. The intensely personal nature of von Trier's apocalypse is achieved via a depersonalising spiral of events that leave Justine feeling abandoned, helpless, and finally contemptuous of the opulence that surrounds her. In this regard, *Melancholia* is bound up with the financial crisis both temporally and figuratively, in that it presents a looming outside threat that will render all other considerations, be they social, economic, or political moot. A 'magic cave' she erects for her nephew Leo (Cameron Spurr) lends added poignancy to the film's closing scene where Justine, Leo, and Claire sit helplessly inside the crude tepee-like wooden structure as Melancholia crashes into the earth. Knowing fully well their fate, they nevertheless seek solace in the familiar. Their symbolic gesture towards a unifying domestic space testifies to the hollowness of the recognisable, the local, and the self-contained when set against the maelstrom of an external threat that is oblivious to human-imposed boundaries.

Iron Sky

Seeking solace in the familiar is a charge that can readily be attributed to Timo Vuorensola, the Finnish director of the avowedly silly 2012 release *Iron Sky*. Set in the near future of 2018, Vuorensola's film imagines a world under attack from a colony of Nazis who had fled to the moon in the aftermath of the Second World War. Although hampered by a reliance on 1940s technology, the moon Nazis plot to invade the earth, with the ultimate goal of establishing a Fourth Reich. Leaning heavily on familiar parody sf tropes (its premise notably borrows strongly from Corrado Guzzanti and Igor Skofic's *Fascists on Mars/Fascisti su Marte* (2006)), *Iron Sky* lampoons the self-interest and internecine squabbling of the international alliance charged with facing down the Nazis, just as it sends up the adolescent morbidity of the Third Reich. Vuorensola himself has remarked on the film's intention to essay 'the stupidity of the human race, from the Nazis all the way to our wonderful international leaders today' (Ward, 'Nazis on the Moon' 63), and while Europe itself is largely marginalised in favour of drawing links between the Nazis and the US Republican Party, it does raise the spectre of larger power struggles in an arena where the EU is but a smaller player. Sure enough, after the UN alliance, under the command of a Sarah Palinesque-US president, eventually defeats the Nazis, the Americans claim on the moon's gas reserves triggers a firefight among the UN fleet who proceed to blow one another to smithereens at the film's conclusion. Furthermore, Vuorensola insists upon the film's thematic relevance by pointing to a resurgence of far-right movements across Europe in recent times, one he attributes to the financial crisis, which, he notes, 'has always been a great breeding ground for fascist ideologies' (Rosenfeld, *Hi Hitler!* 202). In this vein, while *Iron Sky*'s success as a comedy is open to question, its ridiculing of authoritarianism seems apropos given the present moment's vogue for political strongmen who, like all autocrats, exude more than a faint whiff of the ridiculous.

Especially interesting is the film's production: in addition to monies from Eurimages, *Iron Sky* benefited from crowdfunding as well as studio backing from Finland, Germany, and Australia. After a protracted seven-year advertising and funding drive, which included Vuorensola shopping a trailer for his then-prospective film at the 2006 Cannes Film Festival, *Iron Sky* sourced €1.2 million of its overall budget of €7.5 million from crowdfunding, €300,000 of which came from investors who were required to spend a minimum of €1, the rest from those ready to spend upward of €1,000 on the production (Baranova and Lugmayr, 'Crowd Intelligence in Independent Film Productions' 184). Accordingly, the film's narrative and production strategies coalesce, a point convincingly put forward by Chuck Tryon in a detailed account of *Iron Sky*'s production history entitled 'Iron Sky's War Bonds: Cult Sf Cinema and Crowdsourcing', wherein he writes that 'while *Iron Sky*'s narrative makes use of what might appear to be a prefabricated cult approach, the filmmakers also positioned the project as a cult artefact at the level of production and distribution' (125). In conversation with Pietari Kääpä, Vuorensola emphasised a hope that his film's use of crowdfunding in particular would serve as an 'inspiration and a way forth that will encourage Finnish, European and universal film production to combat the overpowering presence of the US film industry' ('A Culture of Reciprocity: The Politics of Cultural Exchange in Contemporary Nordic Genre Film' 256). Therefore, where *Melancholia* and *Time of the Wolf* are very much of the auteurist tradition and thus go to considerable lengths to circumvent generic codes, *Iron Sky* avowedly locates its narrative within both Hollywood sf canons (its tagline 'The Reich Strikes Back' most obviously channelling both Nazism and *Star Wars*) and, more curiously, within a history of European genre cinema that stumbles on often in pastiche form. In the latter instance, one need but think of Sergio Leone and Sergio Corbucci's initially cheap and cheerful ruminations on the Western, for example, or of the farcical 'alternate worlds' offered up by Eastern bloc directors in the 1980s (a prototypical example being Juliusz Machulski's *Sexmission/Seksmisja* (1984), which locates its critique of the ruling Polish communists in a post-nuclear future world governed entirely by women).

More specifically still, in its flirtation with Nazi chic, and in particular in its sexualised depiction of its central female protagonist Renate Richter (Julia Dietze)—an impressionable young moon Nazi who falls in love with an American astronaut (Christopher Kirby)—*Iron Sky* follows in the footsteps of the 1970s European 'Nazisploitation' subgenre, which began promisingly enough with Liliana Cavani's divisive *The Night Porter/Il portiere di notte* (1974) before reaching a nadir with the likes of *The Gestapo's Last Orgy/L'ultima orgia del III Reich* (Cesare Canavari 1977) and *SS Girls/Casa privata per le SS* (Bruno Mattei 1977).

Despite its fantastical premise then, *Iron Sky* can certainly be located within European cinema history. A salient difficulty with the film, however, stems in large part from its drawn-out production history. Upon release *Iron Sky*'s political critique already seemed hopelessly dated, not least in its fixation with Sarah Palin some four years after her failed turn as a vice presidential nominee.[14] The Palin obsession undermines Vuorensola's rebuke of American cinema, all the more so because his film is wholly reliant upon viewers' appreciation of Hollywood films for its comedy.[15] Furthermore, Europe's diminished place in the new world order is confirmed by the Nazis' decision to focus their attack on New York, and while the United States and its international allies succeed in overcoming their enemy, they turn on one another at the film's end, a nuclear war seemingly obliterating the planet in a direct lift from *Dr. Strangelove* (Stanley Kubrick 1964), which, of course, also featured a cartoonish Nazi struggling to come to terms with a post-Reich world. Although *Iron Sky*'s quirkiness may link it to modern-day Scandinavian auteurs such as von Trier, Aki Kaurismaki or Nicolas Winding Refn, directors whom, Kääpä observes 'also display playful uses of commercial genre conventions', its highly derivative narrative owes just 'as much to early Sam Raimi and Peter Jackson' as to its 'national cultural and cinematic histories' ('A Culture of Reciprocity' 245). While *Iron Sky*'s political skewering lacks focus, however, its central premise of an unwieldy, incoherent alliance warding off the threat of extreme nationalism should be familiar enough to contemporary European audiences, not to mention its backers at the CoE and Eurimages.

FUNDING THE DREAM

The role of Eurimages in financing European sf is by no means pervasive and while the body has funded several sf productions, it has done so rather sporadically. Furthermore, it has shown a certain propensity for hedging its bets, as a cursory glance at some of its sf films illustrates. The names of

Michael Haneke and Lars von Trier, as discussed earlier, of course lend prestige to prospective investors and it is probably true that Haneke, in particular, could shoot a sequel to the live action version of *The Smurfs* and still enjoy CoE backing. That said, in the global context, Eurimages is but a minor player, given its €25 million annual budget and its reliance upon member states to contribute financially to the fund. Certain directors will therefore always be attractive to Eurimages, just as prospective films need to prove their financial independence by guaranteeing the support of at least two production companies before qualifying for consideration. A pragmatist in this situation would bet against sf, for although the genre has proven immensely profitable in the United States, any European consideration needs to be seen against the wider contexts of the continent's often troublesome relationship with genre in general. Unlike private investors, Eurimages' aim is to support the European film industry, and thus we should not be overly surprised that it chooses to do so largely to the exclusion of sf, a traditionally marginalised genre in Europe (even if, as this book aims to demonstrate, this is beginning to change). Indeed, the genre refuses to die, and in this context, institutionally embedded dystopian critiques of Europe such as *Time of the Wolf*, *Melancholia*, and *Iron Sky* are to be welcomed, all the more so given their scarcity. Like that of the EU, the CoE's public mission statement is one of inclusiveness, prosperity, and fraternity, and Eurimages seeks to perpetuate these same ideals, not through a hard-line editorial stance on content but via an insistence on cross-border co-production. Therefore, while films such as those analysed here may at times fly in the face of such aspirations, their existence alone tacitly endorses the European project on a macro-industrial level.

NOTES

1. As Liz writes: 'since its establishment, Eurimages has supported 1266 European co-productions for a total amount of approximately €375 million—a sum which represents half of the budget for MEDIA's last phase' (*Euro-Visions* 37).
2. Membership fees are supplemented by additional sources. In its most recent financial regulations document which was agreed in 2016, Eurimages includes amongst these sources: 'voluntary contributions, sums derived from reimbursements or cancellations of support, the interest earned on the Fund's financial assets, miscellaneous receipts and all other payments, donations or legacies' ('Financial Regulations').

3. Such as Rosalind Galt notes, she writes that Haneke's 'choice [to make his major films in French] speaks to the dominance of France not only in film funding but as the privileged language of international European cinema' ('The Functionary of Mankind' 234–235).
4. Stated artistic criteria used to decipher the quality of a project include 'story and theme (originality of content, subject); characters and dialogue; narrative structure'; and 'style (director's intention, cinematic vision, genre, tone)'. The feasibility of completion, in turn, is measured against the experience and track records of the director and writer, producers, and cast and crew. Stated production criteria, meanwhile, take into account 'artistic and technical co-operation; circulation potential (festivals, distribution, audience)' and 'consistency and level of confirmed financing' ('Eurimages Support' 9).
5. Eurimages President Catherine Trautmann hailed Canada's membership of the fund, declaring that 'it will bring new opportunities for producers on both sides of the Atlantic in a sector that increasingly works on a global scale' ('Canada Strengthens Its Cultural and Economic Ties with Europe').
6. The outward figure of €500,000 is a new limit set by Eurimages, as prior to 2013 the figure was potentially higher (as was the case with *Melancholia*, which received €600,000).
7. *Mr. Nobody* grossed a paltry $3622 domestically, while its overseas gross was tallied at little over $2 million ('Mr Nobody').
8. Despite the promise offered by its full title of *Das weiße Band—Eine deutsche Kindergeschichte* and its depiction of a generation that would vote Hitler into power, *The White Ribbon* takes pains to avoid direct reference to Germany. As I argue elsewhere, 'it takes a particular kind of director to make a film about a nation without once mentioning it by name. Yet, this same refusal to identify is at its core a salient tenet of Haneke's work' ('Dance Me to the End of Love: Community and Impending Doom in Michael Haneke's Das weiße band and John Ford's West' 120).
9. All of Haneke's French language films (*Code Unknown/Code inconnu: Récit incomplet de divers voyages* (2000), *Time of the Wolf*, *Hidden/Caché* (2005), *Love/Amour* (2012), *Happy End* (2017)) feature central characters called Georges and Anne, with the exception of *La pianiste/The Piano Teacher* (2001), which, though shot in French, is based in Vienna. As such, we should, in Michael Lawrence's terms, view these characters as 'incarnations or reincarnations rather than distinct fictional human individuals realistically represented in consecutive films' ('Haneke's Stable' 75).
10. Azerbaijan, which has been part of the CoE since 2001, is one of several member states to openly flout the body's seeming commitment to transparent democratic values (Russia and Turkey being two other obvious examples). A recent investigation into the Azerbaijan-related activities of the Parliamentary Assembly of the Council of Europe, which was published in

April 2018, seemingly corroborates long-held suspicions about alleged corruption in the body. The report states that members of the assembly are strongly suspected of accepting bribes from the Azerbaijani government, which, the German broadcaster *Deutsche Welle* reported, conducted 'lobbying activities' to 'silence criticism from the human rights body in exchange for gifts and money in what the report termed "caviar diplomacy"' (Burack, 'Ex-President of Council of Europe Assembly Under Fire for Azerbaijan-linked Corruption').

11. For Caroline Bainbridge, author of *The Cinema of Lars von Trier*, the ultimate goal of what she describes as von Trier's 'encyclopaedic oeuvre' and 'eclectic intertextuality' is to both display the director's 'extensive knowledge and appreciation of film' and to align himself 'with the magisterial qualities associated with the greatest moments in cinema history' (1).

12. French and Shacklock single John out for special mention in their analysis of the film, writing that '*Melancholia* is critical of the hollowness and meaninglessness of contemporary bourgeois society, embodied in the film by the figure of John and his grand estate situated on an 18-hole golf course' ('The Affective Sublime' 350).

13. Allowing for seasonal adjustment, the EU's own figures state that unemployment figures rose from 9.0 per cent in 2002 to 9.6 per cent by 2010, while in Sweden the figure is more acute still given the post-1990s strength of its economy, rising from 6.0 per cent to 8.6 per cent in the same period ('Statistics Explained').

14. Writing in *Sight and Sound*, for example, Kim Newman noted that 'the film has been in production so long that some of its best jokes are now backlist items – like the North Korean delegate mocked in the UN when he claims that the unidentified attacking spacecraft were personally designed and built by his "great leader"' ('Moon Kampf' 44).

15. Iron Sky's *IMDb* page alone cites references to *Dr. Strangelove*, *The Great Dictator* (Charlie Chaplin 1940), *THX 1138* (George Lucas 1971), *Jaws* (Steven Spielberg 1975), *Star Wars: Episode IV-A New Hope* (George Lucas 1977), *Apocalypse Now* (Francis Ford Coppola 1979), *Crocodile Dundee* (Peter Faiman 1986), and *The Matrix Revolutions* (Lana and Lily Wachowski 2003).

Bibliography

Bainbridge, Caroline. 2007. *The Cinema of Lars von Trier*. London: Wallflower.

Baranova, Darya, and Artur Lugmayr. 2013. Crowd Intelligence in Independent Film Productions. In *Proceedings of the 17th International Academic Mindtrek Conference*, ed. Artur Lugmayr et al., 182–186. ACM.

Brunette, Peter. 2010. *Michael Haneke*. Urbana: University of Illinois Press.

Burack, Cristina. 2018. Ex-President of Council of Europe Assembly Under Fire for Azerbaijan-Linked Corruption. *DW*, April 26. www.dw.com/en/ex-president-of-council-of-europe-assembly-under-fire-for-azerbaijan-linked-corruption/a-43540198. Accessed 1 May 2018.

Canada Strengthens Its Cultural and Economic Ties with Europe. 2017. *Market Wired*, March 15. www.marketwired.com/press-release/canada-strengthens-its-cultural-and-economic-ties-with-europe-2203168.htm. Accessed 1 May 2018.

Co-Production Funding in 2010. 2010. *Eurimages*, December 21. www.coe.int/en/web/eurimages/co-production-funding-in-2010#M2010. Accessed 1 May 2018.

Diehl, Karen. 2012. A Conflicted Passion. In *Europe and Love in Cinema*, ed. Luisa Passerini, Jo Labanyi, and Karen Diehl, 239–262. Bristol: Intellect.

Elsaesser, Thomas. 2005. *European Cinema: Face to Face with Hollywood*. Amsterdam: University of Amsterdam.

———. 2012. European Cinema and the Postheroic Narrative: Jean-Luc Nancy, Claire Denis, and Beau Travail. *New Literary History* 43 (4): 703–725.

Eurimages Support for Co-production: Feature-Length Fiction, Animation and Documentary Films. 2018. *Eurimages*, January 1. sf.coe.int/t/dg4/eurimages/Source/Regulations/Co-ProductionRegulations2015_EN.pdf. Accessed 1 May 2018.

Feehily, Gerry. 2011. European Press Reaction: Papandreou's Referendum and the Euro Crisis. *Guardian*, November 2.

Financial Regulations of the Support Fund for the Co-Production and Distribution of Creative Cinematographic and Audiovisual Works. 2016. *Eurimages*, October 21. rm.coe.int/eurimages-financial-regulations-of-the-support-fund-for-the-co-product/16807327d5. Accessed 1 May 2018.

French, Sarah, and Zoë Shacklock. 2014. The Affective Sublime in Lars von Trier's Melancholia and Terrance Malick's The Tree of Life. *New Review of Film and Television Studies* 12 (4): 339–356.

Galt, Rosalind. 2010. The Functionary of Mankind: Haneke and Europe. In *On Michael Haneke*, ed. Brian Price and John David Rhodes, 221–242. Detroit: Wayne State University Press.

Grundmann, Roy. 2010. Haneke's Anachronism. In *A Companion to Michael Haneke*, ed. Roy Grundmann, 1–50. Oxford: Wiley-Blackwell.

Halle, Randall. 2014. *Europeanization of Cinema: Interzones and Imaginative Communities*. Urbana: University of Illinois.

Hazelton, John. 2012. Michael Haneke. *Screen Daily*, November 23. www.screendaily.com/michael-haneke/5049313.article. Accessed 1 May 2018.

Higgins, Charlotte. 2011. Lars von Trier Provokes Cannes with "I'm a Nazi" Comments. *Guardian*, May 18.

Hofmann, Katja. 2017. Eurimages Tries to Cut the Red Tape. *Variety*, November 21.

Kääpä, Pietari. 2015. A Culture of Reciprocity: The Politics of Cultural Exchange in Contemporary Nordic Genre Film. In *Nordic Genre Film: Small Nation Film Cultures in the Global Marketplace*, ed. Tommy Gustafsson and Pietari Kääpä, 244–261. Edinburgh: Edinburgh University Press.
Kern, Stephen. 1983. *The Culture of Time and Space, 1880–1918*. Cambridge, MA: Harvard University Press.
Liz, Mariana. 2016. *Euro-Visions: Europe in Contemporary Cinema*. New York: Bloomsbury.
Lykidis, Alex. 2010. Multi-Cultural Encounters in Haneke's French Language Films. In *A Companion to Michael Haneke*, ed. Roy Grundmann, 455–476. Oxford: Wiley-Blackwell.
Mr Nobody. 2013. *Bomb Report*. bombreport.com/yearly-breakdowns/2013-2/mr-nobody/.
Newman, Kim. 2012. Moon Kampf. *Sight and Sound* 22 (5), May.
Pasha-Robinson, Lucy. 2017. Marine Le Pen says France Should Seek to Renegotiate EU Membership. *Independent*, January 5.
Rivi, Luisa. 2007. *European Cinema After 1989: Identity and Transnational Production*. New York: Palgrave Macmillan.
Rosenfeld, Gavriel D. 2014. *Hi Hitler!* Cambridge: Cambridge University Press.
Schengen: Enlargement of Europe's Border-Free Area. 2018. *European Parliament*, February 23. www.europarl.europa.eu/news/en/headlines/security/20180216STO98008/schengen-enlargement-of-europe-s-border-free-area. Accessed 1 May 2018.
Sinnerbrink, Robert. 2014. Anatomy of Melancholia. *Angelaki: Journal of the Theoretical Humanities* 19 (4): 111–126.
Sobchack, Vivian. 1999. Cities on the Edge of Time: The Urban Science Fiction Film. In *Alien Zone II: The Spaces of Science-Fiction Cinema*, ed. Annette Kuhn, 121–143. London: Verso.
Statistics Explained. 2014. *Eurostat*, May. ec.europa.eu/eurostat/statistics-explained/index.php/Unemployment_statistics. Accessed 1 May 2018.
Torner, Evan. 2010. Civilization's Endless Shadow: Haneke's Time of the Wolf. In *A Companion to Michael Haneke*, ed. Roy Grundmann, 532–550. Malden: Wiley-Blackwell.
Tryon, Chuck. 2015. Iron Sky's War Bonds: Cult Sf Cinema and Crowdsourcing. In *Science Fiction Double Feature: the Science Fiction Film as Cult Text*, ed. J.P. Telotte and Gerald Duchovnay, 115–129. Liverpool: Liverpool University Press.
Ward, James J. 2015. Nazis on the Moon! Nazis Under the Polar Ice Cap! And Other Recent Episodes in the Strange Cinematic Afterlife of the Third Reich. *Horrors of War: The Undead on the Battlefield*, ed. Cynthia A. Miller and A. Bowdoin van Riper, 53–74. Rowman & Littlefield.

CHAPTER 3

SF in the EU's Newest Member States

Not all EU stories are bad ones. Whilst anti-EU sentiment has swelled much populist discourse across the continent in recent years, it is worthwhile to remember that EU membership and the access it provides to the common market are for many a desirable, if not coveted, commodity. Amidst the voluminous clamour that has accompanied the escalation of Brexit, as well as the ultimately unsuccessful efforts of France's Front National to place EU membership front and centre of their electoral mandate,[1] it is easy to forget that since 1957 the collective has known only growth, with Croatia becoming its 28th member state in 2013. In the twenty-first century, moreover, and following the ratification of the Nice Treaty in 2001,[2] the EU has undergone three rounds of expansion: the first occurring in 2004 with the accession of the Central and Eastern European states of the Czech Republic, Estonia, Hungary, Latvia, Lithuania, Poland, Slovakia, and Slovenia as well as the Mediterranean islands of Cyprus and Malta; the second in 2007 when Bulgaria and Romania attained membership; and the third on 1 July 2013 with Croatia's accession. After the dissolution of the Soviet Union and latterly of Yugoslavia, the prospect of joining the EU held clear appeal for newly liberated states in the former Eastern bloc. An obvious reason for this, aside from the economic benefits that may have accrued, was the recognition of nationhood in a European and world sphere and the security that comes with membership status, for nominally an attack

© The Author(s) 2018
A. Power, *Contemporary European Science Fiction Cinemas*,
Palgrave European Film and Media Studies,
https://doi.org/10.1007/978-3-319-89827-8_3

on one member constitutes an attack on the collective. It is unsurprising therefore that Serbia and Montenegro are currently candidates for accession, while further east, negotiations over mooted Turkish membership have been ongoing for over a decade, even if they now look highly unlikely to survive Recep Erdoğan's increasingly despotic presidency. In the Baltic States meanwhile, EU integration partially signals a desire to stave off future advances from a resurgent Russia, with membership offering the reassurance of safety in numbers. Eastward NATO expansion coupled with Vladimir Putin's ruthless consolidation of power since his first appointment as Prime Minister in 1999 has lent urgency to the situation. It should be noted, for example, that Russia's cynical annexation of Crimea came at the height of the Euromaidan protests that emerged in opposition to former President Viktor Yanukovych's suspension of an association agreement with the EU, one that would have seen Ukraine edge closer to eventual membership. Eager to insulate itself from regional upheaval that could affect its access to natural gas supplies, the EU was not above cynicism itself, and its subsequent disjointedness in the face of Russian aggression hinted at a level of pre-existent indifference towards Ukraine.[3] In such an environment, nervousness evident in geopolitically strategic locations such as Estonia and Poland is entirely understandable. For Russia instead, a marked antipathy towards closer European integration has led to exponential increases in cyberattacks and backing for Eurosceptic and far-right political parties across the EU. Whilst the terms of engagement may have evolved since the cessation of the Cold War, mutual enmity consistent with the EU's rise in opposition to Russian interests owes much to the drive for European integration which was conceived of in large part as a bulwark to Soviet expansion. Thus, in reductionist terms, the EU has from the outset literally defined itself in opposition to Russia, with its modern-day borders ending where Russia begins. More accurately still, we can say that the EU has defined itself in opposition to communism, with the collapse of Czechoslovakia and Yugoslavia in the early 1990s paving the way for EU membership status for the Czech Republic, Slovakia, Croatia, and Slovenia, with Macedonia, Montenegro, and Serbia currently recognised candidates for future membership, as is Albania, formerly the most isolated communist nation in Europe. We have seen already how modern-day Europe emerged out of pragmatic necessity, and the swiftness with which Britain, France, and Germany were able to set aside hostilities in the aftermath of the Second World

War was in large part due to mutual fear of the USSR. Implicit in this unanimity was an imaginary construction of Eastern Europe that would both stand in opposition to and offer validation for the construction of Western Europe, as Luisa Rivi has observed:

> World War II created Europe, or better yet, Western Europe: The unspoken assumption that by Europe we refer to Western Europe dates to recent times. By the same stroke, Eastern Europe became the 'other Europe,' comprising the satellites of the USSR in Eastern Europe, as well as the USSR itself. The Treaty of Yalta, the Cold War, the Iron Curtain and later the Berlin Wall restructured a Europe ravaged by war according to the principles of a geopolitical bipolarism, splitting the continent in two opposing blocs for decades. (*European Cinema After 1989* 14)

This implicit imposition of opposing blocs persists today even if nominally all EU member states are equal. The reality, however, is somewhat different with Bulgaria, Croatia, and Romania yet to be granted membership of the Schengen Area, despite an EU mandate that all are legally obliged to become members ('Schengen: Enlargement of Europe's Border-Free Area'). Moreover, the moment when one outlines a nominal core of an entity is precisely the moment when a periphery is simultaneously designated in opposition. Poland, for example, is a Central European nation that shares a 467 km-long border with Germany along the Oder–Neisse line, yet it is frequently othered as 'Eastern' in a European context: witness, for example, widespread claims from Brexit campaigners about the supposedly deleterious impact of Polish labourers upon the British economy. While a degree of historic enmity towards Germany may still linger under the surface of British life, it is somewhat difficult to imagine a comparable othering of German workers, even if they may have grown up in view of the Polish border. In Europe then, East is not necessarily East. Although the collapse of communism allowed for new freedoms, the changing of outside perceptions of former communist nations remains an obdurate challenge. In this vein, Yonka Krasteva argues that while 'postcommunist society has vastly extended the possibilities for people to redefine themselves', it does not automatically follow 'that they are fully free to choose a new identity, or even to articulate their sense of identity' ('Western Writing and the (Re)Construction of the Balkans' 97). Instead, their self-conception is 'shaped by the way in which the West perceives them, and by the images that Western media and culture disseminate for global consumption' ('Western Writing' 97). 'The centre', Krasteva continues, 'though claiming to be in disintegration, still functions as a centre circulating systems of codes in its attempt to define unprecedented historical developments and marginal, non-Western cultural identities' ('Western Writing' 97). In turn, a further marginalisation is increasingly salient in the region. While ex-communist nations are frequently othered and designated as peripheries by their 'Western' European counterparts, growing numbers of people in Hungary, Poland, and the Czech Republic imagine themselves as being at the vanguard of new cultural and civilisational clashes that at once accentuate their own uniqueness as Europeans and in turn cast refugees seeking European sanctuary as incompatible others. This residual displacement and recentring plays upon the tactile mutability of constructions of Europe itself, for as Krasteva observes, in 'striving to eliminate one kind of a periphery, it inadvertently creates new ones in order to sustain the opposition of "us" versus "them"' ('Western Writing' 97). For Thomas Elsaesser, such spikes in nationalism are linked to an identity crisis caused by the collapse of the Soviet Union, as 'the postnational condition has led neither to a credible post-heroic narrative [...] nor to a whole-hearted embrace of globalization' but has instead left the region turning 'obsessively inward, towards the past, towards commemoration and collective nostalgia' ('European Cinema into the Twenty-first Century' 36).

Undermining things further was the vulnerability of newly opened-up post-communist economies, with tightly regulated, centrally planned models giving way in many instances to untethered venture capitalism. Ewa Mazierska, Lars Kristensen, and Eva Näripea are unequivocal in their view that this, in turn, has led to the replacing of one cultural and economic hegemony with another. Drawing upon David Harvey who charts the links between decolonisation and capital flight, they note that while the collapse of the Soviet Union had the positive effect of granting Eastern European nations freedom from colonisation, virtually all have been affected by a 'new global order that coordinates the circulation of cultural values, commodities and wealth, and which is not very different from the old-style colonialism' (*Postcolonial Approaches* 14). Independence then is partial, and post-communist Europe, as Harvey himself argues in *A Brief History of Neoliberalism*, was uniquely susceptible to rapid-fire privatisation which has created 'enormous stresses that reverberate to this day' (71). The USSR's demise provided an existential conundrum for sf too, leading to the near death of the genre for a time amongst its former satellite states, for as Matthias Schwartz has noted, on the one hand, it 'lost its function as systemic critique', while on the other, 'remaining studios were no longer able to keep up with Hollywood financially or technologically, so there was hardly a chance to produce science fiction films that were even marginally commercially successful' ('Archaeologies of a Past Future' 115). Indeed, to some extent the film industry serves as a microcosmic example of wider events, as nationally subsidised film studios were suddenly shorn of both finance and purpose and thus especially prone to venture capitalism. Perhaps appropriately then, this chapter will begin with an examination of the impact of privatisation and foreign investment upon a former communist nation, taking the Nu Boyana Film Studios in Bulgaria as a case study. This production studies-based analysis will then give way to an examination of the Croatian film *The Show Must Go On* which engages with Europe's reaction to the Yugoslav Wars while depicting a future where Croatia's accession to the EU ultimately leads to its virtual eradication. I will then examine rising xenophobia in Hungary via Kornél Mundruczó's *Jupiter's Moon/Jupiter holdja* (2017), the plot of which centres on a young Syrian refugee with supernatural powers who is seeking refuge in Europe, before closing with an analysis of the Lithuanian film *Vanishing Waves/Aurora* which, through its self-conscious engagement with modernist cinema, will return us to key historical features of European sf, most saliently the relationship between arthouse and genre film. Where the earlier case study of Bulgarian-based sf aims to illustrate how American studios capitalised on the collapse of communist-era infrastructure, my analysis of *Vanishing Waves* will also consider the extension of European film funding structures into new markets. The cross-section of nations chosen reflects a desire to sample as wide an area as possible while allowing for significant sociocultural and political differences amongst the EU's newer member states. That I am unable to engage sf from all of the nations to have joined the EU since 2004 is due to several factors, the most pressing of which is a lack of space. Another practical consideration is that there is an uneven scattering of contemporary sf films to emerge from the same nations. Poland, for instance, despite a long history with the genre, has produced few sf films in recent years.[4] It follows then that this chapter is not intended as being prescriptive of post-communist Europe as a whole, rather it aims instead to survey some of the pressing contemporary issues in post-Nice Treaty European states and comprises analysis of Bulgaria to the South East, Croatia in the Balkans, Hungary in Central Europe, and Lithuania in the Baltic region.

Bulgaria

As with all sectors of society, the collapse of communism in Bulgaria had serious implications for the native film industry. Concurrent with other nations across Central and Eastern Europe, Bulgaria was pressured into holding open elections after the collapse of the Berlin Wall, soon after which, in late 1989, Communist leader Petar Mladenov pledged to hold multiparty elections for the first time since the outset of the Second World War. The gradual opening-up of the country's economy was a rocky process, however, with a collapse in communist-era state infrastructure leaving a large vacuum to be filled. Dina Iordanova, for example, notes that the transition 'was not a planned one with a clearly defined and supervised outcome' but rather 'a somewhat cluttered and rambling period of reassessment and self-interrogation' ('Bulgarian Cinema: Optimism in Moderation' 14). Geography complicated things further, for bordering both Turkey and the Black Sea, Bulgaria is at a considerable remove from Europe's centres of power, occupying, in Temenuga Trifonova's words, 'one of the positions furthest from the sun in the solar system known as the European Union' ('Between the National and the Transnational' 34). Amidst the uncertainty, the domestic film industry was left in dire straits, with Iordanova observing that the total output of Bulgarian films between 1990 and 2005 averaged four to five productions a year, while not 'a single Bulgarian feature title was released in 1999' ('Bulgaria' 97). Shorn of state support, the country's geographical and political isolation left few options open to Bulgarian filmmakers during this time. The nation joined Eurimages in 1993, yet according to Maya Nedyalkova, 'the unstructured changeover to an open market economy which began in 1989 sent the Bulgarian film industry into serious crisis …[for]… without state regulation, appropriate film business education, and international contacts, film professionals proved ill-equipped to face the trends of international commercialisation governing the global film trade' ('Festivals Gone Digital: A Case-Study of Netcinema.bg and the Online European Film Festival in Bulgaria' 138). The Bulgarian experience is not unique in a post-communist context and nor are the solutions that the market subsequently imposed,[5] yet the country remains an intriguing test case. Attracted by the low cost of shooting in Bulgaria and by the country's varied topography, which includes seaside resorts, mountainous terrain, and the urban landscapes of Sofia, Hollywood investors swooped into the void left by a collapsed native film industry that in turn left a generation of filmmakers in its wake.[6] In the interim years, a whole host of Hollywood films have been shot in the country, a good many of them glorified b-movies that nevertheless enjoy budgets that vastly exceed anything on offer within the European film industries. Some of the more noteworthy recent examples of this trend include *Conan the Barbarian* (Marcus Nispel 2011), *300: Rise of an Empire* (Noam Murro 2014), and *The Hitman's Bodyguard* (Patrick Hughes 2017). Nispel's critically panned reboot of the *Conan* series alone should grant us some perspective about the attraction of hosting such productions, for its reputed cost of $90 million is over three times Eurimages' entire annual budget. All three films were shot at Nu Boyana Studios in Sofia, which today vies with Barrandov Studios in Prague for the honour of being the largest facility of its kind in post-communist Europe. Established by the communist government as the state-owned National Film Centre in 1963, the studio re-emerged from a lengthy period of uncertainty largely because of a growing business relationship with the Los Angeles-based independent company Nu Image, which first started making films in Sofia in 1999. Following protracted and highly controversial negotiations, the state formally sold the studio to Nu Image in 2006.[7] Initially keen to attract what Iordanova calls 'runaway productions' from other Eastern and Central European nations, the studio has in recent years focused increasingly upon US co-productions ('Bulgarian Cinema' 11). By 2014, David Varod, the studio's chief executive, who was centrally involved in the purchase of Boyana, boasted to the *New York Times* that he 'put Bulgaria on the map', despite what he perceived as the country's unwillingness to provide sufficient tax breaks for his company (Ewing, 'Making Films in Bulgaria'). The same article reports that Nu Image spent upwards of $50 million developing the studios and that the once stagnant film industry now generates thousands of jobs in a country with 'highly skilled workers available at salaries far below those in Los Angeles or London' (Ewing, 'Making Films'). The suspicion lingers that these developments run the risk of relegating Bulgarian cinema to the status of a mere Hollywood satellite, and Iordanova appears prescient when observing in 2007 that Boyana's sale was the 'final step in shaping the parallel industries' where the 'servicing of large runaway productions from Hollywood and elsewhere has become the default arrangement, whereas work on domestic productions will need to be negotiated on a per project basis' ('Bulgaria' 107). Unsurprisingly, contemporary Bulgarian sf cinema may be all but non-existent then, but as we will now see, a plethora of multinational b-movie sf productions have been shot in the country since Nu Image first entered the picture in 1999.

I should point out to begin with that the sheer volume of sf films shot in Bulgaria in recent years mitigates against in-depth filmic analysis of a kind that I will carry out elsewhere in this chapter. Additionally, few of these films are 'European' in any discernible sense of the word, and it is doubtful that the average American viewer would conceive of them as being foreign in any meaningful way. Even in a film such as *Man with the Screaming Brain* (Bruce Campbell 2005), wherein Bruce Campbell's character William Cole actually travels to Bulgaria, the focus is very much on the novelty value of a rich American visiting a supposedly backward ex-communist state which he clearly finds repellent. Given the unique niche that he has carved out for himself within the Hollywood firmament, Campbell's films tend to be exceptions anyway, yet in the same year that he directed *Man with a Screaming Brain*, Campbell also starred in *Alien Apocalypse* (Josh Becker 2005), another Bulgarian-shot sf which follows an astronaut's attempts to free the world from alien overlords. Both films were produced by the Sci-Fi Channel, an American cable channel owned by NBC Universal which was later rebranded as Sci Fi and then Syfy (its current incarnation). Keen to capitalise upon the success of their regular Saturday night sf b-movie screenings and obviate the need to buy in films from elsewhere, the channel's executives elected to commission their own productions in 2002.[8] To keep costs down, Syfy made a host of such films in Bulgaria, providing a welcome stream of business for the then-struggling Boyana studio. In addition to the Bruce Campbell films, sf productions filmed at Boyana include *Mansquito* (Tibor Takács 2005), which details the transformation of a convict into a mosquito-human hybrid, and alien films including *Alien Lockdown* (Tim Cox 2004), *Alien Siege* (Robert Stadd 2005), and *Deep Shock* (Paul Joshua Rubin 2003), as well as the post-apocalyptic films *Path of Destruction* (Stephen Furst 2005) and *Annihilation Earth* (Rafael Jordan 2009). These Syfy productions followed formulaic narrative structures that were calculated to be both risible and fast moving, with writers encouraged to divide their films into seven acts ('six cliffhangers, plus a climax') and to ideally include 'a death every eight minutes' (Wolf, 'We've Created a Monster!'). Despite fears over rising costs,[9] Syfy's initiative paved the way for others to shoot sf films in Bulgaria, with relevant examples including *Post Impact* (Christoph Schrewe 2004), *Index Zero* (Lorenzo Sportiello 2014), and *Autómata* (Gabe Ibáñez 2014). The latter film was co-produced by Nu Image which has expanded considerably since its purchase of Boyana in 2006.

The studio had previously co-produced *Alien Hunter* (Ronald Krauss 2003) and *The Black Hole* (Tibor Takács 2006), the latter a joint venture with Syfy, through its subsidiary Millennium Films. Nu Image has continued their relationship with Syfy in the interim and in 2014 announced a deal to make a further four films with the channel (Frater, 'Nu Image, Active To Make Four Syfy Movies'). Given that all of these films were shot in English, produced by predominantly US companies, and feature moderately recognisable Hollywood actors, they can scarcely be classed as European. Nonetheless, their sheer quantity alone makes them noteworthy in a European context, while the conditions that begat their existence demonstrate the susceptibility of post-communist Bulgaria to transnational capital.

Nu Boyana's appeal as a film studio was recently summed up by its current CEO, Yariv Lerner, who explained to the *Sofia Globe* that 'If you spend one dollar here, it makes it look like ten dollars, you get value and the money ends up on the screen' (Marcus, 'Yariv Lerner: The man who runs Nu Boyana Film Studios'). The studio has grown from strength to strength and offers what Lerner refers to as an 'end-to-end service', which covers every aspect of production from location to crew to equipment to a full complement of post-production facilities.[10] This facility, to essentially complete a film on site, ensures the studio's physical presence in Bulgaria and a resultant degree of permanency that foreign-owned enterprises in other tax incentivised sectors cannot always provide. Its continued success, however, will depend on being able to offer comparatively low overheads, predicated, among other considerations, upon keeping labour costs down and thus maintaining a level of inequality between Bulgaria and its fellow EU member states. It is hardly coincidental that Boyana's rise in prominence has coincided with Bulgaria's EU membership: the completion of its takeover by Nu Image taking place in the run-up to Bulgarian accession in 2007. Yet while eligibility for European funding has been a boon for floundering native film industries across ex-communist nations, 'at the same time, European integration has further exposed Eastern Europe to neoliberal deregulation, weakening the political and economic power of nation-states and reinforcing existing geopolitical inequalities within Europe' (Imre, *A Companion to Eastern European Cinemas* 5). In the case of Bulgaria, this results in a quintessentially neoliberal paradox: a nation that at once houses one of the most prolific sf film industries in Europe and yet produces no 'Bulgarian' sf at all.

CROATIA

Film: The Show Must Go On (Nevio Marasović 2010)

Reflecting upon four years of Croatian EU membership in 2017, former Prime Minister Jadranka Kosor, who signed the nation's accession treaty with the EU, observed that joining the EU was 'in a figurative sense a departure from the painful past as well as the acknowledgement of our achievements' (Pavlic, 'Croatia Marks Four Years as EU Member State'). While stressing the economic benefits of access to a market of 500 million people, as well as pledging EU support for major infrastructural projects, Kosor was keen to emphasise another key consideration, namely, that 'the European Union is founded on the idea of preserving lasting peace and stability in Europe' (Pavlic, 'Croatia Marks'). *The Show Must Go On*, a debut feature by Zagreb-born director Nevio Marasović, instead paints a near-future Croatia confronted by an opposing reality, one where EU membership draws the nation into the Third World War. The first film from Croatia to be distributed solely in digital format, *The Show Must Go On* is also the first Croatian sf production of any kind since Dušan Vukotić's *Visitors from the Galaxy/Gosti iz galaksije* (1981) (Petkovic, 'The Show Must Go on with the Widest Local Roll-Out Ever'). Topically, the film places Croatia's membership of the EU front and centre of its narrative and is set on the seventh anniversary of the nation's accession to the collective. We learn this early on, when reality television producer Filip Dogan (Sven Medvesek), who produces a *Big Brother*-like programme called 'Housed!', enquires about the latest episode of his ex-wife's current affairs programme. This collision between low-brow trash TV and current affairs as embodied by Filip on the one hand, and his producer ex-wife Helena (Natasa Dorcic) on the other, neatly synopsises the film's central aims of being at once a satire on the power of the media and a dystopian sf that imagines the end of Europe as we know it. The premise is relatively straightforward: mid-way through a season of Housed!, war breaks out between a NATO alliance and an unnamed Asian enemy, yet instead of cancelling his show and informing its contestants of the conflict, Filip elects to keep Housed! on air and its participants in the dark. An all-Croatian affair, the film was funded by local production companies Copycat Production House and Vizija SFT as well as by the Academy of Dramatic Art in Zagreb from where Marasović graduated. Shot for an estimated 200,000 kuna (circa €26,000), *The Show Must Go On*'s micro-budget mitigates against the use of expensive special effects, yet the film's war scenes in particular are nevertheless impressively handled (Jelić, 'Information Technology' 88).

With war reaching Croatia, the escapism offered by watching people sequestered from the real world proves to be a welcome distraction, and sure enough, Housed! becomes a huge commercial success. Capturing the prevailing pessimism, Helena caustically explains to Filip that this is because 'people want to get away from what is happening in the world and what will most likely happen to us'. She advocates sending the estranged couple's son to Sarajevo to avoid the conflict, arguing that Bosnia should be safe as 'it's not in the EU' and 'Sarajevo is a Muslim town'. The immediacy of the threat is underscored in the very next scene when a fighter jet bombs the television studios where Filip and Helena both work. The irony here is considerable: Croatia is suddenly exposed to war because it is part of the EU, in a direct inversion of Jadranka Kosor's stated benefits for joining the collective. As such, on one level, *The Show Must Go On* plays upon entrenched attitudes that have long positioned the Balkans as a '"Third World" waiting to "return to Europe"' and juxtapose 'Western Europe as the epitome of civilization' against the 'primitiveness and barbarity of the Balkans' (Trifonova, 'Between the National and the Transnational' 34–35). Joining the EU will not 'civilise' the once warring Croats, the film posits, but instead will lead directly to its involvement in further bloodshed.

A Bleached Europe

As we have seen in Chap. 2, the European community evinced considerable helplessness in the face of mass slaughter during the 1990s wars across what was once Yugoslavia. Such helplessness extended to Sarajevo, which was subjected to the longest siege in the history of modern warfare by Bosnian Serb forces. The siege, which accounted for the deaths of almost 14,000 people, lasted from April 1992 to February 1996 and was perpetrated by the Bosnian Serb Army of Republika Srpska, a force also responsible for the mass genocide of Muslim Bosniaks at Srebrenica in 1995. The Srebrenica massacre occurred on the EU's doorstep and despite the UN's designation of the region as a 'safe area'. As Ivana Maček, a social anthropologist who chronicles the events extensively in *Sarajevo Under Siege: Anthropology in Wartime*, writes: 'Bosnia had been part of Europe, but it seemed so no longer. Many westerners may have come to regard Bosnia as outside of Europe because they did not want to acknowledge that forces within their own societies and nation-states could lead to such a situation' (27). As mentioned in the introduction, EU membership is undoubtedly a fillip to smaller nations keen to safeguard their security, and unsurprisingly, Bosnia and Herzegovina formally applied for EU membership in 2016. It currently remains a candidate country for consideration. Nevertheless, the EU's indifference to carnage in its midst points to sharp demarcation lines between being a member of the EU and being merely European. The EU's eastward expansion in 2004 and 2007 was no doubt facilitated by such considerations, yet as Vlastimir Sudar has noted, a side-effect of the latter expansion in particular—which incorporated the majority Orthodox Christian nations of Bulgaria and Romania—was the unintentional crushing of 'long-established prejudiced beliefs about not only geographical positions, but also the belief that Catholic countries have precedence in EU membership over Orthodox Christian ones' (Sudar, 'New Neighbours, Old Habits' 243). Like nearby Albania, Bosnia and Herzegovina remains statistically a Muslim majority country and as such would be an anomaly within traditional EU configurations. In *The Show Must Go On*, however, its othering as non-EU and Muslim ironically renders it safe, whereas the EU's very integration makes of it an amorphous mass target for the shadowy Asian enemy coalition.[11] By estranging this one element of perceived wisdom, the film forces us to question the assumption that European integration is automatically synonymous with peace.

Unlike its fleeting yet telling reference to Bosnia, *The Show Must Go On* makes no mention of Croatia's erstwhile nemesis Serbia, an absence that in the context of European integration is hardly incidental. Following on from his infamous and frequently misunderstood maxim that the 'Gulf War did not take place', one that, for all the criticism it received for perceived callousness, sought to deny equivalence between knowledge garnered from media imagery and actual lived experience, Jean Baudrillard argued that Serbia's very exclusion from European society at the time of the Yugoslav Wars allowed Serb forces to reinforce age-old ethnic and religious conceptualisations of Europe:

> In carrying out ethnic cleansing, the Serbs are Europe's cutting edge. The 'real' Europe is a white Europe, a bleached Europe that is morally, economically, and ethnically integrated and cleansed. In Sarajevo, this Europe is victoriously in the making [...] By banishing them from the human community, we are actually protecting them and continuing to let them carry out their work. ('No Pity for Sarajevo; The West's Serbianization' 82)

Baudrillard's inversion of the perceived logic that Serbia had no place within a peaceful European configuration exposes the assumption that the EU is, in fact, inherently peaceful and not simply the pragmatic response of a continent finally exhausted from centuries of internecine conflict. Constructions of monstrous Eastern European others in opposition to a civilised West, after all, while frequently invoking the horrors of Nazism as a precedent run the risk of erasing from history the many heinous acts perpetuated in the name of European colonisation. No matter the EU's rhetoric and conception of itself, Stjepan Meštrović concludes that 'when one has reviewed all the many rationalizations for the West's actions and inactions in relation to the Balkan War that began in 1991, one is still left with the sobering conclusion that the West allowed Serbia to win and to commit crimes against humanity that were not supposed to be tolerated ever again' (*Balkanization of the West* 86). Despite the EU's paralysis, the Yugoslav Wars were a large-scale media event, one that reintroduced the spectre of ethnic cleansing to European soil. The Balkans were at once depicted as both local and other, a society at war in a manner that, in Maček's words, 'empties out meanings and causes a vacuum of norms' (*Sarajevo* viii). The problem with Western media reports, as Maček sees it, was 'that they rarely filled this vacuum with anything except politically empowered actors on the highest international institutional levels' (*Sarajevo* viii). As such, ordinary people were left voiceless and denied agency, and it is here that we get to the core of *The Show Must Go On*: namely, Filip's struggle to sustain the relevance of a reality TV show, as war rages outside his television studio.

Once Filip first hears of a declaration of war upon 'Europe and her allies' while at his mother's apartment, Marasović immediately cuts to the inside of the Housed! studio, where participants are having a farewell drink in honour of a contestant who has been voted off the show. Following banal platitudes and farewells, the contestant in question is given a goofy, oversized stovepipe hat of a kind worn by football supporters, chequered red and white and embroidered with the Croatian coat of arms. Jubilantly making his way up a dark passageway from the studio, he emerges noisily into daylight only to be confronted by a war zone. The hollowness of his nationalist performativity is immediately put into sharp relief as a soldier tasked with rescuing him is gunned down. Yet far from being abandoned due to the outset of war, the Housed! studio is instead fortified by the army, and the programme becomes a sensation, with Filip feted for creating the most watched reality TV show of all time. Even as casualties pile up (a nuclear attack on an unnamed Asian city is said to have resulted in the death of millions), the show continues, with frontline soldiers cheerfully recounting the exploits of their favourite participants to television war correspondents. On a current affairs programme where his work is lauded, Filip accounts for his success by observing that 'people have simply had enough of war. They are assaulted with the image of war relentlessly for twenty-four hours a day'. Like the near contemporaneous Gulf War, the Yugoslav Wars became outsized media events as they coincided with the astonishing development of satellite news channels that were multinational in ownership and thus no longer anchored to strictly national concerns. In such a context, Stjepan Meštrović observes that 'the major implication is that media coverage of the current Balkan War did not lead to a compassionate desire to end the slaughter, but to a passive state of vicarious sadism vis-à-vis the consumption of truly horrifying images and concepts' (*Balkanization* 83). Although the hatreds were distinctly local, the methods deployed were sadly familiar to European audiences to the point that mass rape, slaughter, and ultimately genocide were not quite enough to forestall a conflict that raged through Europe's 'peripheries'. Returning the conversation to the war, one of Filip's co-panellists on the current affairs programme decries the actions of Croatia's allies, closing out the show with the resigned observation that 'our destiny is in the hands of superpowers, and not only our destiny, but that of the whole world'. His pessimism it transpires is well founded, with the world's superpowers seemingly content to wipe one another out. Closing with shots of contestants emerging into an empty, scorched Zagreb, *The Show Must Go On* thus configures a post-apocalyptic future where Croatia's accession to the EU results in the nation's ruination. Whether intentionally or not, this turn of events has historical significance, given that like much of the rest of Central and Eastern Europe, Croatia has a long history of foreign occupation. By the early nineteenth century, the nation was split between territorial France—as a consequence of the Napoleonic Wars—and the Austro-Hungarian Empire. After the First World War, it was merged into the Kingdom of Yugoslavia, before being invaded by the Axis powers in 1941 after which, and despite its nominally monarchical status, the bulk of modern-day Croatia became a fascist state under the control of the Ustaše locally and the Nazis ultimately. In the aftermath of the Second World War instead, the country was subsumed as a constitutive unit of the Socialist Federal Republic of Yugoslavia. Accordingly, like its neighbours in Central and Eastern Europe, Croatians have cause to be weary of Europeanism, given that prior to declaring independence in 1991, it enjoyed limited autonomy. Therefore, unlike in Western Europe where 'it was the legacy of the colonial empires that shaped encounters with the non-European world, Central European states were born of the disintegration of Europe's continental empires—Germany, Austro- Hungary, Russia—and the processes of ethnic cleansing that followed' (Krastev, 'Western Writing' 48). Given such a history, it is perhaps not altogether that surprising that *The Show Must Go On* harbours reservations about automatic equations between European integration and peace.

Hungary

Film: Jupiter's Moon (Kornél Mundruczó 2017)

Jupiter's Moon is Hungarian film and theatre director Kornél Mundruczó's seventh feature film in a career that began in 2000 with *This I Wish and Nothing More/Nincsen nekem vágyam semmi* and that has gained considerable momentum in recent years. A follow-up to *White God/Fehér isten* (2014)—winner of the Prize Un Certain Regard at the 2014 Cannes Film festival and Hungary's official entry for the Best Foreign Language Film for the 2015 Academy Awards—*Jupiter's Moon* is the newest release studied in depth in this book and is also arguably the most thematically apposite, focused as it is, upon the experiences of Aryan Dashni (played by Hungarian actor Zsombor Jéger), a young Syrian escaping the Civil War in his homeland and seeking refuge in Europe. Usefully for a book about sf, Aryan can also fly. Cowritten by Mundruczó and Kata Wéber, who worked together on *White God*, *Jupiter's Moon* unsurprisingly shares several thematic connections with the former film and is similarly concerned with the fantastic. Indeed, *White God*, which depicts a canine uprising against abusive humans on the streets of Budapest, has clear political subtexts that *Jupiter's Moon* shares and amplifies. Both films ask us to reflect upon questions of humanity, both in terms of those who we apportion it to and those for whom it is denied. In *White God*, the presence of upwards of 250 real dogs in the cast, to say nothing of their anthropomorphic adventures, is offset by an absence of humanity in the film's humans, save for a young girl named Lili (Zsófia Psotta), whose dog Hagen is cruelly set loose on the streets by her disapproving father. In one of the more unlikely screen Bildungsromane of recent years, the film follow's Hagen's exploits as he is physically abused and neglected, becomes a prize fighter, then a freedom fighter, and ultimately a violent revolutionary leader. In *Jupiter's Moon* instead, Aryan is shot at by border police, imprisoned by the state, and exploited by locals, and ultimately it is only when he takes to the skies of Budapest that incredulous Hungarians begin to acknowledge his humanity. Notable for Mundruczó's deployment of dizzying special effects, long takes, and mobile, handheld cameras, *Jupiter's Moon* is less accomplished than its predecessor, an observation that most of the film's early reviews bear out, yet in its blending of superhero movie tropes with social critique of the EU's most stridently anti-immigration regime, it is in many ways a remarkably timely release.

A QUESTION OF PURITY

In both *White God* and *Jupiter's Moon*, a state obsession with 'purity' is largely to blame for Hagen and Aryan's respective predicaments, with the government's imposition of an extortionate 'mongrel tax' prompting Lili's father to dispense of Hagen in the former and rampant anti-immigrant sentiment forcing Aryan to flee for his life in the latter. The subtexts that inform both films are concurrent with Mundruczó's calling for 'new kinds of moral stories' in a post-9/11, economically troubled world, when explaining that *White God* reflects the fact that 'the majority creates the minority [and that] *we* create our monsters, and we label them as monsters, street dogs, minorities or what have you'.[12] A nation of paradoxes, Hungary has been both coloniser and colonised since its founding in 895, and in its various iterations has been invaded by the Mongols, the Ottoman Empire, and the Soviet Union. Not unlike other ex-communist European states, it has endured something of an identity crisis since the fall of the Berlin Wall, with Lesley C. Pleasant observing that 'since the 1990s, Hungarian national identity has had several iterations from being a member of the Eastern Bloc, to becoming a transit country for migrants from the Eastern Bloc, a member of the EU, and a transit and sometimes destination country for migrants from Afghanistan, Libya, Syria etc' ('Seeing Beings: "Dog" Looks Back at "God"' 3). Nonetheless, in common with neighbours Poland, Slovakia, and the Czech Republic, Hungary has undergone a nationalist revival since joining the EU on 18 May 2004. Currently both Poland and Hungary are presided over by populist right-wing governments that maintain a conspicuous line of Euroscepticism, particularly in relation to EU migration policies. Since Viktor Orbán's re-election as Prime Minister of Hungary in 2010 (a post he had previously held at the turn of the century),

Hungarian politics have shifted notably rightward, with Orbán's ruling Fidesz party volubly railing against migration and a host of perceived slights visited upon the country by the EU. Eager to present himself as a defender of traditional values, Orbán has consolidated his grip on power by diluting the powers of the judiciary, curbing press freedom, and rewriting the Hungarian constitution.[13] Under the auspices of 'law and order', Fidesz has also clamped down upon universities, reserving particular opprobrium for the business magnate and Europhile George Soros, whose charitable foundation once funded Orbán's own third-level education in Oxford.[14] Orbán, who has also proposed the reintroduction of the death penalty in Hungary, has in recent years overseen the fortification of the nation's borders, building razor wire-topped fences where its southern flank adjoins Serbia and Croatia, before evoking Donald Trump in demanding that the EU foot half of the construction bill (Than, 'Hungarian PM Orban to ask EU to help Foot Bill'). As in Poland, which is currently governed by the PiS, or Law and Justice party, Fidesz has been emboldened by the actions of extremist parties to their right. While PiS has benefited from a surge of nationalist sentiment that has led to the largest annual far-right demonstration in the world, a Warsaw-based march held every November nominally to mark Poland's independence in 1918, Fidesz has profited from groundwork put in place by the far-right Jobbik, who routinely espouse anti-Roma and anti-Semitic rhetoric in their avowal of Hungarian nationalism and nativist economic policies.[15] Moreover, policies initially pursued by Jobbik in Hungary have passed into law under Orbán's watch.[16] Keen to perpetuate the tenets of what he has since described as 'illiberal democracy', Orbán has been swift to paint the EU as an existential threat and as an 'institution that interferes with sovereign state business and is not able to understand the situation in Hungary' (Hyttinen and Näre, 'Symbolic and Ritual Enactments of Nationalism' 238). Above all, Orbán has portrayed himself and his party as defenders of Hungarian values, finding common ground with fellow Visegrád Group members Poland, Slovakia, and the Czech Republic, in arguing that Europe's 'Christian identity' is under threat from 'Muslim invaders', namely, refugees from Syria whose presence in Europe he has described as 'the Trojan horse of terrorism' ('Brunsden, Orban: EU's 'Christian Identity' Under Threat from Muslim Migrants'). Accordingly, Fidesz's anti-migrant sentiment is routinely framed within entreaties to the country's Christian heritage, which can be traced back to the coronation of Grand Prince Stephen I in the year 1000, and provides us with an opportune point of departure for analysis of *Jupiter's Moon*.

White Christian Identity

From its opening scene onward, it is made abundantly clear that refugees are not welcome in Hungary in *Jupiter's Moon*. Crossing into the country from Serbia, Aryan, his father Mourad, and their fellow travellers are accosted by border police who open fire upon the prone group, killing several of their number. László (György Cserhalmi), the patrol's leader then, hunts down the fleeing Aryan and shoots him three times, only to be later left gazing in astonishment at video footage of his would-be-victim rising from the dead, taking flight and hovering above the border before being captured and detained in a refugee camp. László's brutality, though tantamount to murder, does not earn him reproach, however. Instead, his actions are revealed to be in keeping with state policy, as a brief scene at the refugee camp makes clear. After inspecting the corpse of a migrant killed by a colleague, László congratulates the man for earning a promotion, the reasons for which, though clearly related, are left unsaid. Whilst such scenes may lack subtlety, Mundruczó can be forgiven on the basis that real-life Hungarian border activities have of late been anything but refined. The Hungarian border with Serbia was militarised by Orbán in 2015, as was the border with Croatia at the same moment that punitive anti-asylum laws were added to the constitution, events described thusly by Liz Fekete:

> Soldiers, prison labourers and those on workfare were drafted in to erect a 109-mile razor-wire fence at the border with Serbia. The cost was a staggering €98 million, at least three times the €27.5 million budget of the Office of Immigration and Nationality for 2015. And along Hungary's border with Croatia, armoured vehicles (equipped with machine guns) and heavily armed soldiers took up position, prior to its being totally sealed off on 17 October 2015. On the same day that emergency measures were officially introduced, amendments to the Criminal Code and the Asylum Law came into force, making it a crime to enter Hungary through a border fence with up to three years in prison for anyone caught so doing, and with children subject to the same procedures and penalties as adults. ('Hungary: Power, Punishment and the Christian National Idea' 41)

Fekete also notes that emergency legislation authorised the army to support Hungarian border police, clearing both forces to 'use rubber bullets, tear-gas grenades and pyrotechnical devices', while a parliamentary resolution unequivocally backed the use of 'all available measures to defend Hungary's borders' ('Hungary' 41). Accordingly, in *Jupiter's Moon*, maltreatment and exploitation are rife within the camp as Aryan swiftly discovers. Still wounded, he encounters Gábor Stern (Merab Ninidze), an ethically suspect doctor, who, upon examining the three large bullet holes in his patient's chest and torso, senses the possibility for a financial windfall. Gábor offers to help Aryan escape the camp in exchange for his agreeing to use his superpowers to validate the doctor's prowess as a 'spiritual healer' and in the process help defraud vulnerable patients in Budapest. Once in Budapest, Aryan must do Gábor's bidding, outwit László, and later survive a national manhunt after being inadvertently implicated in a terrorist plot to bomb the Budapest metro system. Therefore, although *Jupiter's Moon* strives to equate Aryan's gifts with the divine, it also makes clear that where László considered him to be sub-human, Gábor initially views him solely as a commodity to be exploited, before later reversing his position after being overcome with remorse upon hearing that Mourad died during the border crossing. Gábor's eventual change of heart will in time be shared by ordinary Hungarians in the film who are awed by Aryan's ability to fly. Such are his gifts that it will ultimately prove impossible to deny his humanity, with even László declining an opportunity to shoot him as he floats above the centre of Budapest in the film's concluding scene. With traffic stopped by onlookers gazing up in wonderment, László aims directly at Aryan, before unexpectedly pausing, lowering his gun and turning to face the camera. Staring directly at the audience, the faintest hint of a smile discernible on his face, László appears to defy us not to be similarly affected, a challenge underscored by Mundruczó's decision to not to cut away for a full ten seconds. If somebody as zealously opposed to refugees as László can change, the message appears clear, then so can anybody.

A difficulty with accepting such a reading verbatim, however, is that in order to be acknowledged as human, Aryan first must demonstrate superhuman abilities. In this sense, he is not unlike Sidney Poitier's Dr John Wayde Prentice in *Guess Who's Coming to Dinner* (Stanley Kramer 1967) in that he is forced to prove himself extraordinary just to gain the acceptance of his distinctly ordinary peers. Mundruczó and Kata Wéber clearly have wider motivations for creating a refugee character whose wondrous gifts make him impossible to ignore. After all, the spectre of thousands of ordinary refugees being assaulted by riot police at the Hungarian-Serb border in 2015[17] did little to quell popular support for Fidesz.[18] Aryan then is a clear challenge to some of the assumptions upon which Fidesz's reactionary ideologies are based. Most saliently, Aryan is carefully calibrated to evoke Christ, a strategy that implicitly problematises Hungary's Christian identity and with it Orbán's official reasons for rejecting 'incompatible' Middle-Eastern migrants. His name alone challenges notions of authenticity, undermining a basic building block of white supremacy: 'Aryan' being adopted by the Nazis to classify Nordic racial purity, despite originally referring to Indo-Iranians and thus people from the Middle East (just as early swastikas have been found throughout Mesopotamia). Aryan is thus a true member of the Aryan race in its original form, even if we should not overlook the rider that he is played by a Hungarian actor. Mundruczó's often heavy-handed depiction of Aryan—he is a carpenter's son who rose from the dead—wilfully complicates the conflation of Christianity with white supremacy by reminding us that Christ too came from the Middle East, a fact that today would almost certainly bar him from entry into Hungary. When Gábor asks him why he is in Hungary, Aryan is cryptic, stating only that everybody has a specific purpose in life. Having fled Homs, which was devastated during the Syrian Civil War, Aryan is redeemer and avenging angel rolled into one, and accordingly, the screenplay is awash with references to angels and god. Like the angels in Wim Wenders' *Wings of Desire* (1987), Aryan occupies a liminal space, capable of rising above the fray and observing, and yet is not entirely human either, at least not in the minds of his pursuers. Lamenting the state of modern Hungary, Gábor at one point speculates that Aryan was resurrected to bring a much-needed message to a country where 'people forgot to look up'. Gábor's redemption will come when he sacrifices his life to save Aryan from László, who in turn will spare Aryan, but others will not be so lucky. When Gábor and Aryan attend to a skinhead patient, for instance, the man in question expresses revulsion that his doctor would hire a 'gyppo', before confronting Aryan and calling him a 'filthy pig'. Adorned with neo-Nazi tattoos and spewing racial insults, the patient is an obvious cipher for extreme nationalism and is thus beyond redemption. Ergo, as Aryan demonstrates his powers, in this case creating a vortex that destroys the man's living room, Gábor blithely announces that 'The Lord has sent his angel…And the Lord will punish you now.' By repeatedly framing Aryan in Christian terms, therefore, *Jupiter's Moon* highlights an absence of Christianity in Fidesz's espousal of Christian identity while conversely suggesting that Judgement Day is coming to those who fail to recognise the error of their ways.

Europa

A suspicion lingers that for all Fidesz's Euroscepticism, Hungary needs the EU more than it lets on, even if only to play the part of surrogate other in the absence of the Soviet Union. More pragmatic reasons are in play too, not least a major discrepancy between what Hungary receives in annual funding from the EU and what it contributes.[19] Additionally, and not at all insignificantly, an absence of actual refugees in Hungary to scapegoat is handily offset by the presence of the EU, which functions as a de facto aggregation of miscellaneous anxieties. On this point *Jupiter's Moon* notably demurs, with an expository intertitle simultaneously explaining the film's title and painting Europe as a bountiful space, ripe for new beginnings:

> Jupiter has 67 known moons. The four largest were discovered in 1610 by Galileo Galilei. One moon is presumed to have a saltwater ocean under its icy surface. This could be a cradle of new life forms. That moon has been named Europa.

Tensions between Hungary and the EU came to a head in 2015, when the Council of the European Union drew up a 'European Agenda on Migration', issuing a call for immediate action to relieve the pressure on Greece and Italy, who were receiving the bulk of migrants escaping conflicts in Syria and Libya. The Council, a distinct body that represents EU member states' executive governments, called for a suspension of the Dublin Regulation, a mutually agreed EU directive which stipulated that asylum seekers be processed within the country in which they first claimed asylum. Citing the humanitarian crisis in the Mediterranean, the Council called for 'a temporary distribution scheme for persons in clear need of international protection to ensure a fair and balanced participation of all Member States to this common effort' ('Proposal for a Council Decision Establishing Provisional Measures in the Area of International Protection for the Benefit of Italy, Greece and Hungary'). The proposals would have allowed for the relocation of up to 160,000 people across the EU but were challenged by Hungary and Slovakia, who were later joined in opposition by Poland. In 2017, the European Court of Justice dismissed this challenge while separately launching action against Hungary and Poland for a refusal to take in any refugees as part of the Council's plan (Kroet, 'ECJ Rejects Slovakia, Hungary Refugee Challenge'). While thousands of migrants have passed through the nation in recent years, many of whom were en route to Germany, it is estimated that by 2017, there were less than 700 migrants in Hungary, a significant number of whom were detained in militarised camps near the Serbian border (Dunai, 'Hungary Builds New High-tech Border Fence'). The veracity of such estimates is endorsed by the scale of the Council of the European Union's agenda, which had called upon Hungary to accept 1,294 migrants from Italy and Greece. As of April 2018, the European Commission notes that Hungary has refused to accept a single migrant ('Member States' Support to Emergency Relocation Mechanism'). Like Orbán before him, Hungarian Foreign Minister Péter Szijjártó sought to frame the EU's agenda in ethnopolitical terms, labelling it a 'rape of European law and values' (Thorpe, 'Hungary rages at EU Asylum Verdict'). This espousal of European values by an avowedly Eurosceptic government would be ironic, were it not suffused with strongly ethnonationalist and exclusively Christian undertones deliberated to resonate in Prague, Warsaw, and Bratislava as much as Budapest.[20] *Jupiter's Moon*'s opening nod to Galileo, therefore, is surely calibrated to underline the fallacies of such religious fundamentalism in a European sphere. Branded a heretic by a Roman Inquisition affronted by the very notion of heliocentrism, the 'father of modern physics' was sentenced to a lifetime of house arrest, a further reminder, lest we need it, of the dangers of confusing 'European laws and values' with selective religious dogma.

Lithuania

Film: Vanishing Waves/Aurora (Kristina Buožytė 2012)

The southernmost of Europe's Baltic States, Lithuania was the first Soviet Republic to declare independence and, along with near neighbours Estonia, Latvia, and Poland, joined the EU in 2004. Once the largest country in Europe,[21] today Lithuania is one of the EU's more sparsely populated member states, with its total of almost three million citizens putting it ahead of Latvia, Estonia, and Slovenia but behind every other mainland EU nation bar Luxembourg. Perhaps unsurprisingly then, dedicated scholarship of Lithuanian cinema remains comparatively thin on the ground, a reality which Bjorn Ingvoldstad suggests may be due in part to a need to recalibrate inadequate definitions of Lithuanian cinema history.[22] As was the case in Latvia and Estonia, a localised Lithuanian film culture was 'launched under the Russian empire, gained relative independence in the interwar period' but was then 'forcefully incorporated into the centralized film industries of the Soviet Union after World War Two' (Imre, *A Companion to Eastern European Cinema* 10). Kristina Buožytė's *Vanishing Waves/Aurora*, therefore, is not only independent Lithuania's first sf production, it is also the first Lithuanian film of any kind to be theatrically released in the North American market (Hough, 'Sensory

Deprivation and Cinema'). Shot at Tremora Studios in Vilnius and cowritten by Buožytė and Spanish writer/director Bruno Samper, the film was released internationally under the former title, most likely to avoid confusion with the Romanian drama *Aurora* (Cristi Puiu 2010). A self-consciously arthouse sf, *Vanishing Waves* explores the uncomfortable 'relationship' between Lukas (Marius Jampolskis), a violently misogynistic scientist for Aurora—a European experimental research project specialised in 'human neuron research'—and a young woman (Jurga Jutaite) rendered comatose by a drowning accident, whose thoughts the project is attempting to access. Journeying within the deepest recesses of her mind—a journey he likens to 'lucid dreams'—Lukas swiftly falls for the woman and inserts himself into her increasingly detailed sexual fantasies, a fact he keeps hidden from his unsuspecting colleagues. Although she will remain comatose for the duration of the film, her dream-state is brought vividly to life by Buožytė in a series of visually arresting scenes which seemingly blur Lukas' desires with his subject's supressed memories. *Vanishing Waves*' ethical heft therefore comes from deciding who is ultimately controlling who, as Lukas swiftly becomes obsessed with the woman (whom he also refers to as Aurora) and attempts to lead her back to consciousness.[23]

A Dialogue with European Modernism

A Eurimages co-production featuring a Lithuanian/English screenplay,[24] *Vanishing Waves* gained considerable traction on the European film festival circuit, winning the Méliés d'Or award in 2012[25] and Best Film at the 2013 Dublin International Film Festival, while its penetration of the American market stemmed from a premiere at the 2012 Fantastic Fest in Austin, the largest film genre festival in the United States.[26] National exposure would follow at the 2013 Lithuanian Silver Crane Awards, where *Vanishing Waves* won Best Film (as did Buožytė's 2008 debut feature *The Collectress/Kolekcioniere*) and Buožytė best director, cementing her place as one of Lithuania's pre-eminent up-and-coming filmmakers. At first, *Vanishing Waves* appears quite straightforward, framed as an intrepid voyage of discovery undertaken by Lukas, one which soon offers sexual possibilities that he proves eager to pursue. Isolated in a sensory deprivation pool, Lukas is connected to Aurora via neuron-transferring wires affixed to skullcaps in time-honoured sf fashion.[27] His journeys from the lab into Aurora's mind are depicted visually as dives into the depths of a lake, from where he follows a light to the surface, a motif that will be repeated throughout the film. From there he must swim to unknown shores, a leap of faith necessary for him to reach Aurora, even as her physical body reposes in the lab and as such is little more than a human test case for the observing team of scientists. With each journey, Lukas delves deeper into Aurora's past, finding out what makes her tick and learning more about her innermost desires. As such, Lukas and his colleagues in the European research team recall the European Commission's close observation of Lithuania's candidacy for EU membership, a process that took several years and was not without its problems.[28] Although some 90 per cent of Lithuanians voted in favour of joining the EU during a referendum held in May 2003, the process was not altogether straightforward as Ida Harboe Knudsen has noted:

> Europeanization entails a new class of marginalized citizens; the geopolitical belonging that came about with the membership not only fuelled political and economic processes, but likewise forged a reconceptualization of recent history and national identity. In Lithuania, citizens were expected to arise from the Soviet breakup as no longer Soviet-minded citizens, but internationally minded "New Lithuanians". (*New Lithuania in Old Hands* 4)

While much pre-accession debate in the Baltic States of Lithuania, Latvia, and Estonia focused upon the opportunities afforded by EU membership, Daunis Auers notes that 'these early debates did not envisage how long and how traumatic the economic and social transformation would prove', and while all three have experienced significant GDP growth in the interim, it remains the case that 'a quarter century after the break with the Soviet Union all three Baltic states are still much poorer than their Nordic neighbours and incomes remain well below the European Union average' (*Comparative Politics and Government of the Baltic States* 156–157). Sure enough, Aurora's unconscious mind in time becomes a contested space, as trauma from her past collides with Lukas' efforts to exert control over her ever-shifting desires. The scientific reasoning behind this spatial contestation is later provided by one of Lukas' superiors who attributes it to 'the observer effect', wherein an observer 'influences the observing system', meaning that because of Lukas, Aurora's unconscious mind is in a state of flux and signifies an interstitial space between her past and possible future.[29] To this end, Buožytė's choice of title is hardly coincidental: Aurora being the Latin word for dawn as well as the goddess of dawn in Roman mythology. In *Vanishing Waves*, Aurora's past traumas come to the surface as her thoughts meld with those of Lukas the observer and her unconscious experiences a host of ruptures. Framed, as we will now see, within repeated references to modernist European cinema, these ruptures link Aurora with Lithuania and the trauma she encounters with the rapid changes experienced by Lithuanian society in keeping with the nation's embrace of a new post-communist, pro-EU dawn.

Modernist Cinema and the Uncanny

In interview, Buožytė has been vocal about the influence she drew for *Vanishing Waves* from European modernist cinema, expressing particular admiration for Michelangelo Antonioni, whose work she describes as being 'all about inner mood' and 'more than storytelling but a way of being', a description that we could just as easily apply to *Vanishing Waves* ('Lithuanian Director Kristina Buožytė on Vanishing Waves'). Beyond Antonioni, however, the film explicitly draws upon Robert Wiene's masterwork of German Expressionism *The Cabinet of Dr. Caligari/Das Cabinet des Dr. Caligari* (1920) and Luis Buñuel's Surrealist satire *The Golden Age/L'Âge d'or* (1930), for reasons that I will shortly explore. Additionally, *Vanishing Waves* owes a debt to Rainer Werner Fassbinder's *World on a Wire/Welt am Draht* (1973), a film which also depicts the attempts of an emotionally unstable lab-bound male to come to terms with new ontological contingencies that decentre his privileged assumptions.[30] It is the links to the first two films that are particularly telling, however, for they explicitly foreground the collapse of the contested, transitional dream world and force both Lukas and Aurora to abandon the comforts (and traumas) of the past and adjust to a new world order where things will never quite be the same again, a metaphor, should we chose to accept it, for the rapid-fire transition of Lithuania from Soviet state, to fledgling independent nation, to fully fledged member of the EU.

Although Lukas and Aurora are initially exhilarated by one another's company, things begin to unravel when Lukas stumbles upon a large abstract approximation of a house, all angles and jutting wood, and seemingly bereft of windows and doors (see Fig. 3.1). Inside, the rooms are bare and mutable and he struggles to find his bearings. Buožytė likens the house to Norman Bates' residence in *Psycho* (Alfred Hitchcock 1960), calling it an extension of Aurora, one that encapsulates: 'a little of her memory, a little of her imagination, a little of her surroundings. It's an image of how we remember' (McCabe, 'Interview: Kristina Buožytė'). Whilst the house bears a resemblance to Bates' home, its abstract configurations more convincingly recall the unsettling angular dwellings of Wiene's otherworldly *The Cabinet of Dr. Caligari*,[31] themselves evocative of Sigmund Freud's theorisation of the 'unheimlich', most commonly interpreted in English as the 'uncanny'. Unheimlich literally translates as 'un-home-like', a description that perfectly captures the 'house' that suddenly confronts Lukas (Freud, 'The "Uncanny"' 219). Freud's 1919 essay, the publication of which was more or less coterminous with the release of *Caligari*, describes unheimlich as being something oddly familiar yet unsettling, belonging 'to all that is terrible—to all that that arouses dread and creeping horror' ('The "Uncanny"' 219). Yet like the house, the word itself is ambiguous, thus eliciting the very dread its meaning connotes, with Freud stating that 'it is equally certain, too, that the word is not always used in a clearly definable sense, so that it tends to coincide with whatever excites dread' ('The "Uncanny"' 219). Freud's essay does not mention film specifically, but as Ara H. Merjian has noted, 'the Uncanny coincided with the wider diffusion of Metaphysical painting in European modernism' and modernist art stemmed perhaps above all, from crises in the representation of reality consistent with rapid technological and industrial advances in early twentieth-century European society ('Purity and Putrefaction' 123). By rejecting mimesis, or the 'realistic' imitation of reality, modernist art problematised humankind's place in a rapidly changing world, privileging instead the presentation of the unpresentable. Nowhere was this more evident than with the Surrealist movement of the 1920s and 1930s, and it is telling therefore that *Vanishing Waves* also draws heavily upon *The*

Fig. 3.1 'The Uncanny'

Golden Age, Buñuel and Salvador Dalí's Surrealist film par excellence. Surrealist art, as Elizabeth Wright has argued, gains its shock value through its use of 'patterns of discontinuity' which provoke 'that sense of "where I have I seen this before?", the Heimlich (homely and familiar) combined with the unheimlich (hidden and secret)' (*Speaking Desires Can Be Dangerous: Poetics of the Unconscious* 20). Drawing upon Theodore Adorno's essay 'Looking Back on Surrealism', where, she writes, Adorno 'maintains that the affinity of Surrealism and psychoanalysis depends not on their common interest in the symbols utilized by a truth-seeking unconscious, but rather on the way in which they both focus on the images of our childhood', Wright observes that 'the uncanny effect is brought about because we are confronted with a subjectivity now alien to us, having had to move on' (*Speaking Desires* 20). Such is the function of Aurora's 'house' in *Vanishing Waves*, for it at once presents the unpresentable ('a little of her memory, a little of her imagination, a little of her surroundings. It's an image of how we remember') while forcing Lukas to confront the reality that Aurora (and Lithuania) as he knew her is no more but instead on the verge of a rapid transformation.[32] Accordingly, Adorno suggests that surrealism's rejection of 'normal representation becomes threatening, leading to a kind of death, either because objects become rigid and unchanging, or because they melt, flow and dissolve' (*Speaking Desires* 20). It is significant then that the house is also the site at which Lukas' sense of control begins to unravel.

An Interstitial State of Being

In the 'real world' which, as a linear construction, provides a counterpoint to the experimentation of the unconscious world, Lukas' behaviour grows increasingly monstrous. Enraged, for example, that his girlfriend refuses to have sex with him during her period, Lukas attempts to rape her before returning to the lab to live out his fantasies with Aurora instead. Here in this interstitial space, he can indulge behaviour deemed taboo by society, and it is at this point that Buožytė channels *The Golden Age*, a film that begins with a close-up of scorpions and develops into a depiction of amour fou between two lovers that scandalises the bourgeois society in which they reside. Just like Buñuel's nameless lovers, Lukas and Aurora dance wildly, gorge gluttonously on food, and gleefully suck one another's toes, in scenes interspersed with images of scorpions and insects. It is not immediately clear to him, but we soon realise that Lukas himself is also being observed. Forced to take a break from the experiment, he once more channels his frustration upon vulnerable women, this time assaulting a prostitute in a pique of anger after he is unable to sustain an erection. He soon returns to the lab, eager to compensate for his sexual inadequacies and regain control of Aurora's unconscious. Yet once there, he is confronted by the abstract approximation of the house, a dissolving, melting image of the kind that Adorno argues 'are fetishes, objects once invested with emotion but now estranged, left over from the past, dead substitutes for what is no longer.' (*Speaking Desires* 20–21). Lukas desperately seeks to force his way into the house, tearing frantically at its façade, before spying from a distance a shadowy male figure (played, in a brief cameo, by the renowned Lithuanian director Šarūnas Bartas) whispering in Aurora's ear. It is unclear if this figure represents a lover from Aurora's past or an observing scientist, yet regardless, Lukas is enraged by the apparent threat to his ascendency. He beats the man senseless, gouging, biting, and punching his face until it in turn is devoid of distinguishing features and, like the house before it, transformed into an abstract approximation of a face, or an uncanny object. Observing the assault, Aurora squats in the corner of the distorted room like a distressed child, as angular steaks of light and shadow emerge from the cracks in the uneven walls, in another direct allusion to *The Cabinet of Dr. Caligari*. Traumatised by Lukas' violence, Aurora breaks down and begins to scream uncontrollably. Her comatose state had heretofore enabled her to pursue her unconscious desires free from the shackles of socially imposed notions of propriety, and while she flirted with sadomasochism, her actions to date had been consensual. Lukas' unfettered violence instead forces her to confront both his true nature and the artificiality of her 'existence'. A high-pitched frequency assails the soundtrack as he assaults the stranger, foreshadowing a heart monitor back in the lab where Aurora's body has gone into a state of cardiac arrest.

For Freud, 'an uncanny experience occurs either when repressed infantile complexes have been revived by some impression, or when the primitive beliefs we have surmounted seem once more to be confirmed' ('The Uncanny' 17), and in this respect, Lukas' actions shatter all socially acceptable parameters of sexual experimentation and operate as a return of the repressed, reminding Aurora of the violence visited upon her in real life when a drowning accident put her into a coma. A resultant breakdown in her self-conception occurs when she looks at the featureless face, and she is 'beset by abjection', to invoke Julia Kristeva, which occurs when one is confronted by a 'something' that they do not recognise as a thing

(*Powers of Horror: An Essay on Abjection* 2). Kristeva's conceptualisation of the abject draws upon Freud's uncanny, positing that 'there looms, within abjection, one of those violent, dark revolts of being... opposed to 'I'...A massive and sudden emergence of uncanniness, which... now harries me as radically separate, loathsome' (*Powers* 2). Accordingly, abjection 'disturbs identity, system, order' and problematises space, occupying 'the in-between, the ambiguous, the composite' (*Powers* 4). Aurora is thus between entities, just as Lithuania found itself after the collapse of the Soviet Union and before its accession into the EU.[33] When next we see her, Lukas is frantically chasing her through near darkness, but it is too late: the vistas once provided by her unconscious swiftly dissipating into nothingness as the filmic space literally begins to disappear. They hold one another on a beach where Lukas apologises for his actions, but Aurora asks that he let her go, stating that he has 'absorbed her' and that she 'is no longer a separate entity'. The reappearance of the uncanny has shattered the unconscious world, and though Lukas attempts to save her, the whole world in which she resides is literally disappearing. Lukas awakens back in the lab where a team of scientists are closely observing him. Aurora instead has died, her traumas and memories little more than data now to be picked over by the group of European scientific researchers.

Notes

1. As part of her electoral mandate, Marine Le Pen stated a desire to hold a referendum on continued French membership of the EU within six months of her being elected President of the Republic.
2. The Nice Treaty essentially replaced the Maastricht Treaty and paved the way for the EU's eastward expansion. It passed into law in 2003 following considerable opposition, most saliently in Ireland, whose population initially rejected the treaty in a 2001 referendum, before then accepting it in a second referendum the following year.
3. Writing in the aftermath of its 2004 expansion, Hryhoriy Nemyria argued that the EU was unlikely to welcome Ukraine any time soon for several reasons: 'Ukraine's biggest problem was its image of a country that is too big in the sense that Ukraine is larger in geography than France, and is the fifth largest country in Europe by population; too poor in the sense that GDP per capita is just slightly more than a third of the average of the ten new EU members; and, of course, too Soviet to elicit serious consideration of its chances' ('The Orange Revolution: Explaining the Unexpected' 57).

4. While the 1980s saw films such as *O-bi, O-ba: The End of Civilization/o-bi, o-ba: koniec cywilizacji* (Piotr Szulkin 1985), *Sexmission/seksmisja* (Juliusz Machulski 1984), and *On The Silver Globe/na srebrnym globie* (Andrzej Żuławski 1988) emerge, the twenty-first century has been surprisingly barren, rare exceptions being the Japanese/Polish production *Avalon* (Mamoru Oshii 2001) and the animated multinational co-production *The Congress* (Ari Folman 2013), which received some Polish financing and was based on Stanisław Lem's 1971 novel *The Futurological Congress*.
5. In the introduction to their edited collection *Cinemas in Transition in Central and Eastern Europe After 1989*, Peter Hames and Catherine Portuges note the repetition of the same pattern: 'At different times, and in different ways, the nationalized systems have collapsed and the numbers of cinemas and audience sizes have been drastically reduced. The era of cultural globalization has arrived, signalling the dominance of English-language (mainly US) cinema. However, the notion that the degree of such domination is a response to public demand is highly questionable' (3).
6. Dina Iordanova writes: 'The directors of the generation that came to the profession in the 1990s faced a difficult situation: because of non-existent distribution, their names never reached wider Bulgarian audiences; only those who worked for television are known in Bulgaria today' ('Bulgarian Cinema' 12).
7. For a detailed history of Boyana, see Dina Iordanova's chapter 'Bulgaria' in Mette Hjort and Duncan Petrie's *The Cinema of Small Nations* (2007).
8. Syfy executive Ray Cannella outlined to *Wired* how the company elected to move away from outsourcing films in order to take control of the means of production. Doing so, he reasoned, would initially be more expensive but would give the company full rights over the finished film, enabling them to rescreen it as often as they pleased ('We've Created a Monster!').
9. As early as 2004, Ken Badish, then president of the LA-based production company Active Entertainment—a frequent collaborator with Syfy—expressed doubts as to the sustainability of shooting in Bulgaria, stating that 'In Bulgaria, you can get good technical labor and all the other things you need for production. But ironically, the business these guys have created in Bulgaria is reducing the benefit of working there. Other producers come in, the costs rise, and soon you are looking for someplace else' ('We've Created a Monster!').
10. Adam Garstone writes: 'Nu Boyana is able to provide everything required for a production, from equipment to crew to sound stages to locations, through editing, VFX and grading, sound design and final mix. A producer can hand off a script to one of the in-house Unit Production Managers, who will return a full budget and will source everything possible, for

instance the company has cameras and lens packages from most of the major manufactures' ('Nu Boyana Film Studios, The East European Hollywood').
11. The nebulous nature of this 'Asian Alliance' is rather problematic insofar as it seemingly plays into Occidentalist East/West binaries, yet if we choose to give Nevio Marasović the benefit of the doubt, we could point towards George Orwell's deliberately hazy descriptions of East Asia in *Nineteen Eighty-Four* as an sf precedent, all the more so if we consider *The Show Must Go On*'s focus on a *Big Brother*-like TV show.
12. In an interview with *Film Comment*, Mundruczó stated: 'I think that after the economic crisis, and after September 11, there's been a huge moral crisis. And this new kind of cinema or cinematic language, and these new kinds of moral stories are important nowadays, because you can't find your way in conservative art anymore' (Talu, 'ND/NF Interview: Kornél Mundruczó').
13. In March 2018, *The New York Times* reported that Orbán's administration had gone so far as to amend schoolchildren's history textbooks to reflect his policies, including the contestation that 'it can be problematic for different cultures to coexist' (Kingsley, 'How Viktor Orban Bends Hungarian Society to His Will').
14. The long-standing relationship between Orbán and Soros—an American-based billionaire and Holocaust survivor—is a complex one that spans the length of contemporary Hungarian democracy. Writing for *The Washington Post*, Griff Witte elaborates: 'Orban was a young democratic activist in the dying days of communist control in the late 1980s. Soros funded a scholarship for him to study at Oxford and even helped with the launch of Fidesz, which began as a liberal student movement'. Measures taken to undermine Soros included a nationwide survey posted to every home in Hungary which, Witte reports, 'asked a series of leading questions, including whether respondents supported the "Soros plan" to "resettle at least one million immigrants from Africa and the Middle East annually on the territory of the European Union, including Hungary' ('Once-fringe Soros Conspiracy Theory Takes Center Stage in Hungarian Election').
15. Whilst Fidesz nominally stood to lose ground to a party that attracted over a million votes in the 2014 Parliamentary Elections (over 20 per cent of the overall vote), Jobbik's rise contributed to a significant lowering of the tone of national discourse which in turn has served to normalise Fidesz's move further to the right (Paterson, 'Concerns as neo-Nazi Jobbik Party wins 20% of Vote'). This phenomenon is by no means exclusive to Central and Eastern Europe of course; witness, for example, how the emergence of UKIP precipitated a rightward swerve by the British Conservative Party which ultimately contributed to the Brexit referendum.

16. As Anniina Hyttinen and Lena Näre explain: 'publically Fidesz condemns most of the proposals of Jobbik, but has later on implemented some of them', a case in point being the first law amendment put forward by Fidesz in 2010 which granted Hungarian citizenship to all ethnic Hungarians living in neighbouring countries ('Symbolic and Ritual Enactments of Nationalism' 238).
17. Describing the moment that the 2015 refugee crisis arrived directly on Hungary's borders, Liz Fekete writes: 'Disturbing images relayed across the world showed riot police at the Hungarian-Serb border dispersing exhausted refugee families with tear-gas and water cannon while a video, uploaded onto Youtube, exposed guards throwing food at detainees in metal pens as though they were animals in cages' ('Hungary: Power, Punishment and the 'Christian-National Idea' 39).
18. On the contrary, Fidesz's immigration stance arguably only contributed to increased electoral gains, with the party returning to power in the 2018 Hungarian general elections. It should be noted, however, that not all Hungarians are enamoured with Orbán, and a protest march the week after his re-election drew an estimated 100,000 people onto the streets of Budapest. In addition to its size, the crowd was noteworthy for its diversity, with *Politico* reporting that 'young liberals, far-right Jobbik supporters, and pensioners all marched together [while] European Union flags could be seen alongside the red and white Arpad flag, associated with Hungary's murderous World War II-era Arrow Cross regime' (Bayer, '100,000 Hungarians March Against Viktor Orbán').
19. In 2016, for example, the EU spent €4.546 billion in Hungary, with Hungary instead contributing less than a quarter of that figure (€0.924 billion) to that year's EU budget ('European Union: Hungary').
20. In policy terms, a practical result of Orbán's cultivation of closer relationships with Hungary's fellow Visegrád members is the group's ability to veto EU disciplinary sanctions against fellow members, for any such measures are dependent upon the consensus of all 28 member states.
21. Ida Harboe Knudsen writes that during the fourteenth century, the then Grand Duchy of Lithuania comprised 'Belarus, Ukraine and parts of Poland and Russia. In 1569 Poland and Lithuania formed a new state, the Polish-Lithuanian Commonwealth' which endured for over two centuries before eventually being incorporated into the Russian Empire (*New Lithuania in Old Hands* ix).
22. In 'Paradox of Lithuanian National Cinema', Ingvoldstad argues that 'the political and economic structure of Soviet film production calls for a rethinking of how we understand the function of national cinemas. Paradoxically, it appears that "Lithuanian national cinema" did in fact exist and was viable—but only at a time when the Lithuanian nation was still subsumed within the Soviet state' (140).

23. As Jeannette Catsoulis writes in a review of the film for *The New York Times*: 'Whatever else is going on in the psychedelic science-fiction tale "Vanishing Waves", an unflattering portrait of the male psyche is front and center. With Aurora struggling for sensation and Lukas beginning to feel too much, we're left with a single question: Who is awakening whom?' ('Lustful Pursuit of Sensory Overload').
24. *Vanishing Waves* was part-funded by the Lithuanian Cultural Ministry and the Vilnius-based production company Tremora Films as well as production companies from Belgium (Les Films 2 Cinema) and France (Acajou Films). Eurimages, in turn, allocated €150,000 towards the film's overall budget of €1,175,000, which also benefitted from the backing of the EU's MEDIA programme ('Co-Production Funding in 2010').
25. The Brussels-based European Fantastic Film Festivals Federation, which draws its votes from 22 film festivals, created the Méliés d'Or awards in 1996 to 'highlight the creativity and quality of European fantastic films, stimulate production and promote them worldwide' ('European Fantastic Film Festivals Federation'). Focussing upon European genre film, the federation links established festivals such as the Trieste Science+Fiction Festival, the Lund International Fantastic Film Festival, and the Brussels International Fantastic Film Festival and grants international exposure to sf and fantasy films that may otherwise be overlooked.
26. Festival exposure was central to *Vanishing Waves*' rise in prominence, and on the back of such success, it got picked up by Philadelphia-based Artsploitation Films which oversaw the film's distribution in America (Galetski, 'Lithuanian Sci-Fi Film Gets U.S. Distribution').
27. Here the film draws heavily upon iconography from films such as *The Matrix* (Lana and Lili Wachowski 1999) and *Minority Report* (Steven Spielberg 2002).
28. In 1999, the European Commission presented its second 'Regular Report on Progress Towards Enlargement', concluding that 'formal accession negotiations with Lithuania should begin as soon as possible'. Previously, the commission had recommended that Lithuania not be among those countries with whom accession negotiations should be opened due to a need to stymy corruption and oversee continued reform of the Lithuanian judiciary ('Briefing No 11 Lithuania and the Enlargement of the European Union').
29. A simple example of the observer effect occurs when we consider that in order for us to see an object, we need to allow the same object to be hit by light, thereby at least nominally altering the conditions in which it exists.
30. At one point Lukas finds Aurora sitting in front of two mirrors, one reflecting her image and another his own, the symbolism underscored by her remarking that 'sometimes I don't recognise you. I like that'. The struggle

for recognition and with it a claim on reality is reflected in the scene's mise en scène which directly recalls arguably *the* key scene in *World on a Wire* when Fred Stiller (Klaus Löwitsch) is informed by his lover Eva Vollmer (Mascha Rabben) that his whole world is a simulation. Before them on the dressing table are three mirrors, none of which reflect the images of Stiller and Vollmer at the same time. Stiller, whose all-action, sexually aggressive persona suggests the caricature of a man in control, has his worst suspicions confirmed, namely, that he can be erased from the world with the press of a button, a turn of events Vollmer explains to him while she brushes her hair.

31. In her book, *Movies and the Modern Psyche*, Sharon Packer describes the aesthetic effects of *The Cabinet of Dr. Caligari* thusly: 'Diagonal lines generally induce unease because they lack the stability of horizontal lines and are not grounded like vertical lines projecting from a surface. Everything in Caligari is set at an angle, and a deliberately disorienting angle at that' (69).
32. Tellingly, Buožytė also links Lukas' journeys into Aurora's unconscious to his childhood, stating that 'every connection was built on Lukas and what he experienced as a child. The bath—when the child comes up from the water—or when he sees very abstract shapes' (Hough, 'Sensory Deprivation and Cinema').
33. Central to this reading is the striking image of Aurora that featured heavily in the marketing campaign for *Vanishing Waves* (adorning film posters, DVD, and Blu-ray covers). The image in question stems from an orgy scene at a party, which Aurora attends wearing a dress of deep EU blue. At her feet, an entangled physically indeterminate mass of naked bodies lays writhing on the floor, and although Lukas succeeds in prising himself away from the bodies, Aurora is grabbed at by random hands, her elusive form slowly subsumed by the collective. Naked from the waist up and standing above a mass of interlinked bodies, she pauses momentarily and stares defiantly ahead, a visual embodiment of Eugène Delacroix's iconic French Revolutionary painting *Liberty Leading the People* (1830) amidst a sea of abject bodies.

Bibliography

Adorno, Theodore. 1991. Looking Back on Surrealism. In *Notes to Literature: Volume 1*, ed. Rolf Tiedemann, 86–90. Trans. Shierry Weber Nicholsen. New York: Columbia University Press.

Auers, Daunis. 2015. *Comparative Politics and Government of the Baltic States: Estonia, Latvia and Lithuania in the 21st Century*. New York: Palgrave Macmillan.

Baudrillard, Jean. 1996. No Pity for Sarajevo; The West's Serbianization; When the West Stands in for the Dead. In *This Time We Knew: Western Responses to Genocide in Bosnia*, ed. Thomas Cushman and Stjepan G. Meštrović, 79–89. New York: New York University Press.

Bayer, Lily. 2018. 100,000 Hungarians March Against Viktor Orbán. *Politico*, April 15. www.politico.eu/article/100000-hungarians-march-against-viktor-orban/. Accessed 1 May 2018.

Briefing No 11: Lithuania and the Enlargement of the European Union. 2000. *European Parliament*, October 24. www.europarl.europa.eu/enlargement/briefings/11a3_en.htm. Accessed 1 May 2018.

Brunsden, Jim. 2017. Orban: EU's "Christian Identity" Under Threat from Muslim Migrants. *Financial Times*, March 30.

Catsoulis, Jeanette. 2013. Lustful Pursuit of Sensory Overload. *New York Times*, March 14.

Co-Production Funding in 2010. 2010. *Eurimages*, December 21. www.coe.int/en/web/eurimages/co-production-funding-in-2010#M2010. Accessed 1 May 2018.

Dunai, Marton. 2017. Hungary Builds New High-Tech Border Fence. *Reuters*, March 2. ec.europa.eu/home-affairs/sites/homeaffairs/files/what-we-do/policies/european-agenda-migration/backgroundinformation/docs/communication_on_the_european_agenda_on_migration_annex_en.pdf. Accessed 1 May 2018.

Elsaesser, Thomas. 2015a. European Cinema Into the Twenty-first Century. In *The Europeanness of European Cinema: Identity, Meaning, Globalization*, ed. Mary Harrod, Mariana Liz, and Alissa Timoshkina, 17–33. London: I.B. Tauris.

———. 2015b. European Cinema into the Twenty-first Century. In *The Europeanness of European Cinema: Identity, Meaning, Globalization*, ed. Mary Harrod, Mariana Liz, and Alissa Timoshkina, 17–33. New York: I.B. Tauris.

European Fantastic Film Festivals Federation. www.melies.org. Accessed 1 May 2018.

European Schemes for Relocation and Settlement. 2015. *European Commission*, April 8.

European Union: Hungary. *Europa.eu*. europa.eu/european-union/about-eu/countries/member-countries/hungary_en. Accessed 1 May 2018.

Ewing, Jack. 2014. Making Films in Bulgaria Can Bring Pleasures and Frustrations. *New York Times*, July 7.

Fekete, Liz. 2016. Hungary: Power, Punishment and the "Christian-National Idea". *Race and Class* 57 (4): 39–53. filmireland.net/2014/01/22/interview-kristina-buozyte/. Accessed 1 May 2018.

Frater, Patrick. 2014. Nu Image, Active to Make Four Syfy Movies. *Chicago Tribune*, May 13.

Freud, Sigmund. 2001. The "Uncanny". In *The Standard Edition of the Complete Psychological Works of Sigmund Freud, Volume XVII (1917–1919): An Infantile Neurosis and Other Works*, 217–256. London: Vintage.

Galetski, Kirill. 2013. Lithuanian Sci-Fi Film Gets U.S. Distribution. *The Hollywood Reporter*, February 4.

Garstone, Adam. 2015. Nu Boyana Film Studios, The East European Hollywood. *Definition*, July 17. www.definitionmagazine.com/journal/2015/7/17/n61qzxhua5ri7j58a6gytj1vd4vx1q. Accessed 1 May 2018.

Harvey, David. 2005. *A Brief History of Neoliberalism*. Oxford: Oxford University Press.

Hough, Q.V. 2014. Sensory Deprivation and Cinema: A Chat with Kristina Buožytė and Bruno Samper of "Vanishing Waves". *Vague Visages*, December 16. vaguevisages.com/2014/12/16/sensory-deprivation-and-cinema-a-chat-with-kristina-buozyte-and-bruno-samper-of-vanishing-waves/. Accessed 1 May 2018.

Hyttinen, Anniina, and Lena Näre. 2017. Symbolic and Ritual Enactments of Nationalism–A Visual Study of Jobbik's Gatherings During Hungarian National Day Commemorations. *Visual Studies* 32 (3): 236–250.

Imre, Anikó, ed. 2012. *A Companion to Eastern European Cinema*. Chichester: Wiley.

Ingvoldstad, Bjorn. 2008. Paradox of Lithuanian Cinema. *Place and Location: Studies in Environmental Aesthetics and Semiotics* 7: 137–154.

Iordanova, Dina. 2007. Bulgaria. In *The Cinema of Small Nations*, ed. Mette Hjort and Duncan Petrie, 93–110. Bloomington: Indiana University Press.

———. 2013. Bulgarian Cinema: Optimism in Moderation. In *Cinemas in Transition in Central and Eastern Europe After 1989*, ed. Catherine Portuges and Peter Hames, 10–39. Philadelphia: Temple University Press.

Jelić, Marcella. 2013. Information Technology as Basis for the Changes in the Social Role of Film. In *4th International Conference "The Future of Information Sciences: INFuture2013 – Information Governance"*, 6–8 November, 85–94.

Kingsley, Patrick. 2018. How Viktor Orban Bends Hungarian Society to His Will. *New York Times*, March 27.

Knudsen, Ida Harboe. 2012. *New Lithuania in Old Hands: Effects and Outcomes of EUropeanization in Rural Lithuania*. New York: Anthem Press.

Krasteva, Yonka. 2004. Western Writing and the (Re)Construction of the Balkans. In *The Balkans and the West: Constructing the European Other, 1945–2003*, ed. Andrew Hammond, 97–109. Hampshire: Ashgate.

Kristeva, Julia. 1982. *Powers of Horror: An Essay on Abjection*. Trans. Leon S. Roudiez. New York: Columbia University Press.

Kristina Buožytė. *Lithuanian Cultural Institute*. lithuanianculture.lt/atlikejai/kristina-buozyte/?lang=en. Accessed 1 May 2018.

Kroet, Cynthia. 2017. ECJ Rejects Slovakia, Hungary Refugee Challenge. *Politico*, September 16. www.politico.eu/article/ecj-rejects-slovakia-hungary-refugee-challenge/. Accessed 1 May 2018.

Landau, Arlene. 2016. White God. (2014). Directed and Co-written by Kornél Mundruczó. *Psychological Perspectives* 59 (1): 149–151.
Lem, Stanisław. 1971. *The Futurological Congress*. New York: Seabury Press.
Lithuanian Director Kristina Buožytė on Vanishing Waves. 2015. *Cineuropa*, July 31.
Lithuanian Director Kristina Buožytė on Vanishing Waves. 2015. *Cineuropa*, July 31. walkthisway.cineuropa.org/wtw.aspx?t=article&t2=news&l=en&did=295070. Accessed 1 May 2018.
Maček, Ivana. 2009. *Sarajevo Under Siege: Anthropology in Wartime*. Philadelphia: University of Pennsylvania Press.
Marcus, Imanuel. 2017. Yariv Lerner: The Man Who Runs Nu Boyana Film Studios. *Sofia Globe*, June 23.
Mazierska, Ewa, Lars Kristensen, and Eva Näripea. 2013. *Postcolonial Approaches to Eastern European Cinema: Portraying Neighbours on Screen*. London: I.B. Tauris.
McCabe, Darragh John. 2014. Interview: Kristina Buožytė. *Film Ireland*, January 22.
Member States' Support to Emergency Relocation Mechanism. 2018. *European Commission*, April 30. ec.europa.eu/home-affairs/sites/homeaffairs/files/what-we-do/policies/european-agenda-migration/press-material/docs/state_of_play_-_relocation_en.pdf. Accessed 1 May 2018.
Merjian, Ara H. 2016. Purity and Putrefaction: Salvador Dalí's Apparatus and Hand (1927). In *Modernism and the Avant-Garde Body in Spain and Italy*, ed. Nicolás Fernández-Medina and Maria Truglio, 113–131. New York: Routledge.
Meštrović, Stjepan. 1994. *Balkanization of the West: The Confluence of Postmodernism and Postcommunism*. London: Routledge.
Nedyalkova, Maya. 2017. Festivals Gone Digital: A Case-Study of Netcinema.bg and the Online European Film Festival in Bulgaria. In *Transformation Processes in Post-Socialist Screen Media*, ed. Jana Dudková and Katarína Mišíková, 138–153. Bratislava: Bratislava, Academy of Performing Arts.
Nemyria, Hryhoriy. 2005. The Orange Revolution: Explaining the Unexpected. In *Democratisation in the European Neighbourhood*, ed. Michael Emerson, 53–62. Brussels: Centre for European Policy Studies.
Packer, Sharon. 2007. *Movies and the Modern Psyche*. Westport: Praeger.
Paterson, Tony. 2014. Hungary Election: Concerns as Neo-Nazi Jobbik Party Wins 20% of Vote. *Independent*, April 7.
Pavlic, Vedran. 2017. Croatia Marks Four Years as EU Member State. *Total Croatia News*, July 1.
Petkovic, Vladan. 2011. The Show Must Go On with the Widest Local Roll-out Ever. *Cineuropa*, April 27.cineuropa.org/nw.aspx?t=newsdetail&l=en&did=202420. Accessed 1 May 2018.
Pleasant, Lesley C. 2017. Seeing Beings: "Dog" Looks Back at "God": Unfixing Canis familiaris in Kornél Mundruczó's Film Fehér isten/White God (2014). *Humanities* 82 (6): 1–21.

Portuges, Catherine, and Peter Hames, eds. 2013. *Cinemas in Transition in Central and Eastern Europe After 1989*. Philadelphia: Temple University Press.

Proposal for a Council Decision Establishing Provisional Measures in the Area of International Protection for the Benefit of Italy, Greece and Hungary. 2015. *European Commission*, September 9. ec.europa.eu/home-affairs/sites/homeaffairs/files/what-we-do/policies/european-agendamigration/proposalimplementationpackage/docs/proposal_for_council_decision_establishing_provisional_measures_in_the_area_of_international_protection_for_it_gr_and_hu_en.pdf. Accessed 1 May 2018.

Rivi, Luisa. 2007. *European Cinema After 1989: Identity and Transnational Production*. New York: Palgrave Macmillan.

Schengen: Enlargement of Europe's Border-Free Area. 2018. *European Parliament*, February 23. www.europarl.europa.eu/news/en/headlines/security/20180216STO98008/schengen-enlargement-of-europe-s-border-free-area. Accessed 1 May 2018.

Schwartz, Matthias. 2017. Archaeologies of a Past Future. In *Future Imperfect: Science, Fiction, Film*, ed. Rainer Rother and Annika Schaefer, 96–117. Berlin: Bertz & Fischer.

Sudar, Vlastimir. 2014. New Neighbours, Old Habits and Nobody's Children: Croatia in the Face of Old Yugoslavia. In *Postcolonial Approaches to Eastern European Cinema: Portraying Neighbours on-Screen*, ed. Ewa Mazierska, Lars Kristensen, and Eva Naripea, 227–251. London: I.B. Tauris.

Talu, Yonca. 2015. ND/NF Interview: Kornél Mundruczó. *Film Comment*, March 20. www.filmcomment.com/blog/ndnf-interview-kornel-mundruczo-white-god/. Accessed 1 May 2018.

Than, Krisztina. 2017. Hungarian PM Orban to Ask EU to Help Foot Bill. *Reuters*, August 31.

Thorpe, Nick. 2017. Europe Migrant Crisis: Hungary Rages at EU Asylum Verdict. *BBC*, September 6. www.bbc.co.uk/news/world-europe-41177420. Accessed 1 May 2018.

Trifonova, Temenuga. 2011. Between the National and the Transnational: Bulgarian Post-Communist Cinema. *Studies in Eastern European Cinema* 2 (2): 211–225.

Witte, Griff. 2018. Once-fringe Soros Conspiracy Theory Takes Center Stage in Hungarian Election. *The Washington Post*, March 17.

Wolf, Gary. 2004. We've Created a Monster! *Wired*, January 10. www.wired.com/2004/10/scifi-2/. Accessed 1 May 2018.

Wright, Elizabeth. 1999. *Speaking Desires Can Be Dangerous: The Poetics of the Unconscious*. Malden: Polity Press.

PART II

Contagion! Responding to the Financial Crisis

CHAPTER 4

PIIGS to the Slaughter

Early on Monday morning, 15 September 2008, the New York-based investment bank Lehman Brothers formally filed for bankruptcy. The largest filing of its kind in US history, the announcement had seismic implications for stock markets around the world, triggering a worldwide economic crisis the likes of which had been unseen since the 1930s. As stocks plummeted, panic quickly spread to Europe and soon threatened the existence of the still nascent euro currency, long trumpeted as a crowning achievement of the 1992 Maastricht Treaty, which copper-fastened the establishment of the EU. Despite stern opposition, most saliently in Britain and Denmark,[1] which both secured opt-outs from adopting the new currency, the treaty was ratified and came into force on 1 November 1993. Within nine years the currency was in full circulation, and by February 2002, the euro had replaced native currencies across the then-12-member states of the Eurozone. Currently 19 of the EU's 28 member states are Eurozone members, with Cyprus, Estonia, Latvia, Lithuania, Malta, Slovakia, and Slovenia adopting the currency in the interim years. Given the euro's subsequent struggles, as well as the attendant opprobrium it has attracted across Europe and beyond, it is easy to forget that at the time of its creation, the currency was held aloft as a pillar that would help shape a more democratic, open, and prosperous union of European states. Mariana Liz captures this optimism neatly, recounting that 'in the early 2000s, the widespread enthusiasm for a project aimed at the democratic and peaceful integration of different peoples, in economic, political and cultural terms, was epitomised by the adoption of the Single Currency, the expansion of the Schengen Area [...] and the launch of the EU's Culture Programme' (*Euro-Visions: Europe in Contemporary Cinema* 2). Given that I look closer at borders (Chap. 7) and European cultural programmes (Chap. 2) elsewhere in this book, the economic crisis in the Eurozone will be the central focus of this double chapter. In real terms, monetary union, itself the de facto crowning glory of the Maastricht Treaty and the logical outcome of the open market, became in time a Trojan horse of sorts that intensified the crisis in the Eurozone. Where once national governments could resort to various corrective measures to stem the bleeding and protect themselves from the fallout—such as the devaluation of their own currencies, for example—[2]the Eurozone's very integration required that, in times of crisis, a multilateral solution would be applied. The nature of the solutions that *were* subsequently applied—as well as their consequences—will be examined in depth in this chapter, which, after outlining the sheer scale of the issue, will focus upon sf films from five of the most affected EU member states: Portugal, Ireland, Italy, Greece, and Spain.

Punishing the Peripheries

Spooked by the global financial crisis, the European Commission announced a €200 billion stimulus plan in November 2008, in the hope of shoring up the increasingly prone Eurozone. By January 2009, several member states—including France, Ireland, Spain, and Greece—had run up budget deficits that exceeded the 3 per cent of GDP threshold nominally imposed by the EU, and the fear lingered that beneath the surface, things could, in actuality, be far worse than they seemed (Baimbridge and Whyman. *Crisis in the Eurozone: Causes, Dilemmas and Solutions*). Specifically, suspicion grew about the underlying soundness of the economies of Portugal, Ireland, Italy, Greece, and Spain, with concerns that the collapse of one could trigger a domino effect throughout the Eurozone. At the core of the problem lay the quandary of how best to proceed, distilled in reductive terms into the question of whether more or less Europe was required, the former requiring a vastly increased role for EU institutions, such as the European Central Bank, the second seemingly flying in the face of the highly interlinked realities of globalisation. This was not a new problem, however, and cut to the heart of an obvious issue with the euro since its launch. Brigitte Young synopsises the predicament neatly when observing that 'setting monetary policy at the European level while leaving fiscal policy in the hands of individual member states was a huge gamble from the inception of the European Monetary Union [EMU], and may have worked during "normal" economic times, but became the Achilles heel during the financial crisis' ('The Role of German Ordoliberalism' 4). As such, Eurozone leaders faced a choice between 'complete disintegration and deep structural reforms of the economic governance structure of the European Union' ('Ordoliberalism' 4). Although the precise cause of the Eurozone crisis remains contested,[3] James A. Caporaso and Martin Rhodes point out that a dominant narrative of 'fiscal misbehaviour' emerged, one that in many instances 'was imposed retroactively' as 'differences among countries in terms of the causal origins of the crisis got submerged in favour of one master narrative of bad fiscal policy' (*Political and Economic Dynamics of the Eurozone Crisis* 3). In short, this thinking had it that the EU's peripheral nations, the so-called PIIGS, were being governed recklessly and threatened to bring down the Eurozone. Such a narrative sat well in Brussels and Berlin and enabled the EU to proceed with punitive measures that separated the 'responsible' member states from the 'reckless' ones, conveniently ignoring systemic fault lines in the currency's adoption as well as the facilitation of unsustainable lending by German banks in the process.[4]

The acronym PIIGS is a semantically loaded one, and before proceeding, it may be fruitful to briefly explore its etymology and demonstrate its pejorative undertones. As Samuel Brazys and Niamh Hardiman have written, PIIGS has been widely used to refer to '"peripheral" European Union countries as they have experienced severe economic downturns, budgetary and debt crises, and interventions by international institutions' ('From "Tiger" to "PIIGS": Ireland and the Use of Heuristics in Comparative Political Economy' 23). The term has its origins in the 'Club Med' label attributed to Portugal, Italy, Greece, and Spain in the early 1990s, albeit the precise composition of the group was seemingly interchangeable, with Belgium and France occasionally included.[5] Over time, the acronym PIGS emerged to refer specifically to Portugal, Italy, Greece, and Spain as concerns grew about their ability to contribute to an increasingly integrated European economy. The term, which has its popular origins in a 1996 Thomas Kamm article for the *Wall Street Journal*,[6] 'took on a new context as it began to be used in discussions about EU enlargement and the proposed/pending EMU, separating Portugal, Italy, Spain and Greece according to their divergent economic history with regards to inflation and government debt and deficits' ('From "Tiger"' 28). Portugal, Spain, and Greece all emerged from totalitarian dictatorships in the mid-1970s, some three decades after Italy, a signatory to the Treaty of Rome, consolidated its transition from fascism to democracy. Whilst Italy's bona fides as a modern democracy were cemented during the *miracolo economico* (economic miracle) of the 1950s and 1960s, Portugal, Spain, and Greece required 'active programmes of institutional reform and of welfare-state building from a low base' to get up to speed with their European counterparts ('From "Tiger"' 30–31). Despite such differences, the designation PIGS cast doubt on the economic viability of all four nations, and its use proliferated with the onset of the financial crisis, when all four teetered on the verge of economic collapse.[7] Ireland, which by late 2008 grew similarly imperilled, was belatedly included, thus adding an additional 'I' to an acronym already straining under the weight of generalisation, as it lumped countries together regardless of the economic specificities of their respective travails.[8] Although the use of acronyms for countries—be it PIIGS, BRICS (Brazil, Russia, India, China, South Africa) or LDCs (least developed countries)—is common, the practice can have potentially damaging consequences and, when used as a 'heuristic to guide risk assessment in inherently unstable conditions, can have a causal effect on the very uncertainties it seeks to model [... causing ...] real consequences for the markets' treatment of the countries in question' ('From "Tiger"' 23). Drawing a correlation between media usage of the PIIGS acronym and fluctuations in bond yields in Ireland, Brazys and Hardiman argue that 'in a world of uncertainty, in which rational risk assessment is extremely problematic and response time is extremely limited, shorthand ideas captured in acronyms guide behaviour in materially significant ways' ('From "Tiger"' 36). The emphasis upon limited response time holds particular relevance if we consider the sheer unpredictability of the financial markets to which the Troika (Russian for 'group of three' consisting of European Commission, European Central Bank, and the International Monetary Fund) found itself reacting to, factors which may explain, in part, the shock and awe economic tactics that it would resort to. Accordingly, the divide between Northern and Southern Europe increased (Ireland's new-found links with its fellow PIIGS notwithstanding), while widely repeated narratives ascribing blame for the crisis upon Europe's unruly 'peripheries' allowed for a retrenchment of Europe's 'core' to occur in opposition.

Institutional Weaknesses

Amidst the fallout, the sight of unelected Troika members arriving in European capitals to instruct national governments on how to proceed amplified popular anxieties about the indelible erosion of national sovereignty and the modern-day role of the EU. Furthermore, it begged the question of how much (and who) was the EU willing to sacrifice in the pursuit of European integration. In this environment, the idea of a two-speed Europe gained ground, one where the strong dictated terms to the weak and where the democratic right of national electorates to choose their own leaders was hijacked. Italian and Greek governments were replaced with unelected technocrats: a development that was 'greeted with euphoria by the financial markets, but alienated many citizens' (Young, 'Ordoliberalism' 4) and begged the question as to whose interests the EU was ultimately serving. As numerous scholars have argued,[9] the EU has long been defined by an uneasy tension between the national and the supranational, one where in good times defects and compromises are accepted nationally as the price of doing business. In times of crisis, however, the strain of such arrangements is laid bare and, in the words of Ulrike Guérot, bears testimony to the reality 'that national sovereignty always collides with the common European interest' ('An Invitation to Bravely Think About the Future of Europe'). As I will argue in the two chapters that comprise this section, such tension was seldom leavened by official EU responses, which, if anything, contributed to the type of nationalist resurgences that European integration was designed to overcome.

Saving the System: Neoliberal Europe

While desperate times may necessitate desperate measures, it is difficult to escape the feeling that the severity of the EU's actions—which included a series of decidedly undemocratic measures—will have long-term consequences that its supporters may in time have significant cause to regret. In 'The Great Recession: Spillover in Europe, Banking Collapse in Ireland', Tony Phillips gets to the crux of the matter when observing that the cost of the EU's austerity policies will be met 'in future debt payments by national taxpayers in the PIIGS economies while the Troika controls the peripheral economy in "recovery"' (20). The ultimate gauge of success, Phillips continues, 'is not whether the patient dies but whether contagion of the core is avoided' ('The Great Recession' 20). A perceived unwillingness to punish and regulate financial institutions exacerbated suspicion of the EU's motives further, whilst a spate of state bailouts of banks blurred the already murky lines between national interests and the maintenance of an out of control system where, by 2017, eight billionaires controlled more wealth than half the world's population.[10] Austerity has served to further dilute the social functions of European states, principally by increased privatisation of state sectors, a recurring theme of neoliberal policies that Mark Fisher, drawing upon a quote commonly attributed to Fredric Jameson: that 'it's easier to imagine the end of the world than the end of capitalism', has labelled 'capitalist realism' (*Capitalist Realism* 6). Whilst Europe's structural weaknesses were in evidence before the 2008 economic crash, the interim period suggests that neoliberal policies have exploited these same weaknesses and redoubled the EU's commitment to austerity. That neoliberal economic practices survived the crisis largely due to state intervention is not without attendant irony for, as Fisher notes: 'neoliberalism surreptitiously relied on the state even while it has ideologically excoriated it [as] was made spectacularly clear during the banking crisis of 2008, when, at the invitation of neoliberal ideologues, the state rushed in to shore up the banking system' (*Capitalist Realism* 6). Yet, before looking closer at the impact of these policies upon the so-called PIIGS and at how contemporaneous sf films from all five nations respond to them, it might be useful to briefly unpack a firmer conceptualisation of neoliberalism itself.

A nebulous term, neoliberalism has been used as something of a catch-all phrase to describe a wide variety of economic phenomena in late capitalist society. As Kevan Harris and Ben Scully relay, 'neoliberalism has been used to describe a specific economic doctrine […] a project by capitalist classes […] a socio-political theory […] a set of cultural practices […] and a technique of power and governmentality' ('A Hidden Counter-Movement? Precarity, Politics, and Social Protection Before and Beyond the Neoliberal Era' 418). First popularised by Austrian economists Ludwig von Mises and Friedrich Hayek in 1938, the term 'neoliberalism' entered the mainstream in the 1970s, buoyed by enthusiastic and high-profile practitioners such as Milton Friedman,[11] before becoming a central plank of the free-market policies pursued by Ronald Reagan and Margaret Thatcher in the United States and Britain during the 1980s. Nominal swings to the left in both countries during the 1990s did little to stall its momentum as both US Democrats and Tony Blair's New Labour movement embraced neoliberal edicts, a trend succinctly summarised by the environmentalist and writer George Monbiot:

After Margaret Thatcher and Ronald Reagan took power, the rest of the package soon followed: massive tax cuts for the rich, the crushing of trade unions, deregulation, privatisation, outsourcing and competition in public services. Through the IMF, the World Bank, the Maastricht Treaty and the World Trade Organisation, neoliberal policies were imposed – often without democratic consent—on much of the world. Most remarkable was its adoption among parties that once belonged to the left. ('Neoliberalism: The Ideology at the Root of All Our Problems')

The inability of the left to present a coherent alternative to the prevailing orthodoxy allowed the impression to deepen that there was no alternative, and so, when tasked with solving the Eurozone crisis, the Troika reverted to default mode through the imposition of austerity: the long-term implications of which, Phillips writes, being 'that the populations in the peripheral nations will reverse recent standard of living improvements and have many state sectors such as social welfare, water, transport and health privatised for "competitiveness"' ('The Great Recession' 20). In a European sphere where the collapse of communism was both contemporary and local—not least in Germany where East/West divisions are still keenly felt—the Troika's actions followed in the slipstream of a consolidated new world order buoyed and indelibly shaped by the supposed 'end of history', or the ultimate triumph of Western capitalist democracy (Fukuyama, *The End of History*). While the precise contours that shape neoliberalism are often blurred due to the hold it has exerted over both the European right and left during the 1990s and 2000s, its very indeterminacy allows it to prosper: 'Imagine', Monbiot writes, 'if the people of the Soviet Union had never heard of communism [...] the ideology that dominates our lives has, for most of us, no name' ('Neoliberalism'). Yet clearly definable neoliberal patterns are nonetheless evident. Harris and Scully endorse the definition put forward by Neil Brenner, Jamie Peck, and Nik Theodore in their article 'After Neoliberalization?', namely, that 'all prevalent uses of the notion of neoliberalism involve references to the tendential extension of market-based competition and commodification processes into previously insulated realms of political-economic life' (329). The upshot of such practices is most frequently the imposition of a Darwinian ethos into the public realm, pitting workers and citizens against one another and, above all, prizing a culture of doing more with less. Prioritising 'market-based, market-oriented or market-disciplinary responses to regulatory problems', neoliberalism 'strives to intensify commodification in all realms of social life', is self-perpetuating, and frequently 'mobilizes speculative financial instruments to open up new arenas for capitalist profit-making' ('After Neoliberalization?' 330). As the Troika of EU, ECB, and IMF (a trinity that both blurs the notion of centralised command and simultaneously recalls the New Testament's radical reconceptualisation of God as the embodiment of three distinct entities) sought to gain control over the Eurozone crisis, the reassertion of a centralised Europe could be glimpsed: one that re-established the peripheral status of the southern member states of Portugal, Italy, Greece and Spain, as well as the Republic of Ireland to the west. Although seldom a unified entity (its constituent parts often clashed over policy), the Troika nonetheless pressed for severe austerity measures to be imposed upon all five nations to recoup the cost of providing them with economic bailouts. Like Fisher, Heiner Flassbeck (a former state secretary in the German Federal Ministry of Finance) and Costas Lapavitsas (a former Syriza MP) have argued that these actions should leave us in little doubt as to the true driving force behind the modern-day EU. As such the treatment of the errant PIIGS follows a wider pattern of punitive measures designed to privilege the market over whole populations. Flassbeck and Lapavitsas write:

> The response of EU authorities to the crisis has cast light on the very nature of the European Union. After an initial period of confusion during which the blame was laid squarely on bad public finances in the periphery (becoming extremely spiteful in the case of Greece), it was realised that the core of the monetary union itself was at risk. Gradually a policy response of 'bailouts' was formulated that took its cue from IMF interventions across the world in previous years as well as from the neoliberal economics that currently dominates thinking within the EU. (*Against the Troika: Crisis and Austerity in the Eurozone* 20)

Flassbeck and Lapavitsas sum up the EU's approach in five steps:

i) Liquidity support was provided to banks by the ECB to prevent banking collapse.
ii) Emergency loans were provided to peripheral states to prevent default but also to ensure that individual states remained capable of injecting capital into their national banking systems.
iii) Austerity was imposed on peripheral countries to stabilise public finances and to reduce national debt.
iv) Deregulation and privatisation were promoted with the aim of reducing wages ('improving competitiveness') and freeing the operations of private capital in the hope that growth would follow.

v) Harsh rules were embedded in the constitution of the EU to ensure discipline in public finances. Some small steps were also taken towards banking union. (*Against the Troika* 20–21)

Although packaged as a series of desperate measures enacted to deal with a specific set of problems at a crucial point in European history, the feeling persists that such policies are the new normal, the shockwaves that reverberate in their slipstream gradually absorbed by dull repetition.

A Crucial Mutation

The dogged pursuance of austerity as a means of repaying ECB loans placed the financial burden squarely on the shoulders of European taxpayers, just as job prospects and working conditions were growing ever more precarious. We can see this trend repeat itself in all five PIIGS countries. So, while Ireland has made an uneven recovery, for example, it remains hopelessly reliant upon multinational corporations and, with them, the capricious whims of the same free market. Greece, instead, has lurched from crisis to crisis and perhaps tellingly has, like Portugal, increasingly turned to China for financial aid, the quid pro quo of which will likely have significant future political ramifications.[12] Portugal, whose then Prime Minister Pedro Passos Coelho stated in 2011 that the country could avert disaster only 'by becoming poorer' ('The True Cost' 3), continued to implement austerity measures well into 2015, until the election of a socialist alliance headed by António Costa, while youth unemployment remains exceedingly high across many regions of austerity-hit Italy and Spain. Furthermore, it is becoming clearer that resentment of austerity measures imposed by the central Spanish government has played a considerable role in the drive for Catalan independence—a potential precursor for the dissolution of Spain itself. J. Magnus Ryner has identified several precedents for the EU's policies—all of which follow a similar neoliberal pattern of rapid privatisation and a resultant hollowing out of societal institutions—arguing that 'the objective of the measures does not seem to be about restoring macroeconomic balance but rather to, à la Naomi Klein's (2007) notion of "shock doctrine", use the crisis as an opportunity to move the limits of the possible even further towards a logic for the commodification of social life' ('The European Monetary Union' 18–19). On this, Ryner is unequivocal, and he describes the EU's actions as befitting a 'neoliberal paradigm that, with local variations, serves as rationale for a finance-dominated transnational capitalism' ('The European Monetary Union' 19). His referencing of Naomi Klein is thus entirely fitting. Klein's conceptualisation of a 'shock doctrine' has its origins in a reaction to Milton Friedman's championing of 'economic shock therapy' as a means of facilitating market freedom, an approach that saw opportunity in near disaster as summed up by Friedman's maxim that 'only a crisis—actual or perceived—produces real change' (*The Shock Doctrine* 6–7). Klein traces the history of the shock doctrine back to 1970s' Chile, where Friedman worked as an advisor for Augusto Pinochet who, when not butchering his own people, implemented 'a rapid-fire transformation of the economy—tax cuts, free trade, privatized services, cuts to social spending and deregulation' (*Shock Doctrine* 7).[13] She has since concurred in identifying the EU's response to the crisis as fitting the above pattern, citing the example of Greece as being a classic example of the shock doctrine.[14]

Intriguingly, in comparing the EU's response to the contemporary financial crisis with the economic resuscitation of post-war Europe, Ryner isolates what he perceives as a crucial mutation in capitalism itself, a 'geopolitical angle to this story, which underlines the tendency toward disaster in the Eurozone' ('Monetary Union' 19). Specifically, Ryner states that while 'both Fordist and finance-led capitalism were sustained through US hegemonic leadership', the 'modalities of leadership were very different' ('Monetary Union' 19). As I have argued at the outset of this book, the drive towards European integration, for all its lofty ambitions, was essentially a pragmatic economic project designed to stimulate newly reopened markets to both facilitate the growth of American exports and provide a bulwark to the spread of communism. A key difference between then and now, however, is that while the stimulus provided by the Marshall Plan had a clearly discernible impact—as illustrated, for example, by the swift revitalisation of Germany or the Italian economic miracle—the contemporary pattern of providing bailouts in exchange for huge cuts owes more to the preservation of the current incarnation of capitalism than to any tangible desire to 'fix' national economies. Ryner continues:

> Whereas, US leadership in the Fordist period was based on support and granting a degree of autonomy to other social formations (the Marshall Plan, capital market regulation provisions in Bretton Woods), leadership in the finance-dominated period was more narrowly self-interested, and based on displacing externalities from the US to other parts of the world. ('Monetary Union' 19)

Unlike then, however, the compulsion or even desire for radical solutions has been retarded by the death of political alternatives: there is no longer an urgency to counteract communism because communism, as we knew it in Europe, is dead, and, at any rate, the US economy itself is hamstrung by shortcomings in the same system. 'For most people under twenty in Europe and North America', Fisher writes, 'the lack of alternatives to capitalism is no longer even an issue. Capitalism seamlessly occupies the horizons of the thinkable' (*Capitalist Realism* 12). The overriding difficulty, it would seem, is that the prevailing neoliberal strain of capitalism is an ouroboros destined to swallow itself whole. Stasis persists amidst an absence of alternatives so that, as Harris and Scully describe it, 'the world economy is plagued by a "zombie" neoliberalism wherein ideological and institutional inertia continue to drive forward processes of commodification' ('Counter-Movement' 415). In its purest form, this is capitalism shorn of social function, and while the Eurozone has survived thus far, the fear remains that further disasters are not just inevitable but hardwired into the very mainframe of the system itself.

Looking at sf films made in Portugal, Ireland, Italy, Greece, and Spain during this time is instructive, for they blend national concerns with wider philosophical questions about the future of Europe. While there have been comparatively few such films, it is striking to note that all of them engage to varying degrees with the crises in capitalism detailed above. Moving through sf releases from all five PIIGS, all of which are contemporaneous with the financial crisis, we will encounter recurring themes relating to EU financial policy such as the twin implementation of bailouts and austerity measures, the political means by which such measures were copper-fastened (the collapse of establishment parties as well as the rise of technocrats), and the ensuing social fallout (unemployment and precarity) as experienced by large swathes of the EU's population. Beginning in Portugal, we will survey how generational gaps have widened across Europe as job security and social benefits, once offered by social democracies, have been gutted by neoliberal policies. Whilst such measures were met with widespread revolt elsewhere (witness the spectacular rise of Syriza in Greece or the populists of the Movimento Cinque Stelle in Italy), the political response in Ireland was surprisingly docile with the centre-right Fianna Fáil party being replaced by the centre-right Fine Gael. Perhaps unsurprisingly, sf films released in Ireland at the time are symptomatic of such complacency, on the surface having little to say about the greatest threat to Irish sovereignty since independence. That they were released to begin with, however, is instructive and following the circumstances of their production can shed light on both the wider issue of Irish sf and the impact of the economic crisis on the Irish film industry. In one of the few sf films to emerge from Italy during the crisis, we will see how precarious work conditions became an everyday feature of life for young Italians and how deteriorating social circumstances contribute to the increased marginalisation of minorities in the same country. Analysis of the Greek co-production *The Lobster* meanwhile will enable us to see how a film can simultaneously endorse European funding models on an industrial level and excoriate EU financial practices onscreen. Lastly, in Spain we will see how the Madrid government's doubling down upon the EU's neoliberal economic agenda has increased calls for Catalan independence, a central theme of *Los últimos días/The Last Days*, a film that itself inadvertently showcases not just the phallocentric nature of much sf but also rampant levels of gender inequality that continues to pervade the Spanish economy.

EAT THE YOUNG: GENERATIONAL CONFLICT AND THE HOLLOWING OUT OF THE PORTUGUESE STATE

Film: Real Playing Game (Tino Navarro and David Rebordão 2013)

Together with neighbouring Spain, Portugal joined the EEC on 1 January 1986. Like Spain, where Francisco Franco reigned until his death a year later, Portugal emerged from dictatorship in the mid-1970s after the collapse of the authoritarian Estado Novo regime in 1974, the same year that the process of Metapolitefsi saw an end to military rule and the restoration of democracy in Greece. All three nations were swiftly welcomed into the EEC, with Greece joining earlier in 1981. EU membership for Portugal would duly follow, with the nation enthusiastically embracing the Maastricht Treaty on the grounds that further integration with Europe would bolster a still-fledgling democracy and provide continued avenues for economic development. It should be stated, however, that the treaty was never ratified by the Portuguese people as the government of the time refused to submit the matter to a public referendum (Cabral and Marques, 'Portugal: 40 Years of Democracy' 3). Despite making strong socio-economic progress in areas such as exports and education levels since its formal adoption of the euro in 1999, Portugal's net external debt, which was close to being balanced in the mid-1990s, grew exponentially, rising to an untenable −118.9 per cent of GDP by 2013 (Cabral and Marques 5). Consequently, the country grew increasingly reliant upon funding from abroad, to the point where at the outset of the financial crisis over three quarters of government direct debt was held by non-residents. By 2009, 'the banking systems of creditor countries (Germany, Holland, etc.) cut back on lending to Portugal' causing a funding crisis meaning that the Portuguese banking system was 'unable to raise new funds to repay old debt that matured' (Cabral and Marques 5). After a succession of measures such as tax increases and pay cuts for public servants failed to rein in the country's spiralling debt levels and budget deficit—which by 2009 was already over three times the EU Stability and Growth Pact limit of 3 per cent—Portugal formally agreed the terms of a €78 billion bailout with the Troika on 17 May 2011 (Lochery, *Out of the Shadows: Portugal from Revolution to the Present Day* 257). Implicit in this arrangement was an agreement to implement €4.7 billion in cuts to public expenditure within three years, the human cost of which resulted in what a 2013 Oxfam report labelled as a 'social emergency' ('The True Cost of Austerity and Inequality: Portugal Case Study'). This figure was met by the imposition of repeated tax hikes, the termination of thousands of public sector jobs, cuts to old-age pensions, and large-scale cuts on education spending (23 per cent in two years) ('The True Cost'). The social impact of such measures was brutal, with unemployment figures peaking at 17.5 per cent in 2013: a tally behind only Greece and Spain in the Eurozone ('Jones, 'No Alternative to Austerity? That Lie Has Now Been Nailed?'). The same year healthcare fees rose in line with inflation in a country where, by 2011, a Deloitte report into Portuguese healthcare stated that '77 per cent of those surveyed said that costs have limited their spending on other essential household items' ('The True Cost' 3). As was the case in Ireland, Italy, Greece, and Spain, social cuts were to have an especially debilitating effect on young adults: disenfranchised millennials for whom job security was a remnant of a past they never knew and hope for the future, a fantasy incompatible with the present they had to endure. Accordingly, as was the case in the other so-called PIIGS nations, increasing numbers of young Portuguese emigrated in search of a better life elsewhere.[15] As Neill Lochery writes, 'the loss of the highly educated young Portuguese adults would prove an additional economic complication [...] put simply, a generation of talent was saying goodbye to their motherland, to which they would only return for holidays and family festivities' (*Out of the Shadows* 260). Prospects for those who elected to remain in the country were bleak.

By 2013, '35.7% of 16–24 year olds were unemployed while restrictions on unemployment insurance meant that only 44% of the unemployed could claim unemployment benefits' (Cabral and Marques 7). Against this backdrop, it is perhaps unsurprising that the only Portuguese sf film to emerge during this period imagines a future where elderly millionaires colonise the minds and bodies of the young for personal gain.

An SF Rarity

Released in 2013, Tino Navarro and David Rebordão's *Real Playing Game* is an sf rarity, although contemporary novels such as Miguel Real's *O Último Europeu/The Last European* (2015) or *EuroNovela* (1997) by Miguel Vale de Almeida do provide evidence of wider Portuguese interest in the genre.[16] Produced by the Lisbon-based MGN Filmes with an estimated budget of €600,000, *Real Playing Game* is set in a near future where a high-line company called RPG offers wealthy elderly clients the opportunity to go back in time and step into the body of a much younger person.[17] Clients pay to embody attractive young adults, of any gender of their choosing, and partake in a very literal role-playing game, the proviso being, as explained by the company's director Mr Chan (Chris Tashima), that in order to 'experience what it is like to be young again, someone has to die'. One such client is the terminally ill Steve Battier (Rutger Hauer) who embodies a young man and swiftly finds himself pitted in a fight for survival against the human surrogates of nine other wealthy contemporaries. In a scenario that owes much to the Japanese film *Battle Royale* (Kinji Fukasaku 2000), only one survivor can remain, and to ensure expediency, contestants are informed that they must kill a person every hour or they themselves will randomly be selected for assassination. Beyond Fukasaku's dystopian film and its most obvious antecedent William Golding's novel *Lord of the Flies* (1954), *Real Playing Game* also calls to mind *Avatar* in providing characters with the scientific means to immerse themselves in the body of another, as well as John Frankenheimer's *Seconds* (1966) in the transhumanistic scope it offers for rejuvenation of the waning male libido (closer to home, it also bears resemblance to Elio Petri's *The Tenth Victim/La decima vittima* (1965)). Unlike *Avatar*, however, where the embodiment of human/Na'vi hybrids is undertaken for expressly commercial purposes, or *Seconds*, where a shadowy organisation utilises plastic surgery to implement the change, the science behind RPG's business is rather obscure, with the filmmakers seemingly more concerned with following the interactions of their attractive, multiracial, young protagonists. Sure enough, like the other contestants, Battier wastes little time in pursuing sexual encounters and in time develops a taste for murder too.

Portuguese produced and directed and featuring a multinational European cast of Portuguese, Albanian, English, Spanish, and Swedish actors, *Real Playing Game* is nevertheless shot entirely in English. Given a limited cinema release, the film made just €113,874 at the box office via 22,855 admissions, despite Hauer's prominence in its trailer (one at odds with the limited screen time he enjoys in the film itself) (*Lumiere*).[18] Opening in 'a near future', the film swiftly touches upon contemporary Portuguese travails through the RPG company's array of potential backdrops for clients to partake in their fight to the death. Outlining the possibilities, Mr Chan cites 'Kenya 1980', 'Greenland 2010', and 'Portugal 2013', before selecting the latter on the basis that 'Portugal in ruins seems just about right'. The differences between Chan's near future and the financially crippled Portugal of 2013 are conveyed to viewers primarily through the directors' use of location shooting, particularly as the film uses only two principal locations. The first is the RPG headquarters, which were filmed in the futuristic offices of the Champalimaud Foundation's 'Centre for the Unknown' biomedical research facility in Lisbon. The centre, which was opened in 2010, embodies modernist architectural influences without being, in the words of its chief architect Charles Correa, 'a museum of modern art' (Frearson, 'Champalimaud Centre for the Unknown'). Its spaceship-like design makes the centre an ideal sf setting, and it works here as a sleek, futuristic counterpoint to the film's other setting, an abandoned rural hotel. In addition to appealing as a positive beacon of Portugal's future, however, the Champalimaud Centre also gestures strongly to the country's colonial past in its visual conceptualisation, which Correa describes as 'three stone ships sailing in a sea of granite' (Frearson, 'Champalimaud Centre'). The centre's location—on the waterfront where the Tagus river meets the Atlantic Ocean—is strategic too, being a site from which Henry the Navigator and Vasco de Gama embarked on voyages of discovery that were to contribute greatly to Portuguese imperial glory while having a ruinous effect on the lands they encountered. Its impressive concrete, steel, and glass façade while nominally gesturing to the future, therefore, is intrinsically tied up with Portugal's lamentable history of colonial subjugation (Fig. 4.1).

Fig. 4.1 'Champalimaud Centre for the Unknown'

Shooting in such a heavily coded site, thereby, affords the film a connection with the past that contextualises the nefarious onscreen deeds of its elderly protagonists. The future, *Real Playing Game* suggests, will be traumatic, with the rich preying on the young whose very bodies become commodities. Such a concept would appear risible were it not suffused with a sense of the historical pathos inflicted by colonialism: after all Europeans have historically commodified the bodies of millions of people, and Portugal, as the first colonial empire of the Renaissance, has been a central player in Europe's long history of slavery. The exploratory journeys of native sons Henry the Navigator, Vasco de Gama, and Ferdinand Magellan, as well as Christopher Columbus who, though Italian, lived in Lisbon for close to a decade and frequently sailed Portuguese ships, were to have major implications for the evolution of colonialism and with it for capitalism itself. Portugal's colonial empire was to last for the bulk of six centuries, with the handover of Portuguese Macau to China in 1999 finally bringing proceedings to a close. An indicator of the vast scale of this enterprise can be grasped from the signing of the Treaty of Tordesillas, after Columbus' 'discovery' of America for the Spanish in 1492. Signed in 1494, the treaty saw Portugal and Spain ostensibly divide the world outside of Europe between them. The biopolitical link between expansion of the colonial project and the resultant commodification and regulation of human bodies became explicit through the slave trade, which was not officially abolished in the Portuguese colonies until 1869, a full century after Michel Foucault locates the origins of biopower in humankind's conceptualisation of itself as a species (*Security, Territory, Population: Lectures at the Collège de France 1977–1978* 1). It was in the eighteenth century, according to Foucault, that an 'event bound up with the development of capitalism' occurred, namely, the 'entry of life into history' (*History of Sexuality* 141–142). By enslaving colonial subjects, colonists literally turned them into commodities: selling them at slave auctions and expending their bodies in the quest for further colonial expansion. Foucault makes the link explicit, writing that 'biopower was without question an indispensable element in the development of capitalism, the latter would not have been possible without the controlled insertion of bodies into the machinery of production' (*History of Sexuality* 142). *Real Playing Game* draws on such developments and imagines their continuation into a post-financial crash future, only this time the moneyed elderly exert biopolitical control over the young. Indeed, Columbus' journey has especial relevance for sf, being a conceptual precursor for fantastical sf voyages, whether they be undertaken by Méliès' earthlings in *Journey to the Moon* or by the crew of the Starship Enterprise seeking new frontiers. Accordingly, and as Peter Fitting has argued, sf's conceptualisation of the 'moment of encounter between humans and aliens' belongs to such a lineage, being 'a moment familiar to us from anthropological investigation and historical accounts; one which, consciously or not, re-enacts the encounters of the European 'discovery' of the New World' ('Estranged Invaders: The War of the Worlds' 127). Istvan Csicsery-Ronay goes further still in locating the origins of sf itself in colonialism, writing that 'even the classical genres to which sf is often traced (the pastoral, the romance, the utopian cityscape) originate in the imperial imagination (specifically from Alexandria, Byzantium, and Rome), as do their shadow-genres, the slave's narrative, the journey through hell, and the dark' ('Science Fiction and Empire' 238). Although the end product is poorly written and highly uneven, Navarro and David Rebordão's decision to focus upon the colonisation of young, multiracial bodies is thus highly telling, for they embody at once

Portugal's imperial, slave-owning capitalist past and a present lost generation whose futures were sacrificed in the name of austerity. Portugal persisted with its colonial project long after it seized to be in any way financially logical, just as it persisted with austerity until 2015, no matter the cost to its unemployed youth. In both instances, illogical and morally bankrupt practices were persevered with, in order to sustain systems that were in obvious decline. The demise of Portuguese colonialism became a fait accompli following the Carnation Revolution of 1974, which led both to the toppling of the dictatorship of the ruling Estado Novo and the withdrawal of Portugal from its overseas colonies—albeit the latter process was terribly mismanaged.[19] Only a year previously, it is estimated that close to 150,000 Portuguese soldiers (the vast bulk of them young adults) were actively deployed in intensive and bloody colonial wars across Angola, Mozambique, and Guinea-Bissau (Cabral and Marques 1). While colonial expansion had once enriched the country immeasurably, by the 1960s funding of overseas wars accounted for over 40 per cent of government expenditures (Cabral and Marques 2). Beyond the barbarity of colonial subjugation lay the cold capitalist reality that colonialism was no longer economically viable. Accordingly, new ideas were called for.

The 12-year period after the Carnation Revolution saw widespread social and political reforms as Portugal readied itself for EEC membership. In marked contrast to the generation they would later produce, young Portuguese stood to benefit from extensive social initiatives, including the establishment of a national health service offering free healthcare and the rapid expansion of the country's free public education system (Cabral and Marques 1). To recalibrate an economy that had undergone extensive shocks in a country that had been under totalitarian rule since 1933—the same year that Hitler became chancellor of Germany—the provisional governments of the revolutionary period pushed through major reforms, which had profound effects on the lives of Portuguese citizens. Specifically, Cabral and Marques note the introduction of social security for all citizens, 'including those that had not paid any contributions, guaranteeing a minimum income for its eldest', the raising of child-care allowances, and the introduction of a minimum wage in May 1974: one 'which has never been as high in real terms since then' ('Portugal' 2). *Real Playing Game*'s central premise then has historical resonance, with the age profiles of both the elderly players and the youthful bodies they commandeer telling. The latter are in their early to mid-twenties and are emblematic of Portugal's college-educated citizens who, shorn of the possibilities and job stability enjoyed by their parents, were forced into either migration or arrested development in the face of increasing austerity. Moreover, whilst the years following the Estado Novo saw the establishment of national unemployment insurance funded in part by the nationalisation of the 'Bank of Portugal, the commercial banking system and leading industrial conglomerates' ('Portugal' 2), the need to meet the Troika's demanded €4.7 billion in cuts saw the Portuguese government turn to privatisation, selling off the public's stake in the energy company Energias de Portugal to China and announcing its intention to privatise one of the nation's two public television companies ('The True Cost' 3). This erosion of public space and ownership tallies neatly with Brenner, Peck, and Theodore's aforementioned definition of neoliberalism as 'the tendential extension of market-based competition and commodification processes into previously insulated realms of political-economic life' ('After Neoliberalization?' 329). Hamstrung by punitive financial obligations, the Portuguese government's sales are textbook examples of the shock doctrine in action and raise numerous concerns about the erosion of state autonomy. The inevitability of such governmental acquiescence to the market is sketched out in *Real Playing Game*. Although Mr Chan stresses that RPG must conduct their affairs in semi-secrecy as 'unfortunately life and death are not on the market', his swift addition of the rejoinder 'yet' suggests that it is only a matter of time before the lucrative private enterprise is granted official sanction.

The 'game' itself is entirely shot in the grounds of the abandoned 1950s-era Hotel do Muxito in the port city of Setúbal. Now derelict and heavily graffitied, the real-life Hotel do Muxito went bankrupt shortly before the Carnation Revolution (Silva, 'A Ocupação Revolucionária do Hotel do Muxito'). Salient amongst the visible graffiti is the legend 'Portugal dies a slow death', and despite initially trying to establish a coalition, Battier and his fellow players degenerate into a Darwinian battle, swiftly developing a flair for manipulation and murder until only Battier remains. The young are sacrificed in the name of self-interest, and a triumphant Battier duly offers his fortune to Chan in exchange for a promise of eternal youth. As he admires his youthful appearance in a car mirror, however, the film cuts to a POV shot from the perspective of the car's driver, revealing that Battier remains an elderly man. Unbeknownst to him, Chan is a con artist pedalling faux-elixirs of eternal youth, even if, like much of the film, the scientific reasoning behind Battier's false perception of himself goes unexplained. He has been duped, and like

Narcissus, he is transfixed by his own reflection, oblivious to the realities that surround him. Eager to capitalise upon Chan's technology, Battier failed to consider that he himself might be vulnerable. Tellingly, Chan closes the film by explaining to his assistant that he perceives of himself as 'a kind of priest' who allows people 'to see what they want to see', a succinct summation of capitalist excess for, while the affluent can exploit the young in an untethered survival of the fittest contest, the game itself is rigged from the outset.

A Rock on the Edge of Europe: SF and the Irish Film Industry

Films: Zonad (John Carney and Kieran Carney 2009) and *Grabbers* (Jon Wright 2012)

Sf film in Ireland is noteworthy for its absence rather than for any real discernible tradition. Indigenous sf film production is thin on the ground, and apart from John Boorman's cult offering *Zardoz* (1974), which was filmed in Ardmore Studios and the surrounding Wicklow countryside, the genre has been largely dormant in an Irish context, until a spate of recent releases—many of which function as parodies that, in Jack Fennell's words, 'make tongue-in-cheek use of the genre while keeping it at arm's length' (*Irish Science Fiction* 1). Significant for Boorman's direction (the film was his first after the commercial success of *Deliverance* (1972)) and Sean Connery's turn as a mankini-wearing futuristic assassin, *Zardoz* was one of several high-profile Hollywood productions shot in Ireland around this time, a sequence that includes *Ryan's Daughter* (David Lean 1970), *The Mackintosh Man* (John Huston 1973), and *Barry Lyndon* (Stanley Kubrick 1975). Nevertheless, the intervening four decades have seen little in the way of sf releases, with solely indigenous production all but non-existent. This curious absence, though by no means exclusive in a European context, cannot be accounted for by any one factor and must be seen in the wider context of a small native film industry that has historically exported much of its best talent to Britain and the United States. Scale is an important factor, for, as Heather MacDougall notes, 'economic conditions coupled with the small size of the industry make it virtually impossible to produce a feature film without either securing financing through the IFB [Irish Film Board] or arranging a deal with a foreign studio' ('Who Needs

Hollywood? The Role of Popular Genre Films in Irish National Cinema' 39). Similarly, in literature, an infinitely more bountiful native sector, sf has largely been sidelined in mainstream discourses: the fantastical inclinations of writers such as Jonathan Swift and George Russell notwithstanding, and while Fennell has sought to redress this imbalance,[20] Irish sf has remained a niche entity to say the least.[21]

The scarcity of Irish sf-related films continued unabated into the new millennium, albeit with rare exceptions such as the Hollywood-backed *Space Truckers* (Stuart Gordon 1996) and the post-apocalyptic *Reign of Fire* (Rob Bowman 2002); and while 1990s' productions *The Boy from Mercury* (Martin Duffy 1996) and *The Butcher Boy* (Neil Jordan 1997) explore the escapist possibilities of sf through the fantastical dream sequences of young male protagonists, both remain anchored to 'real-world' depictions of early 1960s' Ireland. Of late, however, some movement has been afoot, with a wholly unexpected mini-scene emerging, starting with the zombie/apocalyptic hybrid *Red Meat* (Conor McMahon 2004), which profited from the BSE/'mad cow' epidemics of the 1990s. The low-budget *Summer of the Flying Saucer* (Martin Duffy 2008) and *One Hundred Mornings* (Conor Horgan 2009) followed, in advance of a relative flurry of sf-related productions between 2009 and 2014, an occurrence that nevertheless did little to dissuade popular perceptions as to the genre's novelty in an Irish context.[22] A mixture of comic exploitation films (*Zonad*, *Grabbers*), European co-productions (*Collider* (Jason Butler 2013)), independents (*Earthbound* (Alan Brennan 2012), *Dark by Noon* (Alan Leonard and Michael O'Flaherty 2013), *The Quiet Hour* (Stéphanie Joalland 2014), *Pushtar* (Alan Lambert 2015)), and films part-funded by the Irish Film Board (IFB; *Perfect Sense* (David Mackenzie 2011), *The Last Days on Mars* (Ruairí Robinson 2013), *Young Ones* (Jake Paltrow 2014)), none were especially successful commercially, yet collectively they gesture for the first time towards a nascent Irish sf scene. In the cases of *Perfect Sense* and *Young Ones*, however, the links to Ireland are tenuous and attest more to the IFB's desire to attract filmmakers than uncharted levels of depth in Irish sf. The same board's contribution to the Eurimages fund coupled with not inconsiderable tax incentives[23] also led to the filming of Yorgos Lanthimos' award-winning *The Lobster* (2015) in County Kerry, a production I will discuss at length in Chap. 5. Meanwhile, a recent outlier bucks all trends, even if it cannot be conceived of as native, with select Irish locations providing backdrops to the re-emergent *Star Wars* franchise. Competitive tax rates no doubt encouraged Disney to film the concluding scene of *Star Wars: The Force Awakens* (J.J. Abrams 2015) in County Kerry, with filming of the next instalment *Star Wars: The Last Jedi* (Rian Johnson 2017) taking place at several locations along the Atlantic seaboard. While the above occurrences are promising in an Irish context, they evince too disparate a sample to point to a consolidated sf movement per se. Even so, they do gesture towards a gradual emergence of sf in Ireland, a country that like other smaller European nations has long seemed wholly indifferent to the genre. The unlikeliness of their existence, moreover, is amplified when one considers that all bar one (*Red Meat*) were released in the aftermath of the outbreak of the financial crisis in 2008: an event keenly felt in Ireland, where among other factors, a marked overdependence on the property market left the nation prone to volatility in the international markets.

Swollen to bursting point by the fatuity of the 'Celtic Tiger' era—an unprecedented period of prosperity in a historically impoverished nation—Ireland's economy crashed spectacularly in 2008 and, by the following year, was in the throes of a full-on economic depression. Government attempts to stem the bleeding—including the issuing of a disastrous blanket bank guarantee in September 2008—proved fruitless, and in December 2010, Ireland formally accepted the terms of an economic bailout from the Troika, an arrangement predicated upon the implementation of severe austerity measures across Irish society. Amidst widespread public unrest—which nevertheless fell short of the hostility on display in other afflicted Eurozone member states, including Greece and Italy—far-reaching spending cuts were put in place in pivotal sectors such as social services and education, while emigration numbers reached levels not seen since the 1980s (Kenny, 'Emigration Rises to Record High'). Nevertheless, despite recommendations by the government-appointed 'Group on Public Service Numbers and Expenditure Programmes' (more commonly known as An Bord Snip Nua), cuts to the IFB were less pronounced than might have been expected, with the organisation suffering only a 5 per cent cut in funding in 2009 (Tracy, 'Irish Film and Television Review' 205). By the same year, the film industry in Ireland was valued at €557.3 million per annum, while the sector's worth in attracting tourism was flagged by the IFB who claimed that 'almost one in two US tourists to Ireland now state that their decision to come was triggered by seeing Ireland in the movies' (Tracy 205). This latter phenomenon has often been trumpeted by industry insiders, in a nation where the old axiom of Ireland being culturally 'closer to Boston than Berlin' has long held appeal. The granting of permission to Disney to film sections of *Star Wars* at Sceilig Mhichíl—one of only two UNESCO World Heritage Sites in the Republic—is a contemporary manifestation of this trend. Yet, Ireland's historically oleaginous attitude towards American interests has largely been shaped by pragmatic self-interest reflecting the limitations of its local economy. Tax breaks for foreign film production, moreover, need to be viewed in light of wider long-term Irish economic strategies, chief amongst them being the maintenance of low corporate tax levels designed specifically to attract multinational conglomerates, of which Ireland lists close to 1000 in the Republic alone. Such tax strategies are not without controversy, however, and have attracted the ire of fellow European nations, as well as increasing scrutiny from the EU in recent years. Gauging the impact of the financial crisis on the Irish film industry from the standpoint of late 2017, we can say that, although like other sectors it was affected, the damage was not as severe as might have been expected: a claim certainly reflected in sf, given that most of the nation's sf 'canon' was released after 2008. Onscreen instead, things are somewhat different, and while the pervasiveness of the crisis can be felt in *The Lobster* and *The Quiet Hour* (which I analyse in Chap. 6), a curiously apolitical indifference remains overall, as I will now seek to demonstrate with reference to two particularly egregious examples: John and Kieran Carney's *Zonad* and Jon Wright's *Grabbers*, both of which were co-produced by the IFB.

Seeking Solace in the Past

Moving chronologically through sf productions made or financed in Ireland since 2008, one of the first releases, *Zonad*, is perhaps the most curious. Far from being a straight-up sf film, this tame comedy operates as a send-up of 1950s' Hollywood representations of Ireland and follows the sudden appearance of an 'alien' in a fictional Irish village called Ballymoran. The alien in question is in reality Liam Murphy (Simon Delaney), an escaped convict who has little difficulty in convincing the gormless villagers who fete his arrival that he is Zonad, an alien from outer space. An unusual departure for John Carney—whose previous film, the low-budget musical *Once* (2007), won Best Original Song at the 2007 Academy Awards and was a considerable commercial success—*Zonad* is interesting here chiefly because in addition to lampooning sf conventions, it also presents an oddly atemporal Ireland, one that despite evincing contemporary technology and lifestyles is seemingly anchored in the innocence of an idealised 1950s. This is deliberate, with John Carney stating that 'We liked the idea of not being too specific about the period of the film. You know it's probably set in the present, but there are no mobile phones, computers, etc. We wanted the location to be like those small villages you used to find in the 1980s, that were still caught in the 1950s. That's gone in Ireland now, and you just can't escape the 21st century no matter where you go' (Carney, *Movies.ie*). This quandary manifests itself in characters' clothing as well as in the heightened ingenuousness of the villagers. No doubt the intention is to skewer age-old depictions of Ireland in Hollywood films such as *The Quiet Man* (John Ford 1952), or *Darby O' Gill and The Little People* (Robert Stevenson 1959): depictions that themselves seem oddly resistant to the passing of time.[24] Yet, the film's self-reflexivity would arguably be more effective were it not undone by the inherent silliness of its plot. The Carneys channel *The Day the Earth Stood Still* (Robert Wise 1951) in an opening shot of the earth from outer space, one that zooms slowly inward towards Europe and then the west coast of Ireland, before settling above Ballymoran. The village, a narrator informs us, is a 'tiny hamlet hiding from the rest of the world', where famed Irish hospitality is about to be tested by the arrival of a mysterious visitor. We then encounter the Cassidy family who will later invite Zonad, the visitor in question, into their home. The family is attending a stargazing event staged to coincide with the expected passing of a comet, when Dr Ziegler (Brian de Salvo), a German physician, admonishes them for their lack of belief in the extraterrestrial ('surely you're not so vein as to believe that we humans exist alone'). Following a brief interlude that features a town drunk shouting about impending alien invasions and the end of the world, the family returns home to find a drunken man dressed in an alien spacesuit costume asleep on their living room floor. Keen to evade the law, the man (Zonad) stays in character as an 'alien' for the film's duration, winning the affections of the locals until fellow criminal Francis O'Connor (David Pearse) arrives and complicates matters by creating a rival alien named Bonad. Yet, while its premise seems ideally suited to satire, *Zonad* is curiously devoid of any social commentary, and so, one of the IFB's first sf productions can only be seen as a squandered opportunity. The film's occupation of an uneven temporal plateau—which simultaneously shifts between modish contemporary Ireland and an imagined history that takes its cue from Hollywood representations—results in a skewered depiction of a nation at once yearning to prolong the economic advances of the Celtic Tiger years while seeking refuge in halcyon notions of a long-departed past. In creating an Ireland that simultaneously blurs the past, present, and future, *Zonad* inadvertently propagates a temporal no man's land reflective of a national outlook chastened by the fallout from the global financial crisis. Tellingly, in a nod to the wider financial climate, it is an exasperated German doctor who tries to make the locals see the error of their ways, yet they remain stubbornly resistant to reason. Where *Once* focused upon a multicultural, cosmopolitan Dublin, *Zonad*'s Ballymoran features a host of dim-witted, two-dimensional characters who endorse Kevin Rockett's observation that 'the demands of the international marketplace' tend to ensure that native productions all too frequently 'reinforce rather than challenge the inherited stereotypes of the Irish in the cinema' ('Irish Cinema: The National in the International' 24). While culturally Hollywood remains the predominating template for the majority of Irish genre cinema, recent funding efforts by the IFB in conjunction with Eurimages have begun to attract European directors such as Paolo Sorrentino and Yorgos Lanthimos to Ireland: a process facilitated by the increased prominence of local production companies including Dublin-based Element Pictures—a company that in turn co-produced both *Zonad* and *Grabbers* in an endorsement of what the IFB hoped would be a trickle-down effect of foreign film investment.

Jon Wright's *Grabbers* is another case in point. As with *Zonad*, *Grabbers* seeks to be at once a paean to sf and horror mores, as well as a comedy that seeks to deconstruct them. Like the Carneys' film, *Grabbers* is set in a fictional, geographically indistinct, rural idyll, this time a place called 'Erin Island' in the northwest of the country. Shot in counties Donegal and Antrim, even before its release, *Grabbers* was hailed in the local and national press as a boon to a region badly affected by the economic crisis. A feature in *The Irish Times* entitled 'Monster movie brings boost to business in north Donegal', for instance, concluded that the 'monster movie is taking some of the horror out of the recession for one small Donegal community' (McGrory). After the film was screened at the 2012 Sundance Film Festival meanwhile, the regional *Derry Journal* focused upon its potential to attract tourism to the area, speculating that *Grabbers* 'could well do for the peninsula what *Ryan's Daughter* did for Dingle or *The Quiet Man* did for Connemara' ('Director of the Movie They are all talking About says Inishowen was Magnificent'). Such comparisons are of course unfair given that between them David Lean and John Ford amassed six Academy Awards for best director, whilst their respective films were major productions featuring bona fide Hollywood stars in Robert Mitchum and John Wayne. *Grabbers* by contrast, as an independent Irish/British co-production, features no big names but benefits from the financial backing of the IFB, Northern Ireland Screen, and the UK Film Council. The film's plot centres on novice police officer Lisa Nolan (Ruth Bradley) who is seconded to Erin Island for a fortnight of relief duty, just as bloodsucking, squid-like aliens begin to descend from outer space. With the help of alcoholic policeman Ciarán O'Shea (Richard Coyle), English ecologist Dr Smith (Russell Tovey), and village idiot Paddy (Lalor Roddy)—also an alcoholic—Nolan must somehow prevent the aliens from wiping out the island's inhabitants. Despite paying homage to classic horror films such as *Jaws* (Steven Spielberg 1975) and *The Wicker Man* (Robin Hardy 1973), *Grabbers*' opening is defiantly sf in tone: a shot of Ireland from space followed by the hurtling of mysterious, meteor-like, objects into the sea. Although this shot is almost identical to the opening of *Zonad*, the aliens in this instance are real: the celestial objects turning out to be the eponymous 'grabbers', creatures who need water and blood to survive and, therefore, swiftly develop a taste for humans. The film's comedic premise stems from Dr Smith's realisation that the aliens cannot process alcohol, and so a plan is devised to gather the island's population in a pub; the more inebriated they get, the more resistant they become to the aliens (if nothing else, the aliens' fatal intolerance to alcohol updates the role of the common cold in H.G. Wells' *The War of the Worlds*). No doubt seeking to poke fun at Irish stereotypes, Wright and screenwriter Kevin Lehane duly present us with an assortment of naïve villagers reminiscent of the denizens of *Zonad*'s Ballymoran. Wright to his credit freely acknowledged the historical difficulty of achieving such a balance, noting that 'it's always been a source of annoyance to me that English films set in Ireland, they just don't care about the authenticity of it at all [...]. We wanted a film that the Irish could love as well as the rest of the world, rather than the other way around, which is how it often is' (Sugrue, 'Interview: Jon Wright'). Nonetheless, it is highly questionable whether this is achieved: for one thing, the English Dr Smith provides the breakthrough, a character who responds to Nolan and O'Shea's misguided attempts to kill a grabber with the glib observation that 'you really are Irish' and later speaks of the need to attain 'Paddy levels of drunkenness' to fend off the aliens. Moreover, the arduous task of shepherding the endangered locals into the pub is helpfully achieved with a visit to evening mass where, despite myriad scandals in the Irish Catholic Church, the island's entire population is seemingly present. Given its wilfully risible premise, po-faced analysis of

Grabbers may seem itself absurd, yet, beyond the all-too-obvious metaphor of an island community (Ireland) being subject to assault from nebulous outside forces (the Troika), it is possible to locate a deeper level of meaning in the film's apparent eschewal of meaningful social commentary, one that links it closely to *Zonad*.

Like Ballymoran, Erin Island evokes a culturally stagnant and ethnically monochrome Ireland of indeterminate origin, one where the effects of globalisation are virtually nowhere to be seen. This vague sense of place is accentuated by the film's use of location shooting, with Wright and cinematographer Trevor Forrest making ample use of the picturesque Donegal and Antrim coastlines throughout, blurring geographic specificity in a manner akin to the cast's curious *mélange* of regional accents. This indistinctness also applies to the film's relationship with genre, with Katie Moylan observing that 'the crude reflexivity *Grabbers* delivers in the representations of characters and setting also informs the film's use and appropriation of science fiction visual tropes' ('Aliens Dancing at the Crossroads: Science Fiction Interventions in Irish Cinema' 164). Appropriately then, the film's sf influences have their roots in the late 1970s and 1980s, with Moylan further noting that 'the aliens, or "grabbers", of the title are consciously derivative [of] the *Alien* films but also from horror films including the 1980s cult favorite *Gremlins*' ('Aliens' 164). Moylan doubts the critical perspicacity of *Grabbers*, arguing that 'any critical praxis is limited, as the sweeping landscape, the rural complicity, the pub singsong are all depicted semi-ironically on screen, as though simply the activity of display equates interrogation' ('Aliens' 164). In its promulgation of yet another idealised imaginary elsewhere, it is difficult not to see *Grabbers* as a further missed opportunity. Wright himself teases the possibilities offered by Irish sf while promoting the film: 'Why do the aliens always land in America? [...] When aliens look down on Planet Earth they can't see our self-imposed national boundaries, let alone know which language we're speaking' ('I Filmed a Horror Movie in Ireland. Here's Why'). Onscreen, however, national boundaries play no part in the narratives of either *Zonad* or *Grabbers*, while the socio-political and economic turbulence enveloping Ireland at the time of their respective productions is curiously absent. Unlike sf films from the other four PIIGS nations looked at here, all of which engage with the financial crisis, *Zonad* and *Grabbers* forego the genre's innate potential for social commentary and instead opt to focus on remote villages that are microcosms of nothing more than 1950s' Hollywood perceptions of Ireland. This nostalgia for the past runs alongside a marked inability to engage with the present, in a manner redolent of Fredric Jameson's conceptualisation of nostalgia films at large: namely, that they hide their inability to engage with the present behind an iconic representation of a fake past. Nostalgia films, for Jameson, 'restructure the whole issue of pastiche and project it onto a collective and social level, where the desperate attempt to appropriate a missing past is now refracted through the iron law of fashion change and the emergent ideology of the generation' (*Postmodernism, or, the Cultural Logic of Late Capitalism* 19). Jameson traces this phenomenon to George Lucas' *American Graffiti* (1973), a film which 'set out to recapture, as many films have attempted since, the hence-forth mesmerizing lost reality of the Eisenhower era' and which, he suggests, along with the 1950s at large, remains a 'privileged lost object of desire' for many Americans (*Postmodernism* 19). While neither *Grabbers* nor *Zonad* is explicitly set in the past, their ironic engagement with 1950s' Hollywood versions of Ireland and with sf film history serves little critical function, as they are confined by the very framework they set out to expose. Unlike, say, *Attack the Block* (Joe Cornish 2011)—another sf comedy which, as we will see in Chap. 7, deconstructs latent racial and political anxieties in 1950s' sf to skewer discriminatory gentrification processes in twenty-first-century Britain—*Grabbers* and *Zonad* tell us nothing about modern Ireland nor indeed about genre, despite their continued referencing of Hollywood sf and Irish-themed films. This in turn signals a retreat into a postmodern morass, for 'the classical nostalgia film while evading its present altogether, registered its historicist deficiency by losing itself in mesmerized fascination in lavish images of specific generational pasts' (*Postmodernism* 296). In sidestepping the present altogether, neither film tells us anything of note about Celtic Tiger or postcrash Ireland, beyond inadvertently illustrating native complacency about its causes. Such complacency has not gone away. The *Irish Times* reported that the Irish economy grew by almost 5 per cent in 2017, topping EU growth rates for the fourth year in succession and sending per capita GDP to sixth in the world (McManus, 'Why We Keep Making the Same Mistakes over Housing'). Yet, the report notes that 'wages are still subdued, indebtedness remains high and the housing market is harking back to the pre-2008 madness' (McManus, 'Why We Keep Making'). Indeed, by early 2018, Irish house prices were rising nearly three times faster than the EU average and expected to top Celtic Tiger levels within 18 months (Melia, 'Property prices rise by more than €100,000 in a Year'). All the while, social inequality has increased massively, with homeless figures dwarfing those of the Celtic Tiger era and precipitating what even the Prime Minister Leo Varadkar has described as a 'national emergency' ('Taoiseach Declares Homeless and Housing Crisis a National Emergency'). Early warning signs of an overheating economy are in evidence, particularly as the nation remains extremely vulnerable to outside ruptures. Brexit complicates things further, while Ireland's EU partners have grown increasingly voluble about Irish tax loopholes: an issue that came to a head in 2016 when the Irish government took the extraordinary decision of appealing a European Commission ruling that Apple pay €13 billion of unpaid back taxes to the Irish state.[25] Unlike *Zonad* or *Grabbers*, the Italian film *The Last Man on Earth/L'ultimo Terrestre* (Gianni Pacinotti 2011) has much to say about such matters and places the neoliberal commodification of social life front and centre of its narrative as we shall now see.

PRECARITY AND THE COMMODIFICATION OF ITALIAN SOCIAL LIFE

Film: The Last Man on Earth/L'ultimo Terrestre (Gianni Pacinotti 2011)

In her detailed survey of Italian sf cinema entitled 'The Uncomfortable Relationship Between Science Fiction and Italy: Film, Humor, and Gender', Raffaella Baccolini categorises Italian sf films into two groups: 'those made for the domestic market, which are often comedies, farces, and satires' and those made with an eye on foreign markets, 'which are more serious, adventurous dramas' ('Uncomfortable Relationship' 172–173). She identifies films such as *Death Comes from Outer Space/La morte viene dallo spazio* (Paolo Heusch 1958), *The Tenth Victim/La decima vittima* (Elio Petri 1965), and *Nirvana* (Gabriele Salvatores 1997) as being emblematic of the second type, yet notes that the former model has overwhelmingly predominated, boosted in part by the huge domestic appetite for *commedia all'italiana* during the 1950s and 1960s ('Uncomfortable Relationship' 175). A propensity for sf pastiche has persisted through the generations in Italy, with the 1980s, for example, providing cheap knockoffs of American films like *The Warriors* (Walter Hill 1979) and *Escape from New York* (John Carpenter 1981) in *1990: I guerrieri del Bronx/1990: The Bronx Warriors* (Enzo G. Castellari, 1982), *Endgame/Endgame: Bronx lotta finale* (Joe D'Amato 1983), and *2019:*

After the Fall of New York/2019: dopo la caduta di New York (Sergio Martino 1983). Leading up to the millennium, however, Italian sf cinema all but disappeared, a reality attributed by Baccolini to 'increased budget restrictions, but also because it continued to be largely perceived as a "sub-genre" for young people'—Salvatores' *Nirvana* being a rare exception ('Uncomfortable Relationship' 176). This tendency has continued for, unlike elsewhere in Europe, the twenty-first century has been barren territory for Italian sf film: a trend bucked only by Corrado Guzzanti and Igor Skofic's *Fascisti su Marte/Fascists on Mars* (2006), which, as its title suggests, resuscitates the historic native coupling of sf and farce, the low-budget *The Arrival of Wang/L'arrivo di Wang* (Antonio Manetti & Marco Manetti 2011), and Gianni Pacinotti's *The Last Man on Earth/ L'ultimo Terrestre* (2011)—a film that has attracted surprisingly little scholarly attention despite its highly topical, socially conscious narrative.

BACKDROP

Although strongly satirical and not without its comic moments, *The Last Man on Earth* is particularly noteworthy for blending domestic drama with sf and juxtaposes accounts of everyday economic precarity with the wider narrative of an alien invasion of Italy. More commonly known for his work as a cartoonist, for which he uses the pseudonym 'Gipi', Gianni Pacinotti's turn to filmmaking gained considerable publicity due to a viral internet marketing campaign for *The Last Man on Earth*, which channelled Orson Welles' infamous use of an emergency announcement of an alien invasion as part of his 1938 radio adaptation of *The War of the Worlds* (Hooper, 'Italian Alien Film Tries to Ape Orson Welles Radio Play in Web Marketing'). Pacinotti's campaign featured a spoof emergency news bulletin read out by Maria Cuffaro—a real-life newscaster for the public broadcaster RAI—who informed viewers that an alien invasion of Italy was imminent. This blending of reality and sf gives an early indication of the film's playful yet serious engagement with genre; its deployment of an alien invasion narrative balanced throughout with a stern examination of Italian social and political themes.[26] Co-produced by RAI, the Tuscan Film Commission, and the Rome-based production company Fandango at a time when the Italian film industry—like the nation at large—was undergoing considerable hardship, *The Last Man on Earth* follows the travails of Luca Bertacci (Gabriele Spinelli), an introverted bingo hall waiter living out an unfulfilled existence in Tuscany. Alienated from wider society, Luca's only acquaintances are his elderly father, his misogynistic and homophobic co-workers, and his childhood friend, a transvestite prostitute called Roberta, played by Luca Marinelli.[27] Luca quietly lusts after his neighbour Anna (Anna Bellato), yet his distrust of women and incapacity to establish human relationships see him frequent prostitutes instead. One such encounter early in the narrative foregrounds a recurring theme of glass ceilings, when an elderly bourgeois woman, who is seemingly a recent convert to prostitution, laments the life she once led, before denigrating Luca's profession and insisting that they conduct business on a bed that she reserves for waiters. In a nod to contemporaneous Italian political sex scandals that reached a nadir in the Berlusconi era—with the 2010 revelations about the then Prime Minister's 'bunga bunga' parties—one of the larger beds in the woman's home is reserved for politicians. At work, Luca's boss, 'L'americano' (Stefano Scherini), takes perverse pleasure in forcing his employee to undertake the most menial of tasks: at one point insisting that Luca attend to an overflowing toilet until he is literally up to his arms in shit. As his name suggests, L'americano embodies the stereotype of the Italian migrant who has made it big in America, constantly extolling the virtues of his adopted homeland as a means of elevating himself above compatriots, like Luca, who have never left Italy. Throughout the film, Luca struggles to overcome such snobbery and has considerable difficulty breaking through socio-economically imposed hierarchies. Curious, for example, about the pending alien invasion—visuals of which Pacinotti teases but ultimately withholds for the film's opening half hour—Luca attends a seminar where 'scientific experts' speak of humans living like slaves, an injustice that the benevolent aliens will seemingly address. One speaker explains that he used to work long hours in a call centre for little reward before he was chosen by the god-like aliens to better the lives of others, a pretence that is undercut when the seminar is exposed as a ruse to swindle money from gullible attendees like Luca. In such scenes, *The Last Man on Earth*'s rueful engagement with the growing Italian precariat is at its most forceful and speaks to the nation's embrace of neoliberal doctrines at the expense of its own people.

Perpetual Transition/Zero Prospects

Luca's life in *The Last Man on Earth* is one of perpetual transition where a lack of stability makes planning for the future a near impossibility. Like his neighbour Anna, he works in a precarious job that offers few prospects and lives in a crumbling apartment block that has been put up for sale by absentee owners. Precarity, as Kevan Harris and Ben Scully synopsise, 'is broadly used to connote the fragility of social reproduction and working conditions under neoliberalism' ('Counter-Movement' 415), and its effects have been keenly felt in Italy, where the benefits enjoyed by the generation who lived through the economic miracle of the 1950s and 1960s have long since subsided. Psychologically, precarity denudes workers of any hope for economic security, forcing them, in Mark Fisher's terms, to 'develop a capacity to respond to unforeseen events' and to 'learn to live in conditions of total instability [where] periods of work alternate with periods of unemployment' and where, 'typically, you find yourself employed in a series of short-term jobs, unable to plan for the future' (*Capitalist Realism* 35). Where once a single income could sustain a family, mortgage, and car, processes of transformation in the workplace are, according to Annalisa Murgia, 'distinguishable in Italy by the proliferation, which began in the mid-1990s, of what has been defined as non-standard or 'atypical' work—that is, any working situation which is neither dependent nor independent full-time employment' ('Representations of Precarity in Italy' 50). In *The Last Man on Earth*, this same precarity is highlighted further when we find out that Luca's apartment block is for sale and that he could be evicted at any moment. Ignored by an indifferent building superintendent who has little incentive to maintain the property, his predicament foreshadows an issue that would become increasingly pronounced in prone PIIGS nations, where foreign vulture funds took advantage of distressed housing markets. As if to hammer home the point, a garish billboard outside Luca's bedroom window loudly proclaims: 'spend your money well'. Decay and indifference to it are in fact salient tropes throughout *The Last Man on Earth*. On a visit to his father's rural farm, for example, Luca finds the property to be in a state of advanced decrepitude, much to the indifference of its owner. After telling his father that he has been looking for alien spacecraft in the skies, the old man sarcastically retorts that Luca is lucky to be able to afford binoculars in the current economy. Later, when Luca succeeds in striking up a conversation with Anna, she reveals that she works at a highway rest stop restaurant, a transitional space for everybody but employees, yet a job that Luca piously declares her fortunate to have. Anna, who is clearly fatigued from the tolls exacted by everyday life, tersely replies that 'everyone says that': her tone and subsequent comments suggesting exasperation at a system that provides her with little alternative. When their conversation turns to the threat posed by the advancing spacecraft, Anna states that even under alien overlords things could not get much worse, adding that 'we should be afraid of things not changing at all: me at the rest stop and you at the bingo hall forever'.

Denied meaningful social and economic agency, Anna and Luca are reflective of a wider sense of indifference in Italian society in an era where—starting with Berlusconi's monopolisation of the media in the 1980s—the commodification of social life grew apace. Responding to these changes, Murgia notes that activists in the 2004 May Day parades in Italy created the figure of San Precario (patron saint of precarious workers) to shed light upon the issue of precarity, as well as to 'involve in struggle a generation of younger students and workers who had grown up under the image-conscious and depoliticised culture of Berlusconismo' ('Representations' 53). The effects of Berlusconi's commodification of the media, one that would in turn pave the way for his political success, ensured that television, most glaringly, became less a medium for public discourse than a surreptitious mode of mass anaesthesia: intellectually reductive and saturated with misogynistic representations of women.[28] Although Luca does not own a television and largely ignores the media—save for the billboard outside his window that features an obligatory woman in a bikini—Pacinotti routinely deploys background news reports to expatiate the film's narrative. Tellingly, these reports provide little real news but instead focus upon esoterica, such as alien-themed parties on the Adriatic coast or the addition of model spaceships to Catholic processions celebrating the Immaculate Conception. Such banality is not incidental. By November 2011, and with the nation close to financial collapse, Berlusconi himself was offering up non-sequiturs as a means of sidestepping reality, refusing the offer of a low-interest IMF loan on the spurious basis that Italy's 'restaurants are full, the planes are fully booked and the hotel resorts are fully booked as well' (Spiegel and Dinmore, 'Berlusconi Brushes off Debt Crisis'). With yields on Italy's ten-year bonds reaching 6.4 per cent and dangerously close to levels that forced Greece, Ireland, and Portugal to accept economic bailouts,[29] Berlusconi blithely announced that 'Italy does not feel the crisis'—even as he simultaneously ceded to G20 demands that the IMF be allowed closely scrutinise his government's promised financial reforms ('Berlusconi Brushes'). While official unemployment figures hovered around 8 per cent—as distinct from Ireland, where unemployment averaged out at 14.6 per cent, or Spain, where it was closer to 20 per cent—such figures masked a multitude of underlying issues, not least the pronounced economic disconnect between the old and the young and between men and women in Italian society.[30] As a contemporary editorial in *The Economist* starkly noted, over a quarter of Italy's youth was unemployed, while only 46 per cent of women participated in the workforce—the lowest figure in western Europe ('The Man Who Screwed an Entire Country'). Little wonder, then, that Anna is circumspect about her future in *The Last Man on Earth*, even more so when she is enjoined to be grateful for a precarious job that allows her to do no more than scrape by. Her experience is not unique and tallies with Harris and Scully's observation that 'rather than produce an inclusive and sustainable development, the spread of flexible labor processes, subcontracting networks, and transnationalization of production have increased the precarity of waged work' ('Counter-Movement' 423), a downward spiral worsened by the economic crisis, as across Italy and the other PIIGS nations, people grew desperate to secure work of any kind.

Aliens Are Us

After initially keeping their invasion in the background, the aliens' eventual arrival allows Pacinotti to broaden his focus and skewer Italian society from a host of perspectives. The new-found devotion of alien worshippers fearing the apocalypse gently prods at laissez-faire attitudes to Catholicism, for example, while of perhaps greater interest is the role the aliens play in standing in for Italian society's 'others'. This latter motif is foregrounded at the film's outset when a concerned youth football coach calls a radio show to decry the potentially deleterious effect that 'aliens' will have on the composition of the national football team, reflecting widely reported incidents of racism in real-life Italian football.[31] Later, a female alien visits Luca's father's[32] farm and implausibly elects to stay, becoming a surrogate carer to the man: before long his decrepit property is restored to past glories, his crops are tended to and his quality of life is immeasurably improved. Again, the subtext is the reception of migrants in Italy, in this instance the role played by migrant women in the care of the elderly—a highly relevant topic in a country that by 2008 had one of the oldest populations in Europe, with 20 per cent of the population aged 65 or over.[33] Faced with a choice between unaffordable private care and inadequate public facilities, families of the over two million Italians in need of full-time or part-time assistance have increasingly turned to migrant workers to provide informal domiciliary support and care. Migrant care workers, the vast majority of whom are women,[34] thus fulfil a vital role within the Italian economy, one that 'exceeds by far the contribution of 'formal' care supplied by private or public organisations' (Di Santo and Ceruzzi, 'Migrant Care Workers in Italy: A Case Study' 4). All too often, however, these workers face precarious working conditions and little or no job security. Despite the introduction of laws requiring the legal regularisation of care workers in 2009, large numbers of migrant carers remain undeclared, deprived of legal rights and subject to the whims of the black market.[35] Through the coded female alien, *The Last Man on Earth* depicts migrant guest workers as an overwhelmingly positive force, yet Luca's father nevertheless mistreats her and she duly leaves. He subsequently confesses a history of domestic abuse to his son while in a drunken stupor, including the revelation that he murdered his wife who, it was long supposed, had abandoned the family when Luca was a child. The casual nature of his shocking admission echoes an earlier scene where the prostitute Roberta is brutally beaten and murdered by Luca's homophobic work colleagues. Roberta, whose earlier admonishment of Luca's own misogyny enabled a flowering of the latter's relationship with Anna, thus assumes the role of a martyr within the narrative, and his dead body is gently borne aloft by a group of aliens and beamed into a spaceship, in imagery that consciously evokes Christ's ascending into heaven. This in turn continues the theme of linking aliens to outsiders in society and amplifies the film's critique of discrimination based on class, race, gender, and sexuality. Failure to address these issues, it is suggested, will lead to a day of reckoning, as the film's conclusion makes clear.

Upon learning the truth about his mother, Luca leaves his father's farm in obvious distress. On the drive home, he encounters mass hysteria and numerous abandoned cars as, above, a vortex gathers pace in the sky. Arriving at Anna's apartment, Luca pauses to watch a news bulletin documenting the hysteria from inside a hospital. Onscreen, one of the experts from the earlier bogus conference denounces the aliens as 'evil creatures' who abducted him and severely burned his face, before the bulletin cuts away to an interview with a married couple and their young son. The woman states that she and her husband are 'decent people' who 'never hurt anyone', before revealing that their ill son has miraculously been cured of a serious illness. A dichotomy between good and evil is thus established, with the aliens the ultimate arbiters. Before joining the evacuation, Anna kisses Luca, signalling the rehabilitation of someone she had initially dismissed as a 'strange, idiotic monster'. In the film's concluding scene, Luca then turns towards the apocalyptic vortex in the sky before smiling wryly, perhaps hopeful that the aliens may judge him favourably too. A review by Antonella Carone in the blog *Il Buio in Sala* suggests that this final scene serves to put the pettiness of everyday discrimination in context and in so doing render it ridiculous, a summation with which it is difficult to disagree ('L'ultimo Terrestre'). Yet, despite its satirical instincts, *The Last Man on Earth*'s alien invasion remains almost conventional in sf terms, its ascribing of God-like omniscience to the aliens following a lineage that can be traced from *The Day the Earth Stood Still* (Robert Wise 1951), through *Close Encounters of the Third Kind* (Steven Spielberg 1977), to *Arrival* (Denis Villeneuve 2016). At one point, Anna expresses the wish that she would like for the aliens to have the ability to distinguish between good and bad people and the power to sentence them accordingly. The healing of the ill child coupled with the burning of the fake expert/false prophet provides a neat snapshot of this Manichean dichotomy; yet, if Anna's wish has indeed come through, it leaves open the questions of who in turn gets to judge the aliens and what, precisely, entitles them to decide the future of humanity. After all, there remains the possibility that no matter how bleak things appear, they can always get worse, as Italy's subsequent real-life fortunes attest to.

Within days of cheerily diagnosing his nation's economy as being in robust shape, Silvio Berlusconi could no longer ignore the fiscal vortex in his own midst. By 4 November 2011, with Italy amassing close to €2 trillion in sovereign debt, Berlusconi acknowledged in his closing remarks at the G20 summit in Cannes that the IMF had, in fact, offered the nation a rescue package, sending Italian borrowing costs skyrocketing to near 7.5 per cent (Spiegel, 'How the Euro was Saved'). Having failed to gather parliamentary support for the implementation of new austerity measures and failed further to convince his G20 partners that he possessed the will to do so, Berlusconi faced little alternative but to accept IMF oversight of the Italian economy. Within a week, severe austerity measures targeting the Italian people were passed through parliament, and Berlusconi resigned (three days after his Greek counterpart George Papandreou) to be replaced by the unelected technocrat Mario Monti, who was to preside over an unelected 'unity' government. Disgraced, clownish, and incompetent, Berlusconi had nonetheless proven himself a remarkably resilient politician and, despite his frequently odious behaviour, had at the least been democratically elected Prime Minister by the Italian people on three separate occasions. His fall and Monti's ascension left little doubt as to who really called the shots in Italy. Burdened by the fourth largest debt in the world, the EU deemed Italy as being simply 'too big to bail' (Spiegel, 'How the Euro was Saved'), and under the auspices of the IMF, Monti subsequently passed a series of austerity measures designed to stem the bleeding and above all to satiate the market. By 2013, youth unemployment had risen to 37 per cent with large-scale migration from the peninsula fuelling the narrative of a lost generation.[36] Predictably, the 15–34 age group accounted for the largest number of emigrants, with migration patterns and an ageing population further deepening the historic economic divide between the north and south of the country.[37] In other words, the spiral would continue: unemployment, poverty, and more elderly people than ever requiring help from a system that, as *The Last Man on Earth* takes pains to demonstrate, is largely if not entirely indifferent to their plight.

Notes

1. Sweden, which joined the EU in 1995 and did not secure an opt-out like its Danish neighbour, is nominally required to join the European Exchange Rate Mechanism (ERM II) and with it the Eurozone but to date has also shown little inclination to do so.
2. In a book chapter entitled 'The European Monetary Union: An Unfolding Disaster?', J. Magnus Ryner writes of the deflationary debt trap faced by the so-called PIIGS: 'the classical adjustment mechanism in such a situation is devaluation of the currency, but it is of course exactly this that is not possible in a monetary union' (16).
3. Many economists refute the notion that any single factor is alone responsible for the Eurozone's near collapse. For instance, James A. Caporaso and Martin Rhodes write that 'in short, the crises bear all the marks of situations that befuddle analysts: multiple causation, interactions among variables and shifting parameters rather than simple additive causes, and multiple paths to the same outcomes' (*Political and Economic Dynamics of the Eurozone Crisis* 4).
4. Mark Baimbridge and Philip Whyman observe that, while 'the fact that member states in distress were all located in the Eurozone periphery and had large public deficits, suggested to many that the problem had been fiscal profligacy and, therefore, austerity and an enhanced stringency in curtailing national budget deficits were perceived to be significant elements of the solution', the reality is far less straightforward. They continue: 'It is not the case that all struggling member states had pre-existing budget deficits. Indeed, Ireland and Spain had budget surpluses, in the year before the financial crisis, whereas only Greece exhibited the type of budgetary ill-discipline that corresponds to this neo-liberal critique' (*Crisis in the Eurozone* 148).
5. According to Brazys and Hardiman: 'The "PIGS" terminology was preceded by the perhaps less unflattering, but still loaded, "Club Med" label,

that, at times, variously omitted Greece or Italy and included France and/or Belgium. "Club Med" appears to have been coined no later than 1991 in the context of the EU Investment Services Directive (ISD) (Doty 1991) and has since been used to lump the aforementioned countries together' ('From "Tiger" to "PIIGS"' 29).
6. Kamm himself attributed the acronym PIGS to a banker's joke he had heard repeatedly ('From "Tiger" to "PIIGS"' 28).
7. Although initially used sporadically in the press, the term started to 'pervade discourse with dozens of monthly appearances in December 2009 and January 2010, and hundreds of monthly uses from February 2010' ('From "Tiger" to "PIIGS"' 30).
8. As Brazys and Hardiman note: 'The classification cuts across quite different models of capitalism and different institutional configurations of democracy. The Southern European countries shared something in common in that economic growth depended on a strong state presence in the economy, shaping investments and generating demand stimulus, while the Irish growth model depended heavily on a low-tax, market-conforming approach to encouraging foreign direct investment' ('From "Tiger"' 30).
9. Since the turn of the century, many such studies have emerged. See, amongst others that are too numerous to list in full here: Luisa Rivi's *European Cinema After 1989*, Anne Jäckel's *European Film Industries*, Rosalind Galt's *The New European Cinema: Redrawing the Map*, Mike Wayne's *The Politics of Contemporary European Cinema: Histories, Borders, Diasporas*, or edited collections by Tim Bergfelder, Sue Harris, and Sarah Street (*Film Architecture and the Transnational Imagination*), Catherine Fowler (*The European Cinema Reader*), Wendy Everett (*European Identity in Cinema*), and Mette Hjort and Scott MacKenzie (*Cinema and Nation*).
10. In January 2017, CNN reported that analysis conducted by Oxfam to coincide with that year's World Economic Forum in Davos found that Bill Gates, Warren Buffett, Carlos Slim, Jeff Bezos, Mark Zuckerberg, Amancio Ortega, Larry Ellison, and Michael Bloomberg's collective worth totalled a scarcely credible $426 billion, more than the combined wealth of the 3.6 billion people who constitute the poorest half of the world's population (Kottasova, 'These 8 Men are Richer than 3.6 billion People Combined').
11. As David Harvey writes in *Spaces of Neoliberalization: Towards a Theory of Uneven Geographical Development*, neoliberalism 'had long been lurking in the wings of public policy. But it was only during the troubled years of the 1970s that it began to move center stage […]. It gained respectability by the award of the Nobel Prize in economics to two of its leading proponents, [Friedrich August] von Hayek in 1974 and Milton Friedman in 1976' (11).
12. In August 2017, the *New York Times* reported that the Chinese government had invested close to half a billion Euros in the Athenian Port of Piraeus, while that same summer *The Guardian* reported that Chinese

companies were behind an $8 billion resort project outside Athens (Inman, 'Greece Approves $8bn Chinese-Backed Resort Project Outside Athens'). Such investment the *Times* speculated, when coupled with the EU's hardline stance towards Greece, may have played a significant role in the Greek government's voting against EU efforts to issue a unified statement against Chinese activities in the South Seas or its subsequent refusal to condemn human rights abuses in China (Horowitz and Alderman. 'Chastised by EU, a Resentful Greece Embraces China's Cash'). In 2011, meanwhile, China pledged to buy upward of €2.8 billion in Portuguese bonds and has maintained close ties with the country ever since (Coonan, 'Euro Zone Debt Crisis Recovery of "Crucial' Importance to China').
13. Klein identifies Pinochet ally Margaret Thatcher's exploitation of the Falklands conflict as another example of the shock doctrine in action while citing the fallouts from the war in Iraq and Hurricane Katrina as more contemporary examples (*The Shock Doctrine*). Friedman—who died in 2006—advocated for further deregulation of the Eurozone in his final interview that same year, arguing that for Europe to prosper, it should 'imitate Margaret Thatcher and Ronald Reagan; free markets in short' (Friedman, 'Free Markets and the End of History').
14. In an interview with the independent Greek news service *EnetEnglish*, Klein observed that 'Greeks have this particular fear that's being exploited, around the fear of becoming a developing country, becoming a third world country. And I think in Greece there's always been this sense of hanging on to Europe by a thread. And the threat is having that thread cut' (Edmonds, 'Is Greece in Shock?').
15. Statistics compiled in *Oxfam*'s 2013 study illustrate this trend starkly: 'In 2011, the number of new Portuguese emigrants almost doubled compared to 2010, from 23,760 to 43,998. However, the government acknowledged that the real figures might be twice those published officially, which would mean that almost 100,000 people left Portugal in 2011 alone' (*Oxfam*).
16. Although both books were well received, they 'did not change the market' according to the online *Encyclopedia of Science Fiction*, which states 'that in the twenty-first century no other major publisher has been willing to take a gamble on Portuguese SF; even those with a history of translating genre fiction' ('Portugal').
17. *Real Playing Game*'s screenplay is in fact markedly similar to the German production *Transfer* (Damir Lukacevic 2010), which depicts a future wherein the moneyed elderly can extend their lives by swapping bodies with refugees.
18. While Hauer's presence may be calculated to lend the film a tenuous link to the sf lineage of *Blade Runner* (his character's surname Battier mnemonically recalls *Blade Runner*'s Roy Batty), it is probably more helpful to

view the film in terms of other sf b-movies that the Dutchman recently acted in, such as *2047: Sights of Death* (Alessandro Capone 2014) and *The Broken Key* (Louis Nero 2017).
19. As Sally Faulkner and Mariana Liz note: 'After the Revolution, Portugal had to resolve two problems at the same time: first, how to devise a stable new order for itself and, second, how to put an end to its rule in Africa. The former concern was prioritised, which meant the Portuguese process of decolonization in Africa was little short of disastrous. There was no serious attempt to negotiate the terms of the handover for instance, Portugal never insisted on genuine elections being held. With no legal or economic framework in place, civil war was the obvious outcome, and indeed war broke out, first in Angola (1975–2002) and a few years later in Mozambique (1977–1992)' (*Portuguese Film: Colony, Postcolony, Memory* 4–5).
20. In his monograph *Irish Science Fiction*, Fennell argues that 'SF has been written by Irish authors for at least a hundred and fifty years (or longer, depending on the rigidity of one's definition of the genre)' (3): a trend that has, it seems, passed most Irish observers by.
21. A recent literary exception to this rule is Kevin Barry's novel *City of Bohane* (2011), which takes place in a post-apocalyptic Ireland of 2053; yet it remains the case that analogous to the popular reception of auteur sf films in Europe, evaluations of the Irish literary canon tend to downplay the role of genre.
22. Writing about the 2013 release of Ruairí Robinson's part-Irish co-production *The Last Days on Mars*, for example, the *Irish Times* film critic Donald Clarke opined that 'It all seems hard to believe. Only a decade ago, it would have seemed inconceivable that such a project could have such significant Irish involvement. We didn't build aircraft carriers. We didn't launch space probes. And we certainly didn't produce effects-based science-fiction pictures' ('The Irish Martians Launching a Surprise Cannes Invasion').
23. Ireland's 'Film and TV Tax Credit', also known as Section 481 of the nation's tax laws, offers tax relief of up to 32 per cent on Irish-based expenditure and is applicable to 'all cast and crew working in Ireland, regardless of nationality' ('Ireland's 32% Tax Credit').
24. For more contemporary examples of this trend, see, for example, *Far and Away* (Ron Howard 1992) or *Leap Year* (Anand Tucker 2010).
25. The Irish corporate tax rate of 12.5 per cent continues to be a major bone of contention within the EU, and successive Irish governments have strongly resisted moves to introduce a harmonisation of EU corporate tax rates. This issue came to a head in 2016, when a report by the European Commission concluded that Ireland had given illegal tax benefits to Apple amounting to €13billion, a fee that the Commission ordered Apple to repay. Apple, in collaboration with the Irish government, disputes the

Commission's findings and is currently appealing the ruling ('State Aid: Ireland Gave Illegal Tax Benefits to Apple Worth up to €13 Billion').
26. In a review for the Italian magazine *Senza Soste*, Marco Bruciati compares the film's deployment of an alien invasion narrative with Michelangelo Antonioni's idiosyncratic engagement with the mystery genre in *The Adventure/L'avventura* (1960). Nominally the latter film is about the disappearance of a young woman (Lea Massari), yet Antonioni quickly shifts focus from this seemingly central aspect of his plot in favour of essaying wider issues of alienation and existential angst amongst the Italian bourgeoisie ('Ruggine, Terraferma, L'ultimo Terrestre. L'alieno nel cinema italiano').
27. Marinelli also appears in the superhero movie *They Call Me Jeeg/Lo chiamavano Jeeg Robot* (Gabriele Mainetti 2015), a homage to the cult manga series *Steel Jeeg* and one of the few other sf-related Italian films of recent times.
28. Although over the last few years the situation is slowly improving, even on public television stations, such as RAI 1, it is still quite common practice to encounter afternoon quiz shows that fill breaks in the action with close-ups of dancing showgirls.
29. An editorial in *The Economist* credits 'the tight fiscal policy of Mr Berlusconi's finance minister, Giulio Tremonti', for Italy's ability to survive, claiming that 'Ireland, not Italy, is the I in the PIGS (with Portugal, Greece and Spain). Italy avoided a housing bubble; its banks did not go bust' ('The Man Who Screwed an Entire Country').
30. In 2011, Irish unemployment rates varied from 14.4 per cent (April and May) to 14.9 per cent (December) according to figures from the Central Statistics Office ('Seasonally Adjusted Standardised Unemployment Rates'). By the end of the same year in Spain, the Spanish National Statistics Institute said that 5.3 million people were unemployed ('Spain's Unemployment Total Passes Five Million').
31. This conversation satirises Italian football's problematic history with racism and questions pertaining to the 'Italianness' of black players, such as Mario Balotelli, who, despite being born in Palermo, has frequently faced doubts in Italy about his supposed fitness to wear the Italian shirt. The level to which such attitudes are ingrained in Italian football can be gleaned from more recent events such as the banning of Italian Football Association President Carlo Tavecchio by the sport's international executive FIFA in 2014, for allegedly stating that prior to their arrival in Italy, African players were 'eating bananas' ('Italian FA President Carlo Tavecchio Banned Over "Banana Eaters" Comment'), or a year later, when the celebrated former Italy and AC Milan coach Arrigo Sacchi was quoted in the Italian media as saying: 'I would say that there are too many black players. Italy has no dignity, no pride. It should not be possible that our teams should have 15 foreign players in the squad' ('I'm Not Racist But...').

32. Onscreen and in the end credits, Luca's father (who is played by Roberto Herlitzka) is never given a name but instead referred to only as 'padre di Luca'.
33. 'In Italy, which counts as one of the 'oldest' populations in Europe, 18.3% of citizens above the age of 65 (2.1 million people) are in need of full or part-time assistance' (Di Santo and Ceruzzi, 'Migrant Care Workers in Italy: A Case Study' 4).
34. Women make up 87 per cent of all foreign care workers and 96 per cent amongst Italian care workers (Di Santo and Ceruzzi, 'Migrant Care Workers in Italy' 10).
35. 'By 30 September 2009, the legal regularisation of family assistants and housekeeping personnel was concluded. According to the Italian Home Office that had expected between 500,000 and 750,000 applications to be submitted' [only] 'about 295,000 had applied: mainly Ukrainian (42,000), Moroccan (38,000), Moldovan (29,000) and Chinese (22,000) workers. This suggests that a lot of employees decided to keep working in the black economy, either for financial reasons or through fear' (Di Santo and Ceruzzi, 'Migrant Care Workers in Italy' 7). It would be imprudent to suggest, however, that in all instances exploitation by families is a factor. Exploitation, instead, is endemic in the system: for many financially stretched Italian families denied adequate state services, paying additional taxes and social insurance contributions is not possible.
36. A 2013 report in *Reuters* is exemplary: 'Faced with soaring unemployment and declining economic activity, young Italians are following previous generations in seeking their fortunes abroad, disillusioned by an economy in which graduates must often take precarious and menial jobs' (Jucca, 'Italy's Best Are Emigrating at Time of Crisis').
37. A report released by SVIMEZ, the Association for the Development of Industry in the South, noted that if these trends continued, only 5 million people between 15 and 34 will be left in the south by 2050, compared with the current figure of 7 million, meaning over 75s 'would represent 18% of the total population, up from 8% currently' (Ridet, 'Economic Exodus from Southern Italy').

Bibliography

Baccolini, Raffaella. 2014. The Uncomfortable Relationship Between Science Fiction and Italy: Film, Humor, and Gender. In *The Liverpool Companion to World Science Fiction Film*, ed. Sonja Fritzsche, 172–186. Liverpool: Liverpool University Press.

Baimbridge, Mark, and Philip Whyman. 2015. *Crisis in the Eurozone: Causes, Dilemmas and Solutions.* New York: Palgrave.

Barry, Kevin. 2011. *City of Bohane.* New York: Vintage.

Basevi, Giorgio, and Carlo D'Adda. 2014. Analytics of the Euro Area Crisis. In *The Eurozone Crisis and the Future of Europe: The Political Economy of Further Integration and Governance*, ed. Daniel Daianu, Carlo D'Adda, Giorgio Basevi, and Rajeesh Kumar, 9–22. Basingstoke: Palgrave.

Bergfelder, Tim, Sue Harris, and Sarah Street, eds. 2007. *Film Architecture and the Transnational Imagination: Set Design in 1930s European Cinema (Film Culture in Transition)*. Amsterdam: Amsterdam University Press.

Blum, Cinzia Sartini. 1996. *The Other Modernism: F.T. Marinetti's Futurist Fiction of Power*. Berkeley: University of California.

Bondebjerg, Ib, Eva Novrup Redvall, and Andrew Higson, eds. 2015. *European Cinema and Television: Cultural Policy and Everyday Life*. Basingstoke: Palgrave Macmillan.

Brazys, Samuel, and Niamh Hardiman. 2015. From "Tiger" to "PIIGS": Ireland and the Use of Heuristics in Comparative Political Economy. *European Journal of Political Research* 54: 23–42.

Brenner, Neil, Jamie Peck, and Nik Theodore. 2010. After Neoliberalization? *Globalizations* 7 (3): 327–345.

Bruciati, Marco. 2011. Ruggine, Terraferma, L'ultimo Terrestre. L'alieno nel cinema italiano. *Senza Soste*, September 14. www.archivio.senzasoste.it/visioni/l-alieno-del-cinema-italiano. Accessed 1 May 2018.

Cabral, Ricardo and Viriato Soromenho Marques. 2014. Portugal: 40 Years of Democracy and Integration in the European Union. *Heinrich Böll Stiftung*, March 25, 1–13. eu.boell.org/en/2014/03/25/portugal-40-years-democracy-and-integration-european-union. Accessed 1 May 2018.

Caporaso, James A., and Martin Rhodes, eds. 2016. *The Political and Economic Dynamics of the Eurozone Crisis*. Oxford: Oxford University Press.

Carone, Antonella. 2011. L'ultimo Terrestre. *Il Buio in Sala*. www.puntodisvista.net/?s=l%27ultimo+terrestre. Accessed 1 May 2018.

Clarke, Donald. 2013. The Irish Martians Launching a Surprise Cannes Invasion. *Irish Times*, May 21.

Coonan, Clifford. 2011. Euro Zone Debt Crisis Recovery of "Crucial" Importance to China. *Irish Times*, June 18.

Csicsery-Ronay, Istvan. 2003. Science Fiction and Empire. *Science Fiction Studies* 30 (2): 231–245.

de Almeida, Miguel Vale. 1997. *EuroNovela*. Caminho.

Di Santo, Patrizia and Francesca Ceruzzi. 2010. Migrant Care Workers in Italy: A Case Study. *Interlinks*, 1–39.

Director of the Movie They Are All Talking About Says Inishowen Was Magnificent. *Derry Journal*, August 3, 2012.

Edmonds, Lynn. 2013. Is Greece in Shock? *EnetEnglish*, April 30. www.enetenglish.gr/?i=news.en.article&id=766. Accessed 1 May 2018.

Everett, Wendy ed. 2005. *European Identity in Cinema*. Intellect

Faulkner, Sally and Mariana Liz. Portuguese Film: Colony, Postcolony, Memory. *The Journal of Romance Studies* 16 (2): 1–11.
Fennell, Jack. 2014. *Irish Science Fiction*. Liverpool: Liverpool University Press.
Fisher, Mark. 2009. *Capitalist Realism*. Winchester: Zero Books.
Fitting, Peter. 2000. Estranged Invaders: The War of the Worlds. In *Learning from Other Worlds: Estrangement, Cognition, and the Politics of Science Fiction and Utopia*, ed. Patrick Parrinder, 127–145. Liverpool: Liverpool University Press.
Flassbeck, Heiner, and Costas Lapavitsas. 2015. *Against the Troika: Crisis and Austerity in the Eurozone*. New York: Verso.
Foucault, Michel. 1978. *History of Sexuality. Volume 1: An Introduction*. New York: Random House.
———. 2005. *Archaeologies of the Future: A Desire Called Utopia and Other Science Fictions*. New York: Verso.
———. 2007. S*ecurity, Territory, Population: Lectures at the Collège de France 1977–78*. Trans. Graham Burchell. Basingstoke: Palgrave Macmillan.
Frearson, Amy. 2011. Champalimaud Centre for the Unknown by Charles Correa Associates. *Dezeen.com*, June 14. www.dezeen.com/2011/06/14/champalimaud-centre-for-the-unknown-by-charles-correa-associates/. Accessed 1 May 2018.
Friedman, Milton. 2006. Free Markets and the End of History. *New Perspectives Quarterly* 23 (1).
Fukuyama, Francis. 1992. *The End of History and the Last Man*. New York: Free Press.
Galt, Rosalind. 2006. *The New European Cinema: Redrawing the Map*. New York: Columbia University Press.
Golding, William. 1954. *Lord of the Flies*. London: Faber and Faber.
Guérot, Ulrike. 2016. An Invitation to Bravely Think About the Future of Europe. *The New Federalist*, August 12.
Harris, Kevan, and Ben Scully. 2015. A Hidden Counter-Movement? Precarity, Politics, and Social Protection Before and Beyond the Neoliberal Era. *Theory and Society* 44 (5): 415–444.
Harvey, David. 2005. *A Brief History of Neoliberalism*. Oxford: Oxford University Press.
Hooper, John. 2011. Italian Alien Film Tries to Ape Orson Welles Radio Play in Web Marketing. *The Guardian*, August 8.
Horowitz, Jason and Liz Alderman. 2017. Chastised by EU, a Resentful Greece Embraces China's Cash. *New York Times*, August 25.
I Filmed a Horror Movie in Ireland. Here's Why. *The Journal.ie*, August 5, 2012. www.thejournal.ie/readme/irish-horror-movie-grabbers-544954-Aug2012/. Accessed 1 May 2018.
I'm Not Racist But There Are Too Many Black Players in Italian Youth Football. *Evening Standard*, February 17, 2015.

Inman, Phillip. 2017. Greece Approves $8bn Chinese-Backed Resort Project Outside Athens. *The Guardian*, June 2.
Ireland's 32% Tax Credit. *Irish Film Board*. www.irishfilmboard.ie/filming/section-481. Accessed 1 May 2018.
Italian FA President Carlo Tavecchio Banned Over "Banana Eaters" Comment. *Guardian*, November 5, 2014.
Jäckel, Anne. 2004. *European Film Industries*. London: BFI.
Jameson, Fredric. 1991. *Postmodernism, or, The Cultural Logic of Late Capitalism*. New York: Verso.
Jones, Owen. 2017. No Alternative to Austerity? That Lie Has Now Been Nailed. *The Guardian*, August 24.
Jucca, Lisa. 2013. Italy's Best Are Emigrating at Time of Crisis. *Reuters*, February 21.
Kamm, Thomas. 1996. Snobbery: The Latest Hitch in Unifying Europe. *Wall Street Journal*, November 6.
Kenny, Ciara. 2012. Emigration Rises to Record High. *Irish Times*, September 27.
Klein, Naomi. 2003. Fortress Continents. *The Guardian*, January 16.
———. 2007. *The Shock Doctrine*. New York: Random House.
Kottasova, Ivana. 2017. These 8 Men Are Richer than 3.6 Billion People Combined. *CNN*, January 17. money.cnn.com/2017/01/15/news/economy/oxfam-income-inequality-men/index.html.
Liz, Mariana. 2016. *Euro-Visions: Europe in Contemporary Cinema*. London: Bloomsbury.
Lochery, Neill. 2017. *Out of the Shadows: Portugal from Revolution to the Present Day*. London: Bloomsbury.
Lumiere: Data Base on Admissions of Films Released in Europe. *European Audiovisual Observatory*. lumiere.obs.coe.int/web/search/.
MacDougall, Heather. 2009. Who Needs Hollywood? The Role of Popular Genre Films in Irish National Cinema. *The Canadian Journal of Irish Studies* 35 (1): 39–46.
McGrory, Linda. 2011. Monster Movie Brings Boost to Business in North Donegal. *Irish Times*, January 27.
McManus, John. 2017. Why We Keep Making the Same Mistakes over Housing. *Irish Times*, May 17.
Melia, Paul. 2018. Melia. Property Prices Rise By More than €100,000 in a Year Amid Fear of Celtic Tiger-level Hikes. *Irish Independent*, April 14.
Monbiot, George. 2016. Neoliberalism: The Ideology at the Root of All Our Problems. *The Guardian*, April 15.
———. 2017. A Lesson from Hurricane Irma: Capitalism Can't Save the Planet–It Can Only Destroy It. *The Guardian*, September 13.
Moylan, Katie. 2014. Aliens Dancing at the Crossroads: Science Fiction Interventions in Irish Cinema. In *The Liverpool Companion to World Science Fiction Film*, ed. Sonja Fritzsche, 157–171. Liverpool: Liverpool University Press.

Murgia, Annalisa. 2014. Representations of Precarity in Italy. *Journal of Cultural Economy* 7 (1): 48–63.

Phillips, Tony. 2014. The Great Recession: Spillover in Europe, Banking Collapse in Ireland. In *Debt Crisis and Dissent in the European Periphery*, ed. Tony Phillips, 17–73. London: Zed Books.

Portugal. *The Encyclopedia of Science Fiction*. 5 November 2016. www.sf-encyclopedia.com/entry/portugal.

Real, Miguel. 2015. *O Último Europeu/The Last European*. Dom Quizote.

Ridet, Philippe. 2011. Economic Exodus from Southern Italy. *The Guardian*, October 11.

Rockett, Kevin. 1999. Irish Cinema: The National in the International. *Cineaste* 24 (2–3): 23–25.

Ryner, Magnus. 2014. The European Monetary Union: An Unfolding Disaster? In *The Debt Crisis in the Eurozone*, ed. Nicholas P. Petropoulos and George O. Tsobanoglou, 14–22. Newcastle upon Tyne: Cambridge Scholars.

Seasonally Adjusted Standardised Unemployment Rates. *Central Statistics Office*. www.cso.ie/en/statistics/labourmarket/principalstatistics/seasonallyadjustedstandardisedunemploymentratessur/. Accessed 1 May 2018.

Silva, Gastão Brito E. 2012. A Ocupação Revolucionária do Hotel do Muxito. *Publico*, September 23.

Spain's Unemployment Total Passes Five Million. *BBC*, January 27, 2017. www.bbc.com/news/world-16754600. Accessed 1 May 2018.

Spiegel, Peter. 2014. How the Euro Was Saved. *Financial Times*, May 11.

Spiegel, Peter and Guy Dinmore. 2011. Berlusconi Brushes off Debt Crisis. *Financial Times*, November 4.

State Aid: Ireland Gave Illegal Tax Benefits to Apple Worth Up to €13 Billion. *European Commission*, August 30, 2016. europa.eu/rapid/press-release_IP-16-2923_en.htm. Accessed 1 May 2018.

Sugrue, Emer. 2012. Interview: Jon Wright. *University Observer*, September 19. www.universityobserver.ie/film-tv-otwo/interview-jon-wright/. Accessed 1 May 2018.

The Man Who Screwed an Entire Country. *The Economist*, June 9, 2011.

The True Cost of Austerity and Inequality: Portugal Case Study. *Oxfam Case Study*, September 2013. www.oxfam.org/sites/www.oxfam.org/files/cs-true-cost-austerity-inequality-portugal-120913-en.pdf. Accessed 1 May 2018.

Tracy, Tony. 2010. Irish Film and Television Review: 2009. *Estudios Irlandeses* 5: 203–255.

Wayne, Mike. 2002. *The Politics of Contemporary European Cinema: Histories, Borders, Diasporas*. Intellect.

Young, Brigitte. 2014. The Role of German Ordoliberalism in the Euro Crisis. In *The Debt Crisis in the Eurozone: Social Impacts*, ed. Nicholas P. Petropoulos and George O. Tsobanoglou, 2–14. Newcastle upon Tyne: Cambridge Scholars.

CHAPTER 5

PIIGS to the Slaughter II

Dead Ends and Greek Tragedies

Film: *The Lobster* (Yorgos Lanthimos 2015)

The Greek director Yorgos Lanthimos' fifth feature (and first English language) film sees him transpose the dark humour and surrealism of earlier, critically acclaimed productions such as *Dogtooth/Kynodontas* (2009) and *Alps/Alpeis* (2011) to a dystopian near-future world where single people are forced to form couples or risk being transformed into an animal of their choosing. That implementation of this seemingly state-sanctioned policy takes place during a 28-day mating course at a rural luxury hotel (shot in Co. Kerry, Ireland) only adds to the sense of strangeness. Born in 1973, Lanthimos is an Athenian director who first came to prominence in his native Greece as a director of experimental theatre, television commercials, and music videos, while he also worked on the opening and closing ceremonies of the 2004 Olympic Games in Athens. In the years following his 2001 debut film *My Best Friend/O kalyteros mou filos*, which he co-directed with Lakis Lazopoulos, Lanthimos has become synonymous with the so-called Greek weird wave, an unofficial movement of filmmakers which includes Athina Rachel Tsangari and Yannis Economides and is a classification, incidentally, which Lanthimos himself rejects.[1] Following the low-budget

Kinetta (2005), Lanthimos rose to prominence internationally with *Dogtooth*, an intense yet darkly humorous chronicle of domestic imprisonment which was nominated for the Best Foreign Language Film at the 2011 Academy Awards. His next feature *Alps*, a Golden Lion nominee at the 2011 Venice Film Festival, confirmed his ascendency as a rising star of European arthouse cinema. Nonetheless, Lanthimos' emergence as an auteur of note has come despite extreme budgetary limitations, a reality that the director himself has acknowledged. During promotion for *The Lobster*, which was part-funded by Eurimages, Lanthimos ruefully summed up the limitations of working within a crisis-stricken Greece, noting that 'we're making films largely on favours, and friends aren't getting paid the way they should be, if at all [...] We'd pay people by doing free work for them, as there was very little support from the Greek Film Centre or commercial production companies' (Byrne, 'Interview with Director Yorgos Lanthimos'). As such, Lanthimos views his move into English language productions as a pragmatic step, one facilitated by his leaving Greece in 2011 to live in London. Doing so, he reasoned to *Time Out London*, would enable him to build upon the critical success of his earlier ventures, for although he obtained some minor funding from the Greek government, he noted that 'most of the people on *Dogtooth* had to work for free' (Jenkins, 'Yorgos Lanthimos on Dogtooth'). On the face of it, such a transition is consistent with the experiences of other up-and-coming directors from smaller European nations. Filming *The Lobster* in Ireland, which has a long tradition of exporting aspiring actors and directors to the UK, Lanthimos would not have to look far for evidence of this trend. Yet while his reputation may have contributed to him outgrowing the financial limitations of filmmaking in his native Greece, Lanthimos remains adamant that in the case of *The Lobster*, an increase in budget facilitated by the backing of transnational sources was mitigated by a significant increase in overheads, stating that 'in actual numbers, it might look like a much bigger production, but once you actually pay everyone, you end up with pretty much the same budget on the set' (Byrne, 'Interview with Director Yorgos Lanthimos'). Nevertheless, a combination of Lanthimos' reputation coupled with an estimated budget of €4 million did allow for the casting of Hollywood stars Colin Farrell, Rachel Weisz, and John C. Reilly, a turn of events that certainly helped to raise the profile of the production.

An International Affair

As with casting, production of *The Lobster* was very much an international affair, in keeping with Eurimages diktats that supported films must feature prior funding from at least two contributing member states. Going through the film's credits is instructive with no fewer than 16 individuals listed as executive or co-producers, giving an indication of the portmanteau-like nature of much contemporary arthouse European film production. Lanthimos and his producers successfully attracted a variegated assortment of investors, from commercial partners such as Canal+ and Film4, nationally based production companies in Scarlet Films, Protagonist Films, and Element Pictures, to national film boards including Bord Scannán na Éireann, Nederlands Fonds voor de Film, and the BFI Film Fund. Eurimages' contribution to the project amounted to €460,000 meanwhile, or roughly 11.5 per cent of its overall budget ('Co-production funding in 2013'). With its mélange of backers, both private and public, *The Lobster* operates as a ringing endorsement of CoE integrationist ideals that validate national film structures while gesturing towards a pluralist yet cohesive postnational framework. In real terms, such an arrangement had obvious commercial benefits, raising the profile of the film in markets that otherwise may have been indifferent to it. In Ireland, for example, *The Lobster* was screened in mainstream cinema chains in addition to the dedicated arthouse venues that would otherwise have been its sole outlet.

Lanthimos himself allowed that the film's funding model required an open-minded approach to shooting outside of Greece, pragmatically stating that 'you have to go to these countries and shoot some of your film there. It was the only way to put this film together' (Byrne, 'Interview with Director Yorgos Lanthimos'). While such models have been criticised in the past for creating 'Europuddings', that oft-maligned brand of European production that minimises regional specificity and reinforces soft-edged interpretations of European space, Lanthimos in fact makes a virtue of his onscreen non-place, much as Michael Haneke, a director whom Lanthimos has drawn recurrent comparison, revels in the opportunities afforded by geographic haziness in *Time of the Wolf* as we have seen in Chap. 2. A feature of both films is the obliteration of distinct locality, an effective motif that succeeds in heightening social allegory. Just as Haneke's refusal to namecheck cities or other spatial signifiers (a trend that *The Lobster* embraces by referring only to 'the city') allows us to imagine that the events that unfold could conceivably happen anywhere, and have repercussions not solely restricted to readily identifiable conflict zones, Lanthimos' dystopia is at once oddly familiar and foreign, a reality attributable at least in part to the mishmash of British, Irish, American, and mainland European accents on display. This in turn endorses the feeling that the director is extending his familiar satirical methods to encompass a critique of European society and not just distinctly Greek affairs. Moreover, we can say with some degree of confidence that the nature of *The Lobster*'s production, coupled with its international cast, altered the conditions from which reviewers sought to engage with the film, with public anticipation leavened by soft-focus features on the film's production appearing in outlets not renowned for arthouse cinema coverage such as the *Daily Mail* ('What a Happy Set!'). One direct consequence of the Eurimages model is that it allows for multiple national audiences to feel a degree of investment in finalised films, if only for reasons of local curiosity. In Ireland, such curiosity extended to governmental level, with the then Minister for Culture, Heritage and the Gaeltacht Jimmy Deenihan visiting the set of *The Lobster* on the final day of shooting. Yet as Lanthimos himself has indicated, the use of the Kerry location is somewhat arbitrary and stems largely from a need to meet conditions imposed by the film's backers. Such concessions are not unique to *The Lobster* as the case of *This Must Be the Place* (Paolo Sorrentino 2011) illustrates. Sorrentino, another celebrated European auteur whose work has found favour with The Academy, shot considerable sections of his English language debut in Dublin for reasons largely related to funding from Eurimages and the Irish Film Board. Tellingly, such location shoots serve the wider purpose of perpetuating Eurimages' mission statement while enabling national governments and tourist boards to champion native film industries. Encouraged by Eurimages, figures like Sorrentino and Lanthimos feed into this process by becoming brand names, transnational auteurs whose work serves certain modes of European economic integration, irrespective by and large of the actual films that they end up making.

While in production terms *The Lobster* is an exemplary illustration of integrationist European models, onscreen instead the film provides an especially wry commentary upon the financial disasters afflicting Lanthimos' native Greece, despite a curious insistence by critics such as Richard Brody of the *New Yorker* that it does nothing of the sort.[2] David (Farrell), the film's central protagonist, is taken from his home by shadowy operatives and brought to a rural hotel where, he is told, he must find a compatible romantic partner within 45 days or else he will be turned into a lobster, his animal of choice. Indeed, far from being passive, in its depiction of an uncaring bureaucratic society that enforces orthodoxy by relegating dissidents to non-human status, *The Lobster* may well be the most searing sf critique of the EU's policies towards Greece to emerge during the Eurozone crisis. In his recent article 'The Lobster: Debt, Referenda, and False Choices', Kenan Behzat Sharpe detects this potential, observing that '*The Lobster* can give us insight not only into the Greek crisis but into the crises that are determining and limiting political possibilities across the debt-ridden states of the European periphery (Portugal, Spain, Italy, and Ireland)' (2016). Specifically, Sharpe contends that *The Lobster*'s very premise works as a commentary on late capitalism itself, as 'through absurdist exaggeration the film helps render visible a social logic which everywhere confronts us with two equally disastrous options between which we are compelled to choose' ('The Lobster'). Like characters in the film, the Eurozone crisis would force Greece to confront an especially necrofuturist quandary[3] wherein its people could either accept austerity and watch their economy wither on the vine or refuse austerity, leave the EU, and then watch their economy wither on the vine: the very epitome of what Sharpe describes as a false choice. Closer scrutiny of Lanthimos' style can therefore only enrich our understanding of how formal choices in *The Lobster* work to undermine the notion that the EU's treatment of Greece was unavoidable and thus somehow 'normal'.

Anthropomorphism and Nosebleeds

Although he may have encountered wholly new production considerations while filming *The Lobster*, onscreen, the end product is very much a Yorgos Lanthimos film. A predilection for anthropomorphism dating from *Dogtooth* is very much in evidence, as is Lanthimos' penchant for open-ended conclusions. Furthermore, whilst David has a name, most other characters are referred to principally (albeit not exclusively) in wry descriptive form, resulting in a world populated by people such as Nosebleed Woman (Jessica Barden), Limping Man (Ben Whishaw), Lisping Man (John C. Reilly), and Loner Leader (Léa Seydoux). Carrying on from *Dogtooth* and *Alps*, where almost without exception characters remain nameless,[4] this strategy depersonalises protagonists while fostering levels of estrangement encouraged both by Lanthimos and co-writer Efthymis Filippou's wilfully stilted dialogue and by the strategically po-faced delivery of a talented cast. The absurdity of the piece serves a key function of foregrounding a sense of cognitive rupture at *The Lobster*'s core. Taken at face value, viewers must suspend their belief in the rational in order to decode the estranged internal logic of the film (David's brother, for instance, is played by a dog). In an article explaining the mechanics of *Dogtooth*, Angelos Koutsourakis draws upon Bertolt Brecht, arguing that 'a character is not an individual with fixed and unchanged characteristics, but is always defined by the social context in which he/she is embedded' ('Cinema of the Body: The Politics of Performativity in Lars von Trier's Dogville and Yorgos Lanthimos' Dogtooth' 98). In *Dogtooth*, Koutsourakis argues, a process of estrangement is fostered through the actors' embodiment of Brecht's concept of gestus[5] which emphasises the social aspect of characters over the psychological, in addition to a leitmotif of disembodied characterisation, which Lanthimos achieves in part by routinely shooting his actors from the neck down. *The Lobster* is less radical in this regard and makes more use of the high-profile faces of its cast. Yet the argument for social context remains strong, and it is this aspect that leads us closer to the film's sf core. Brecht's influence, of course, is keenly felt in Darko Suvin's conceptualisation of sf's facility for cognitive estrangement in the oft-cited 'On the Poetics of the Science Fiction Genre' (374). Arguing that sf in the twentieth century had evolved to become a 'diagnosis, a warning, a call to understanding and action, and-most important-a mapping of possible alternatives', Suvin posited that a shift had taken place, one he attributed to sf moving from an extrapolative model to an analogic one ('On the Poetics' 378). In sketching the analogical usefulness of the genre in the same essay, Suvin notes that:

> its figures may but do not have to be anthropomorphic or its localities geomorphic. The objects, figures, and up to a point the relationships from which this indirectly modeled world starts can be quite fantastic (in the sense of empirically unverifiable) as long as they are logically, philosophically and mutually consistent. ('On the Poetics' 379)

In its non-specific setting and attribution of human qualities to animals, *The Lobster* certainly fits these categorisations, even if in its unquestioning matter-of-fact depiction of the latter trait it arguably veers closer to magic realism. Moreover, the film may be absurd, but there is no denying that it embodies a certain internal logic that is consistent with

Lanthimos' oeuvre. In abstracting reality Lanthimos seemingly plays by his own rules, yet it is clear in *The Lobster* that characters are subject to stringent societal decrees meaning that those who violate received wisdom will be punished unmercifully.

Even leaving aside its depiction of a punitive state, the world of *The Lobster* is wholly informed by obscure social conventions and practices. Upon joining an insurrectionist, forest-based rebel group called the 'Loners' after escaping from his hotel, David is warned by his new comrades that initiating a physical relationship will result in his being subjected to extreme violence, if not actual death. Taken at face value, the Loners' outlook appears to be little more than an exact reversal of state policy, their methods every bit as brutal. Yet following Koutsourakis, who, drawing upon Brecht, argues that in Lanthimos' work 'what passes as "real" cannot be understood outside socially constructed representational systems' ('Cinema of the Body' 103), I would argue that a wider political critique is in evidence in *The Lobster*, if we can move past the strangeness of its presentation. On a formal level, *The Lobster*'s abstraction of language concomitant with the decision to reduce each character to an aggregation of seemingly random physical or behavioural traits reinforces humankind's primordial nature and emphasises the role of social constructs in tempering our animalistic urges. Despite the Loners forbidding it, David pursues a burgeoning romance with Short Sighted Woman (Rachel Weisz), one made possible by a form of homemade sign language that keeps their intimate conversations private. This strategy is slightly altered from *Dogtooth*, wherein a domineering father and mother keep their children confined within the family home, stoking their fear of the outside world by teaching them a distorted and highly selective vocabulary. A seemingly innocuous word such as 'sea', for example, is altered to refer to an armchair, while 'zombies' become denotative of yellow flowers. As Koutsourakis has observed, the hopelessness of the situation is 'perplexed by the fact that the language system that the kids have inherited from their parents is illogical and has no representational attributes. It is a rather invented vocabulary which attributes different meanings to common everyday words' ('Cinema of the Body' 96). Similarly, language in *The Lobster* is co-opted for oppressive means, with a dull, unyielding technocratic jargon operating as the new lingua franca, one that David and Short Sighted Woman circumvent through sign language.

Permanent Supervision

That David is seemingly blameless for the predicament he finds himself in (his wife left him for another man) is largely beside the point. Lanthimos' native Greece after all was admitted to the EEC in 1981 despite voluble concerns as to its fiscal suitability. Then as now, however, greater security issues were at stake[6] which overrode strictly economic considerations,[7] and Greece was duly granted the opportunity to emerge from dictatorship and conform to EEC expectations. Within the hotel that he is brought to (and later escapes from), David's every activity is closely monitored; his attempts to find a suitable new partner scrutinised for legitimacy. 'If a match based on likeness is not achieved', Sarah Cooper observes, 'the management intervenes to reinstitute norms that are set out within a regulatory structure from the outset: conformity and uniformity (the hotel guests all wear the same clothes) are paramount here' ('Narcissus and The Lobster' 165–166). The terms of this new reality are starkly outlined by the clinically bureaucratic Hotel Manager (Olivia Coleman), who tells David that failure to fit in will result in his being transformed into an animal. Conformity is key in this new world order, and David is advised by the hotel manager to choose his animal carefully, for 'a wolf and a penguin can never live together'. The veracity of this observation is soon put to the test, with residents going to extreme lengths to feign compatibility: Limping Man, for instance, repeatedly bangs his face against a wall to mimic a potential suitor's frequent nosebleeds. Grave of tone and wearing a subdued grey business suit and pearls, the stateswoman-like hotel manager informs David of the gravity of his situation: 'I understand this discussion is a little unpleasant for you, but it is my duty to prepare you psychologically for all possible outcomes'. Subsequently, every action David takes is monitored, his private space invaded to the point that he is expressly forbidden from masturbating. When Lisping Man is later observed doing just that, he is punished by having his hand placed in a warm toaster. To ensure compliance with this and other rules, the hotel manager has guests provide daily reports on their progress. The wider context here speaks of Greece, similarly stripped of self-determination. Tiring of Greek efforts to meet bailout requirements, Angela Merkel was by 2011 pressing for full supervision of the country, stating that 'it's not enough that the Troika comes and goes every three months. It would be desirable to have a permanent supervision in Greece' (Pop, 'Merkel Wants "Permanent" Supervision of Greece, Warns of War').

The very question of statehood and the EU is in fact alluded to in *The Lobster*'s opening scene when David is taken by bus to the hotel. Shot from behind, the bus prominently displays an EU licence plate without a national code or flag, as clear an indication as Lanthimos will give as to his film's wider concerns. In fact, it is difficult to separate artist from context, particularly given that George Papandreou, Merkel's Greek counterpart at the time, concluded a 2011 emergency cabinet meeting by lauding Lanthimos for *Dogtooth*'s Oscar nomination, a landmark that Papandreou asserted was 'based on features that characterize the creative forces which lead Greece to a new era' (V.B. 'Dark, Haunting and Wonderfully Weird'). Before the year was out, however, Papandreou was to pay heavily for electing to put the terms of an EU bailout before the Greek people, with Merkel and other European leaders insisting that any such referendum be tied to continued Greek membership of the EU.[8] Plunged into deeper crisis, Papandreou was replaced as Prime Minister by the technocratic Lucas Papademos, an unelected former vice president of the European Central Bank, who vowed to implement severe austerity measures in exchange for completion of the bailout. If *The Lobster* is scathing of EU policy, however, then it clearly has reservations about the alternatives too, for David's experience with the Loners is no less harrowing than his time at the hotel. After learning of her relationship with David, Léa Seydoux's fanatical 'Loner Leader' orders her followers to blind Short Sighted Woman as punishment. The Loners' refusal to compromise ultimately delimits their effectiveness, and following David and Short Sighted Woman's escape, which necessitates their tying her up, 'Loner Leader' is set upon by dogs and presumably killed. The Loners' fate perhaps echoes that of the left-wing Syriza party in Greece who came to power in 2015 on the back of a wave of anti-austerity sentiment across the beleaguered nation. Despite promises to the contrary, as well as the resounding opposition of the Greek people, 61 per cent of whom voted against doing so in a referendum, the party was ultimately forced to implement further cuts to secure a new bailout deal (Lowen, 'Greek Debt Crisis: What was the Point of the Referendum?'). Yet parallels between the Loners and Syriza would appear to be rather thin on the face of it, even if both would ultimately lose unyielding, yet charismatic leaders, with Syriza's high-profile finance minister Yanis Varoufakis resigning in protest shortly after the referendum.[9] Instead, it may be sufficient to view the Loners as being emblematic of the chaotic nature of Greek politics during this period, an era notable for the collapse of successive governments, the entrenchment of political factions, and the return of the far-right in the guise of the neo-Nazi Golden Dawn party. In one of *The Lobster*'s standout comic moments, Lanthimos encapsulates this chaos in a surreal scene featuring a Loner silent disco in the forest, an event designed to militate against human contact and where oblivious, headphone-wearing participants literally dance to the beat of their own music. Ultimately, however, Lanthimos provides no answers or resolution, perhaps above all because the questions being asked don't make any sense. In the film's final scene set in a roadside cafe, David seemingly agrees to blind himself so that he may stay with Short Sighted Woman, who is no longer fit to continue a life on the run. Doing so will appease the state and prove the couple's compatibility. Yet Lanthimos leaves matters open by cutting away from a shot of David holding a blade to his eye in the restaurant's bathroom and closing instead with a shot of Short Sighted Woman at a table quietly awaiting his return. Either David can still see, in which case he will remain an enemy of the prevailing orthodoxy, or he will be blinded and allowed to remain part of society, a metaphor that neatly encapsulates Greece's ongoing travails.

Panic, Subnationalism, and Male Futures in Spain

Film: The Last Days/Los últimos días (David and Àlex Pastor 2013)

Catalan brothers David and Àlex Pastor place Spain's financial woes front and centre of their 2013 release *The Last Days/Los últimos días*, one of a handful of Spanish sf films to emerge during the financial crisis.[10] Although embodying aspects familiar to fans of the zombie subgenre, most obviously in its reliance upon the plot device of an out-of-control virus, *The Last Days* largely avoids horror clichés and is instead concerned with engaging with the practicalities of surviving in a post-apocalyptic world. The film shares thematic similarities with the US-based Pastors' debut feature *Carriers* (2009) which was shot on location in New Mexico, yet it is markedly different from a production standpoint. *Carriers* was co-produced by Paramount's 'specialty division' Paramount Vantage,[11] shot in English and featured Hollywood stars Chris Pine and Piper Perabo. *The Last Days* instead is a distinctly European affair and acquired its estimated €5.5 million budget from a host of European sources, companies in Catalonia (Televisió de Catalunya [TV3]), Spain (Antena 3 Films), and France (Canal+) amongst them. Like *The Lobster* it also benefited from the collaboration of Eurimages, as well as the EU's MEDIA funding programme. Unsurprisingly, the film's preoccupations are predominantly European too, with a strong emphasis placed upon the fallout from the financial crisis in the Eurozone, a phenomenon it references on numerous occasions. Indeed, *The Last Days*' preoccupation with the financial crisis is abundantly clear from the film's advertising, with cinema posters, DVD, and Blu-ray covers all featuring images of smoke clouds rising from the financial centre of Barcelona. Intriguingly, the Pastor brothers cite financial imperatives as a principal reason for their engagement with sf itself, stating that whilst they were fans of the post-apocalyptic subgenre, *Carriers* and *The Last Days* 'materialized because the theme is fashionable and because it is what the market demands' (Torrano, 'Political Wishful Thinking' 3). On a narrative level, *The Last Days* focuses on the attempts of two office employees, Marc (Quim Gutiérrez) and Enrique (José Coronado), to survive the collapse of society in an alternate present-day version of Barcelona, one where a mysterious virus called the 'Panic'—which reduces its victims to a state of chronic agoraphobia—has broken out. An obvious surrogate for 'contagion' in the Eurozone, fear of the Panic swiftly becomes ubiquitous in *The Last Days*, as exemplified by the leitmotif of characters gathering in front of television screens to obsess over rolling media coverage of the outbreak. Following early scenes of Marc surveying the smouldering city from within the confines of his office building, we learn through flashback sequences that the company he worked for had begun to lay off workers in a bid to streamline services and overcome accruing financial difficulties. Further flashbacks set in his opulent apartment suggest that Marc led a comfortable life, yet subsequent discussions with his partner Julia (Marta Etura) reveal underlying anxieties, with Marc fretting that the couple will struggle to meet rent payments, a not uncommon concern in a nation where property prices tripled in the decade prior to the economic crash (Knight, 'Spanish Economy: What is to Blame for its Problems?'). In a further development—which will incentivise him to survive the impending apocalypse—Marc finds out that Julia is pregnant, a fact she elected to keep from him after he questioned the logic of bringing children into such an unstable world. The film's narrative is thus lent urgency by Marc's need to navigate the Barcelona metro system and reunite with Julia, whose own function in the film is considerably more problematic as we will see in due course.

Financial Paralysis and Subnationalism

The fact that Marc cannot venture outside during his search for Julia is instructive and nods towards the crushing totality of the financial crisis in Spain. In an analysis of the impact of the crisis on Spanish cinema, Víctor Pueyo suggests that 'the problematic of confinement or the impossibility of escape from one's own home' in *The Last Days* raises the wider question of 'how do we free ourselves from a mortgage that, through the logic of absent credit, was at the same time the interior and the exterior, where the fantasy was paradoxically the only way to live outside its limits?' ('After the End of History: Horror Cinema in Neoliberal Spain' 151). Marc's place within his company is under threat from the outset, not least because Enrique, a HR troubleshooter who oversaw large-scale layoffs in his previous role, has been tasked with streamlining operations. Alternately known as 'The Butcher' and the 'Terminator', Enrique quickly warns Marc of the precarity of his situation, observing that he is behind schedule in his work before adding ominously that 'if you get fired, it's not going to be my fault.' The wider context is largely filled in by diegetic onscreen media sources. Television news reports tie the spreading of the virus to smoke clouds originating from erupting volcanoes in Iceland, a considerable source of panic in 2010 that has largely faded from popular consciousness in the chaotic interim. This reference to Iceland also serves to remind us that unlike its European neighbours within the EU, the Nordic island elected not to bail out its failing banks.[12] In keeping with the zeitgeist, a general sense of helplessness pervades the television coverage and the public's reaction to it. Above the caption 'el panico', panellists on a current affairs show survey the wreckage, while Marc's onlooking co-workers voice their dismay ('They're fucking clueless!' 'They're making it up as they go along!'). A further news report features a politician flanked by Spanish and EU flags appealing for calm: 'I assure you that the government is taking all the necessary measures. We ask the public to keep working and shopping', an appeal redolent of similar pleas made by George W. Bush and Tony Blair in the aftermath of 9/11 when, as we will see in Chap. 8, both sought to ensure that a terrorism crisis would not become an economic one. *The Last Days* riffs on the banality of this doomed attempt to foster consumer confidence by later channelling George Romero's *Dawn of the Dead* (1978), when Marc nervously makes his way through an abandoned shopping centre prominently displaying signs offering 20 per cent off (lest the subtext escape us, he later illuminates an abandoned church by setting fire to a €50 note). As the virus spreads, he and Enrique overcome their initial antagonism and elect to stick together, sharing a GPS system that somewhat implausibly still receives a signal in the underground metro tunnels. In this subterranean environment, they encounter violence, death, and perilous refugee camps as the extent of the unfolding catastrophe grows clearer.

Before reading *The Last Days* as a straightforward critique of the collapse of the Spanish and European economies, however, we would do well to consider the film's specific relevance to economic and social concerns in Catalonia. The Pastor brothers are Catalan after all, and the film's setting in Barcelona is hardly incidental. In a persuasive reading, Pere Gallardo Torrano allows for the socio-political universality of *The Last Day*'s post-apocalyptic narrative but also asserts that the film is equally concerned with 'the uncertain future of Catalonia as a political and cultural reality potentially severed from Spain' ('Political Wishful Thinking' 5). Any such severance would have to be economic as well as political in nature, and as the financial crisis worsened, these two concerns became inseparable in much public discourse. The drive towards Catalan independence became increasingly pronounced in 2010, when the Spanish Constitutional Court rewrote 14 sections of the Statute of Autonomy of Catalonia, a reform bill providing for increased Catalan self-governance voted into being by the citizens of Catalonia in 2006.[13] Crucially, the court decreed that usage of the word 'nation' in a Catalan context had no legal basis, a rejection that compounded perceived economic biases against the region and one that would later feature centrally in the contested 2017 Catalan vote for independence. Against this backdrop, Torrano notes that 'for the first time ever since joining the European Union in 1986, in 2014 Spain contributed to the EU economy more than it received' a situation that exacerbated anxieties in Catalonia to the point that 'the idea spread among many Catalans that the Spanish government was not being fair with the economic situation of a community which contributes almost 20% of the Spanish GDP' ('Wishful Thinking' 11). Torrano therefore links Enrique's cost-cutting measures to the Madrid-based government's imposition of austerity in Catalonia, identifying the former as a 'Spanish neocapitalist technocrat bent on controlling the poor panic-stricken Catalan employee who simply tries to survive' ('Wishful Thinking' 11), a reading lent credence by Enrique's reliance upon Marc to translate the film's few dialogues in Catalan, one of which features a dying Catalan worker whom Enrique had earlier fired. Torrano allows that any such sub-nationalist reading of *The Last Days* is partial, yet if we wished to parse the film for a tacit endorsement of the economic tenability of an independent Catalonia, we might note that when Marc and Enrique eventually re-emerge from the subway, they do so in a building that stands directly opposite the Barcelona headquarters of the Catalan Banco Sabadell, one of the few banks in Europe to emerge stronger from the economic crisis.[14] Catalonia's economic recovery in general has set the region apart, for although it retracted at an alarming rate during 2008 and 2009, its GDP growth since 2012 has exceeded that of any other Spanish region to the point where it currently boasts an economy roughly commensurate in size with that of EU member states such as Finland and Portugal (Romei, 'Catalonia's Economic Strength Fuels Independence Push'). On an institutional level moreover, the film was certainly embraced as Catalan, being nominated in 11 categories at the 2014 Gaudí Awards—a Catalan-specific awards ceremony that has existed since 2009—and winning seven awards including 'Best film not in the Catalan language' (it was also nominated for two awards at the Spanish film industry's annual los Premios Goya ceremony). Of course, *The Last Days* can be at once Catalan, Spanish, and European; as we have seen, the funding models imposed by Eurimages actively encourage such pluralist thinking, yet what sets the film apart from many others examined in this study is that it posits a potentially utopian retort to a neoliberal malady that afflicts all three entities, moving from 'a declining late capitalist model to a survivalist one', from 'a postmodern present, to a neo-agrarian future' ('Wishful Thinking' 14). Instead of the unremitting despair, or at best ambiguous bleakness that most commonly bookends contemporary sf films, *The Last Days* concludes with warm images of children roaming vine-covered Barcelona streets in the process of being reclaimed by nature. Torrano sees hope in this vision, writing that '*Los últimos días* stands out as a languid cry for change; a change not to be found in globalized urban centres of postmodern design, inhabited by aggressive CEOs, but rather in rediscovered green spaces that offer reconciliation with the essence of the human being' ('Wishful Thinking' 14). The true test of any utopian vision, however, is how it constructs and treats its others, in other words how utopian it is for *everybody* within its ambit. Closer inspection of *The Last Days*' concluding scenes instead suggests that for approximately half of the population, the future may be far from bright.

Male Futures

While surface readings of *The Last Days* may position the Pastor brothers' film as a parable on the human cost of unregulated capitalism, its sustainability as a critique of neoliberal policies is ultimately hampered by a marked failure to see beyond an all-too-familiar spectre of male suffering and thus to fully comprehend the same policies' hostility to female empowerment, as exemplified most saliently in its systematic frustration of wage equality for women. Christina Scharff, for instance, argues that while neoliberalism has empowered women, it reinforces existing class and racial hierarchies by positioning its subjects as entrepreneurs and thus punishing those women who fail to attain success within the new world order ('Gender and Neoliberalism: Exploring the Exclusions and Contours of Neoliberal Subjectivities'). In exalting entrepreneurship and asserting that every individual has the power to transform themselves, neoliberalism precludes the possibility of systemic patriarchal imbalances that hamper female agency. Such imbalances are obvious even at the apex of capitalist accumulation: that all eight of the billionaires listed by Oxfam in 2017 as controlling more wealth than half of the world's population are men shouldn't surprise us nor should the fact that men constitute 89 per cent of the world's 1810 dollar billionaires (Kottasova, 'These 8 Men are Richer than 3.6 billion People Combined)'. More relevantly for the rest of us, Scharff notes that in championing its victors, neoliberalism apportions fault to its victims, so that 'the empowered, female neoliberal self is often constructed in opposition to allegedly powerless "other" women' ('Gender and Neoliberalism'). Despite tackling the financial crisis' impact upon Spain and Catalonia, however, *The Last Days* remains essentially blind to such considerations, leaving the men in charge and relegating its female characters to the role of bystanders and/or plot devices as we shall now see.

In 2014, the year after *The Last Days*' release, a Europe-wide report on the gender pay gap conducted by the European Commission found that women across the EU earned on average 16.4 per cent less than men ('Women Earned on Average 16% Less than Men in 2013 in the EU'). Compiling Eurostat data from 2013 meanwhile, which was contemporaneous with the film's production, the report noted that not only did the Spanish gender gap of 19.3 per cent exceed the EU average but that Spain was one of the few countries in Europe where wage inequality was actually increasing, having been at 16.1 per cent in 2008 immediately prior to the Eurozone crisis ('Women Earned').[15] Such figures seemingly confirm suspicions that the crisis exacerbated gender inequality in Spain, not that one would guess from watching *The Last Days*, which frames economic suffering as an almost exclusively male phenomenon. Privileging the travails of Marc and Enrique throughout, the film's wider contexts are introduced through a series of scenes containing abrupt male deaths. In addition to a fired office worker whose forcible removal from the building results in his death, we are presented with news footage of an agoraphobic 16-year-old Canadian boy who live-streams his own death in protest at his father's attempts to coax him outside. There are no equivalent scenes of female suffering, instead the film opens with a scene of Julia placidly making her way through a lush, sun-streaked forest, a scene that recurs throughout and that we initially take to be one of Marc's flashbacks. Through this leitmotif of a green rural utopia—a riposte to urban decay and a fragile entity visible only in snatches—*The Last Days* seemingly suggests that another world is possible, or that such a place once existed for Marc and Julia. That it may exist again is a possibility suggested by Marc's possession of a bag of seeds, assiduously collected from assorted fruit detritus by Enrique, who had hoped to give the bag to his father. Instead, Enrique ritualistically gifts the bag to Marc in a belated act of contrition, reminding him as he leaves that 'I was the bastard who was going to have you fired'. In passing on his seeds to a surrogate, Enrique provides Marc with the means to enable regrowth and thus the ability to subsume the role of Mother Nature and obviate the need for any actual mother to be involved. Through the foregrounding of pregnancy in its apocalyptic narrative, *The Last Days* echoes Alfonso Cuarón's *Children of Men* (2006), a film that I will return to in Chap. 8. Unlike *Children of Men*—where the pregnant Kee (Clare-Hope Ashitey) actively takes part in her own storyline, *The Last Days*' Julia instead is seen only through Marc's eyes, first through flashback and then in person, when after an exhaustive search through the metro tunnels, he spots her from afar through the window of an abandoned hospital. In the dramatic three-and-a-half-minute sequence that follows, a pained and bleeding Marc clutches his bag of seeds and heroically fights his agoraphobia to cross the street to a static Julia. He collapses triumphantly at journey's end and is embraced by Julia, in images reminiscent of Mary's cradling of the crucified Christ in Michelangelo's *Pietà*. The film then cuts to a partially closed door, behind which Marc helps deliver the couple's baby boy to an overjoyed Julia in a scene of nine-second duration. In its overwrought glorification of Marc's ordeal and almost comic disregard for Julia's role and suffering, *The Last Days* suggests that the gender imbalances of the present are likely to be projected in perpetuity into the future. In a concluding montage, we witness the couple's son growing into adolescence, as around him Marc's seeds bear fruit, and their apartment is transformed into an Eden-like paradise. As the sun streaks through the leaves, we see Julia smiling, and thus Marc's recurrent 'flashbacks' taking shape in the present unmasked instead as premonitions. Framed from an exclusively male viewpoint, the future has in fact unfolded exactly as Marc envisioned it. The montage ends with the teenaged boy emerging into vine-covered streets in the process of being reclaimed by nature. Impervious to the debilitations of the agoraphobia virus, he leaves his parents behind to set forth into a post-capitalist world, one nevertheless that is envisioned, fashioned, and made possible by men and where the ever-durable cockroach of patriarchy has survived an apocalypse of its own creation.

Notes

1. Speaking to *The Guardian*, Lanthimos was sceptical about the use of 'weird wave' as a descriptive aesthetic term arguing instead that the main commonality between contemporary Greek directors is a lack of funding: 'It's not quite a coincidence, but I'm afraid there is no foundation for this. There is no common philosophy, which is a good thing, I think. The common thing is we have no funds, so we have to make our own very cheap, very small films' (Rose, 'Attenberg, Dogtooth and the Weird Wave of Greek Cinema').
2. Brody writes: 'Greece and Portugal are in deep shit, but Greece is in slightly deeper shit because its leading younger filmmaker, Yorgos Lanthimos—whose film "The Lobster" is now playing here—makes movies that shed no light whatsoever on the country's troubles' ('The Petty Laments of Yorgos Lanthimos's The Lobster').
3. In an article on Bong Joon-ho's *Snowpiercer* (2013) published in *Paradoxa*, Gerry Canavan
    coined the term 'necrofuturism', a phenomenon that 'premediates the unhappy economic and ecological future that will emerge out of current trends, but not in a register that suggests or nurtures alternatives; rather, necrofuturism resigns us to a coming disaster we can anticipate but not prevent' ('If the Engine Ever Stops We'd All Die': Snowpiercer and Necrofuturism' 3). Applying Mark Fisher's theorisation of capitalist realism (the sense that there is no viable alternative to capitalism) and Subhabrata Bobby Banerjee's concept of necrocapitalism (which links capitalist expansion to death production) to bleak sf visions of the future,

Canavan persuasively argues that *Snowpiercer* embodies but ultimately rails against necrofuturist tendencies in dystopian sf.
4. The one exception is the character of Christina (Anna Kalaitzidou), who 'Father' (Christos Stergioglou) pays to sleep with his son in *Dogtooth*.
5. 'Brecht's concept of gestus refers to a physical acting style which opposes the clichéd dramatic one according to which the actor "becomes" the character he/she embodies. For Brecht, a gestic acting minimizes psychological traits and offers a simplification of character through an exposition of attitudes and postures which allow the audience to place emphasis on the social characteristics of the individual instead of the psychological ones' (Koutsourakis 86).
6. Citing fears over the political climate in Italy and Spain, Eirini Karamouzi, writing for The London School of Economics' *EUROPP: European Politics and Policy* blog, notes that 'by the mid-1970s, Western interests in the southern part of Europe appeared to be increasingly under threat. Similar to the spill-over scenarios prevalent in many assessments of the current crisis, the Greek case was never assessed on its own merits, but as part of the Southern European puzzle. Greece's entry into the EEC was therefore a solution to a genuine Cold War problem' ('Does the Greek Crisis Prove the Country's Entry into the EEC in 1981 Was a Mistake?').
7. Indeed, at the very moment it was being othered in a European context through widely voiced doubts as to its economic competency, Greece was paradoxically being enjoined to live up to its obligations as a good European nation by sealing off the Mediterranean to migrants on behalf of the EU as a whole, recalling Naomi Klein's observation that 'if a continent is serious about being a fortress, it also has to invite one or two poor countries within its walls, because somebody has to do the dirty work and heavy lifting' (*The Shock Doctrine* 23).
8. Crucially, Papandreou's mooted referendum never took place. As Ivan Krastev has observed: 'Three days after announcing it, and following a harsh reaction by Berlin and Brussels, the Greek government shelved the idea and the reforms were voted on in the Parliament instead. It was a painfully clear example of "democracy frustrated". Western European leaders were convinced that Greek citizens should not be permitted a say when the outcome of the vote would affect the fate of a currency belonging to everyone living in the Eurozone' (*After Europe* 65–66).
9. The most obvious rebuke to any such theory is that Varoufakis resigned in July 2015, some two months after *The Lobster* was released.
10. Other Spanish sf films of the period include Extraterrestrial/Extraterrestre/ (Nacho Vigalondo 2011), *Timecrimes/Los cronocrímenes* (Nacho Vigalondo 2007), and *EVA* (Kike Maíllo 2011).
11. Major studios' creation of 'speciality divisions' or oxymoronically titled independent wings began as an attempt to exploit and co-opt the success

of independent films such as *Sex, Lies and Videotape* (Steven Soderbergh 1989) and *Reservoir Dogs* (Quintin Tarantino 1991). For a practical everyday illustration of this model, one could do worse than observe how major beer companies have responded to the explosion of interest in the independent craft beer market by seeking to create 'craft' offerings of their own.

12. Although the narrative that Iceland protected its citizens and instead elected to 'burn the bondholders' is less straightforward than is often portrayed (for one thing it had the option of devaluing its own currency unlike nations tied to the Euro), the island's swift recovery is often held up as a counterpoint to arguments that austerity measures are the only way to move beyond a financial crisis. This recovery belied the severity of the nation's crisis. As Matt O'Brien recounted in *The Washington Post*, a widely repeated joke at the outset of the crisis held that the only difference between Iceland and Ireland 'was one letter and six months ('The Miraculous Story of Iceland').
13. Although voter turnout was low (49.41 per cent), 74 per cent of voters supported the implementation of the statute.
14. *The Guardian* reported that since the outset of the financial crisis, the Banco Sabadell has bucked trends across Spain, 'doubled in size and has risen to become Spain's fifth largest bank, mainly through an energetic programme of acquisitions in both Spain and abroad' (Burgen, 'TSB Takeover: the Spanish Buyer Banco Sabadell').
15. An article in *El País* in March 2018 confirms such suspicions and suggests that while matters have seemingly improved in the interim, with the deficit down to 13 per cent according to the most recent data, the truer figure actually reaches 23 per cent when annual earnings are taken into account (Gómez, 'Women in Spain Earn 13% Less than Men for Similar Work, New Study Shows').

Bibliography

Brody, Richard. 2016. The Petty Laments of Yorgos Lanthimos's The Lobster. *The New Yorker*, May 23.

Burgen, Stephen. 2015. TSB Takeover: The Spanish Buyer Banco Sabadell. *The Guardian*, March 12.

Byrne, Paul. 2015. Interview with Director Yorgos Lanthimos. *Movies.ie*, October 15. www.movies.ie/interview-with-yorgos-lanthimos-for-the-lobster/. Accessed 1 May 2018.

Canavan, Gerry. 2014. "If the Engine Ever Stops, We'd All Die": Snowpiercer and Necrofuturism. *Paradoxa* 26: 41–66.

Cooper, Sarah. 2016. Narcissus and The Lobster. *Studies in European Cinema* 13 (2): 163–176.

Co-production Funding in 2013. *Eurimages*, December 20, 2013. www.coe.int/en/web/eurimages/co-production-funding-in-2013. Accessed 1 May 2018.

Cubitt, Sean. 2017. *Finite Media: Environmental Implications of Digital Technologies*. Durham: Duke University Press.

Gómez, Manuel V. 2018. Women in Spain Earn 13% Less than Men for Similar Work, New Study Shows. *El País*, March 9.

Jenkins, David. Yorgos Lanthimos on Dogtooth. *Time Out London*. www.timeout.com/london/film/giorgos-lanthimos-on-dogtooth-1. Accessed 1 May 2018.

Karamouz, Eirini. 2014. Does the Greek Crisis Prove the Country's Entry into the EEC in 1981 Was a Mistake? *EUROPP: European Politics and Policy*. November 26. blogs.lse.ac.uk/greeceatlse/2014/11/26/does-the-greek-crisis-prove-the-countrys-entry-into-the-eec-in-1981-was-a-mistake/. Accessed 1 May 2018.

Knight, Laurence. 2012. Spanish Economy: What Is to Blame for Its Problems? *BBC*, May 18. www.bbc.co.uk/news/business-17753891. Accessed 1 May 2018.

Kottasova, Ivana. 2017. These 8 Men Are Richer than 3.6 Billion People Combined. *CNN*, January 17. money.cnn.com/2017/01/15/news/economy/oxfam-income-inequality-men/index.html.

Koutsourakis, Angelos. 2012. Cinema of the Body: The Politics of Performativity in Lars von Trier's Dogville and Yorgos Lanthimos' Dogtooth. *Cinema: Journal of the Moving Image* 3: 84–108.

———. 2017. Visualising the Anthropocene Dialectically: Jessica Woodworth and Peter Brosens' Eco-Crisis Trilogy. *Film-Philosophy* 21 (3): 299–325.

Krastev, Ivan. 2017. *After Europe*. Philadelphia: University of Pennsylvania Press.

Lowen, Mark. 2015. Greek Debt Crisis: What Was the Point of the Referendum? *BBC*, July 11. www.bbc.co.uk/news/world-europe-33492387. Accessed 1 May 2018.

O'Brien, Matt. 2015. The Miraculous Story of Iceland. *The Washington Post*, June 17.

Peuyo, Víctor. 2017. After the End of History: Horror Cinema in Neoliberal Spain. In *Tracing the Borders of Spanish Horror Cinema and Television*, ed. Jorge Marí, 141–160. Abingdon: Routledge.

Pop, Valentina. 2011. Merkel Wants "Permanent" Supervision of Greece, Warns of War. *EU Observer*, October 26. euobserver.com/economic/114075. Accessed 1 May 2018.

Richard, Maxwell, and Toby Miller. 2012. *Greening the Media*. Oxford: Oxford University Press.

Romei, Valentina. 2017. Catalonia's Economic Strength Fuels Independence Push. *Financial Times*, September 28.

Rose, Steve. 2011. Attenberg, Dogtooth and the Weird Wave of Greek Cinema. *The Guardian*, August 27.

Scharff, Christina. 2014. Gender and Neoliberalism: Exploring the Exclusions and Contours of Neoliberal Subjectivities. *Theory, Culture & Society*, April 1. www.theoryculturesociety.org/christina-scharff-on-gender-and-neoliberalism/. Accessed 1 May 2018.

Seasonally Adjusted Standardised Unemployment Rates. *Central Statistics Office*. www.cso.ie/en/statistics/labourmarket/principalstatistics/seasonallyadjustedstandardisedunemploymentratessur/. Accessed 1 May 2018.

Sharpe, Kenan Behzat. 2016. The Lobster: Debt, Referenda, and False Choices. *Blind Field*, July 1. blindfieldjournal.com/2016/07/01/the-lobster-debt-referenda-and-false-choices/. Accessed 1 May 2018.

Spain's Unemployment Total Passes Five Million. *BBC*, January 27, 2012. www.bbc.com/news/world-16754600. Accessed 1 May 2018.

Suvin, Darko. 1972. On the Poetics of the Science Fiction Genre. *College English* 34 (3): 372–382.

Torrano. 2017. Political Wishful Thinking versus the Shape of Things to Come: Manuel de Pedrolo's "Mecanoscrit" and "Los últimos días" by Àlex and David Pastor. *Alambique* 4 (2): 1–17.

V.B. 2011. Dark, Haunting and Wonderfully Weird. *The Economist*, December 6.

What a Happy Set!. *Daily Mail*, May 6, 2014.

Women Earned on Average 16% Less than Men in 2013 in the EU. *Eurostat*, March 8, 2015. ec.europa.eu/eurostat/documents/2995521/6729998/3-05032015-AP-EN.pdf/f064bb11-e239-4a8c-a40b-72cf34f1ac6f. Accessed 1 May 2018.

PART III

Shut the Gates! Scorched Earth, Fortress Continent

CHAPTER 6

Climate Change, the Anthropocene, and European SF

Travelling through the Alps from Italy last summer, I was reminded of a scene from the mid-1990s' gross-out comedy par excellence *Dumb and Dumber* (Peter and Bobby Farrelly 1994). Midway through a journey to the Rocky Mountains ski resort of Aspen, and exhausted from countless hours of driving, Harry (Jeff Daniels) makes the mistake of entrusting his gormless friend Lloyd (Jim Carrey) to take the wheel, before falling into a deep slumber. Unbeknownst to them both, Lloyd, who is marginally the stronger candidate for the role of 'dumber' advertised in the title, takes a wrong turn, avoiding Colorado altogether and ending up instead in rural Nebraska. Awakening refreshed the following morning, an initially chipper Harry is confronted by the sight of vast Nebraskan plains stretching out into the far-off horizon. Perplexed by the expanse of flat terrain before him, Harry tentatively opines that 'I thought the Rocky Mountains would be a little rockier than this…,' a sentiment Lloyd echoes absent-mindedly, before adding the glorious punchline: 'that John Denver's full of shit man'. Ahead of us on our own journey was Mont Blanc, the highest continental European mountain west of the Caucasus and thus the highest in the EU, and a rock formation that gained its name due to a peak coloured white by millennia of snowfall. Contrary to nomenclature, however, the Mont Blanc in front of us was not white, save for a barely discernible dusting of snow at its very peak. Passing onward through the border and looking back at the French side of the mountain, I was comforted by the sight

© The Author(s) 2018
A. Power, *Contemporary European Science Fiction Cinemas*,
Palgrave European Film and Media Studies,
https://doi.org/10.1007/978-3-319-89827-8_6

of a large glacier glistening in the sun, and yet, the mountain itself looked decidedly grey as I scanned its peaks for other signs of snow. Having passed this way only two years previously, I had expected the white mountain to be a little whiter than this...

Assailed for weeks by the aptly titled 'Lucifer' heatwave, which scorched its way across Southern Europe and led to record high temperatures and several deaths, the iconic mountain bore disturbing evidence of humankind's deleterious effect on the planet. Such impressions were not misguided, for elsewhere in Italy's Alpine region—eastward towards the Swiss border to be precise—reports surfaced that a ski resort on the Stelvio Pass glacier had been forced to close for the first time in 90 years due to an absence of snow. A far more macabre reminder of humankind's boundless appetite for destruction came soon after, with the news that corpses belonging to Italian and Austro-Hungarian soldiers killed during the First World War were emerging from the melting snow in nearby Trentino (Squires, 'Lucifer Heatwave Shuts Down Summer Skiing'). By September, an analysis by the World Weather Attribution concluded that the Lucifer heatwave was made at least ten times more likely by climate change, predicting ominously that 'if greenhouse gas emissions continue to increase in the atmosphere, a summer like that of 2017 will be normal in the Euro-Mediterranean region by the middle of the century' ('Euro-Mediterranean Heat—Summer 2017'). If the ghoulish spectre of dead soldiers being spat from the earth is not sufficiently apocalyptic, then the realisation that the planet itself may *already* be beyond repair is surely the most dystopian scenario of all.

A Looming Catastrophe

Reflecting on 8 November 2016—the day that Donald Trump was elected as president of the United States—Noam Chomsky opined that we had just witnessed a seismic event 'which might turn out to be one of the most important dates in human history' (*Who Rules the World?* 259). Only he wasn't referring to Trump. On 8 November, Chomsky explained, the World Meteorological Organization delivered a report at the annual United Nations Climate Change Conference, wherein it 'declared that the past five years were the hottest on record' (*Who Rules?* 258). Reporting on rising sea levels, 'soon to increase further as a result of the unexpectedly rapid melting of polar ice caps', the WMO stated that 'the area covered by Arctic sea ice over the past five years is 28 percent below the average of the previous three decades, which directly reduces the polar ice reflection of solar rays, thereby accelerating the global warming process' (*Who Rules?* 258). 'Even more alarming', Chomsky added, was 'the unexpectedly rapid destabilization of the enormous West Antarctic glaciers, which could raise sea levels by several feet, while also leading to disintegration of the ice in all of West Antarctica' (*Who Rules?* 258). The geological implications of such findings are plainly shocking; fuelled by avarice, carelessness, and abject stupidity, humans have already damaged the planet irreparably and are now on the cusp of destroying it for good. The social, economic, and political ramifications of our recklessness will be far-reaching and have relevance to many of the topics that feature in this book, none more so than migration. Temperatures across the Middle East, for example, have already hit record levels in the twenty-first century and are projected to keep rising.[1] Compounding matters further, the 'Middle East may experience the painful consequences of global warming particularly astutely because of its limited water resources', according to Jerzy Zdanowski, who notes that the 'region has the smallest water resources in the world' (*Middle Eastern Societies* 21). The knock-on effects will be profoundly felt across the region, for 'apart from Egypt, Iraq, Saudi Arabia and the Sudan, all Arab countries suffer chronic water shortages; in almost half of them, the situation is described as catastrophic' (*Middle Eastern Societies* 21). In the coming decades, as water becomes scarcer and droughts and famines increasingly common, the figure of the climate refugee is likely to dominate European discourses in ways that make current arguments on how best to respond to the Syrian refugee crisis appear quaint.[2] Complicating things further, Elizabeth Thomas Hope writes that 'the global population is estimated to rise from its total of 7.2 billion in 2015 to a projected 9.6 billion by 2050', a growth that will be 'almost entirely in the low-income countries of the Global South, with 49 of the least developed countries projected to double in size from around 900 million people in 2013 to 1.8 billion in 2050' (*Climate Change and Food Security: Africa and the Caribbean* 1). Lest we doubt her sincerity, it should give us pause to note that within two years, it has already risen to 7.6 billion according to figures compiled from the United Nations and the World Health Organization by *worldometers*, a website that provides real-time global population data (*worldometers*). Yet, while it will predominantly be denizens of the Global South who will suffer first and most because of climate change, we should be under few illusions as to where to apportion the largest quantity of blame. Writing about the social and economic impact of climate change on the Global South, the late Australian political economist Del Weston argued that climate change cannot be divorced from historical patterns of Western imperialism:

> The significance of class to global warming is profound. The incessant drive for growth for the benefit of the ruling class-based profits and capital accumulation is directly linked to the exploitation of both labour and land. Capitalism's inherent need to grow and accumulate is directly linked to the economic impoverishment of capitalism's periphery—what are known as the Third World or peripheral countries, in order to supply the material needs of the centre. (*Political Economy of Global Warming: The Terminal Crisis* 80)

While 'traditional' modes of Western colonialism began to die out in the second half of the twentieth century, the hold that foreign banks and multinational corporations exert over former colonies remains resolute. Such a hold is maintained by slavish adherence to the tenets of free markets as we have seen in the previous section of this book, one which places a premium upon eradicating restraints on the movement of capital but forcibly regulates the movement of labour. Thus, the West voraciously exploits the native resources of the Global South, contributing deleteriously to climate change trends that disproportionately affect these same nations while insisting that their people have no place in its societies. Weston is clear on this point, noting that 'the pillage of the periphery continues, and the economies of the periphery are structured to meet the needs of the core nations, the transactions being carried out by multinationals in the framework set by the core-country arbiters' (*Political Economy* 80). Ian Angus is more explicit still, noting that 'climate change and extreme weather events are not devastating a random selection of human beings from all walks of life', but instead the vast majority of victims are poor, as '99 percent of weather disaster casualties are in developing countries, and 75 percent of them are women' (*Facing the Anthropocene: Fossil Capitalism and the Crisis of the Earth System* 243). Hope concurs, stating unequivocally that 'the greatest anthropogenic contributors to climate change are the socio-economic systems of the Global North, but the greatest effects of the change are projected to be most acutely felt in the tropics and subtropics, thus the countries of the South' (*Climate Change* 2). Historically common patterns of colonial subjugation thereby continue apace, and numerous initiatives and accords notwithstanding, we appear locked into a spiral that appears guaranteed to repeat familiar crises, only on ever larger scales. As the world's pre-eminent coloniser, and the birthplace of the Industrial Revolution, Europe has been a major contributor to both climate change and the radical inequality it accelerates, even if we should add the caveat that such is not true of all European nations.[3]

To give the EU due credit, it has been to the fore in recent efforts to combat climate change, even if historically Europe is largely culpable for the crisis. Stavros Afionis, for example, credits the EU with taking 'from the outset a leadership role in the international negotiations on climate change, pushing hard for a legally binding climate regime that would facilitate substantive cuts in greenhouse gas emissions' (*The European Union in International Climate Change Negotiations* 7). Evoking a trend that continues to this day, Afionis suggests that 'US reticence' encouraged the EU to assume a prominent role, noting that since the 1990s, 'the EU has ratified every major international environmental agreement', while the United States, by contrast, 'has refrained from entering into new international environmental regimes altogether' (*European Union* 8). Along the way, there have been noted successes, and in 2012, by way of illustration, six EU member states were ranked in the top ten most committed green countries in the world.[4] Moreover, as Richard Youngs writes in *Climate Change and European Security*, 'progress has been made on each of the EU's flagship '20/20/20' commitments: renewables, emissions and efficiency', with 'most member states on track to meet their target to have 20 per cent of their energy generated from renewables by 2020' (60). In 2000, the European Commission launched the European Climate Change Programme (ECCP) with the express intention of putting in place structural mechanisms that would best facilitate agreements reached in the 1997 Kyoto Protocol, itself an extension of the 1992 United Nations Framework Convention on Climate Change, which, according to Article 2 of the programme, was established to 'prevent dangerous anthropogenic interference with the climate system' ('United Nations Framework Convention on Climate Change'). In real terms, the ECCP set clearly definable national targets for limiting greenhouse gas emissions, even if some have been scaled back in the interim as countries struggle to meet their obligations. The urgency of the situation has been exacerbated by a global failure to meet such targets, with Chomsky noting that in its report to the 2016 UN Climate Change Conference, the WMO 'reported that temperatures are already approaching dangerously close to the maximum target levels established by the Paris agreements of COP21 just the previous year, among other dire analyses and predictions' (*Who Rules?* 258).

The Paris Agreement, which was signed in 2015, aims to 'strengthen the global response to the threat of climate change by keeping a global temperature rise this century well below 2 degrees Celsius above pre-industrial levels and to pursue efforts to limit the temperature increase even further to 1.5 degrees Celsius' ('United Nations: Climate Change'), yet even as critics contended that such measures did not go far enough, the accord was in the process of being severely weakened by Donald Trump's decision to withdraw the United States from the agreement in 2017.[5] Nevertheless, despite making progress on climate change, the EU is far from faultless and is hamstrung by an inability to forge consensus on the issue. As with the refugee crises that have assailed Europe in recent years, the EU's ability to pass through measures to counteract climate change has met with resistance amongst some of its newer member states. Poland, whose Deputy Minister of Energy Grzegorz Tobiszowski praised Trump's decision to withdraw from the Paris Agreement, announced in July 2017 that nearly 60 per cent of the country's energy in 2030 will continue to come from bituminous coal and lignite in direct contravention of the Paris Agreement (Sengupta, Eddy and Buckley, 'As Trump Exits Paris Agreement, Other Nations are Defiant'). The antipathy of Tobiszowski's Law and Justice Party towards all matters environmental was underscored by the administration's recent decision to permit logging in the primeval Białowieża Forest, the nation's sole UNESCO natural world heritage site (Davies, 'My Worst Nightmares Are Coming True'). Amidst a resurgence of nationalism and nationalist economics across Europe and the United States, the possibility exists that consensus on climate change, already so precarious, will be indelibly eroded. In such a scenario, while the Global South will undoubtedly suffer most, the EU will experience a rapid intensification of its existing economic and refugee crises, at which point consensus, let alone solutions, may be nothing more than a pipe dream.

The Anthropocene: A Science Fictional Catastrophe

The anthropogenic, as distinct from the Anthropocene which defines an epoch of human impact upon the earth's ecosystems, dates to 1923, and A.G. Tansley's *Practical Plant Ecology: A Guide for Beginners in Field Study of Plant Communities*, wherein, as Nathan F. Sayre relates, the author speaks of 'anthropogenic climaxes' introduced by a human-caused, 'more or less permanent modifying factor or set of factors' ('The Politics of the Anthropogenic' 60). By 1939, Tansley foresaw the likely result of anthropogenic climaxes shaped by human activity when writing that 'It seems likely that in less than another century none but the most inhospitable regions—some of the more extreme deserts, the high mountains and the arctic tundra—will have escaped. Even these may eventually come, partially if not completely, under the human yoke' (Sayre, 'Politics' 60). Many scholars locate the origins of the Anthropocene in the Industrial Revolution, principally because James Watt's 'dramatically improved steam engine enabled an ever-accelerating use of fossil fuels, releasing carbon that had been sequestered over hundreds of millions of years and thereby disrupting the energy balance of Earth' (Sayre, 'Politics' 58). So far, so dystopian, for in Constance Penley's words: 'The true atrophy of the utopian imagination is this: we can imagine the future but we cannot conceive the kind of collective political strategies necessary to change or ensure that future' ('Time Travel, Primal Scene' 126). While the Anthropocene's linkage of hard science and major planetary destruction naturally lends itself to sf narratives, its origins chime with those of sf too, insofar as the latter's predecessor scientific romance emerged in the aftermath of and partly due to the Industrial Revolution. Sf's simultaneous glorification and fear of large-scale industrial developments and technology owe much to the aftereffects of an era where machinery threatened to at once empower and/or replace workers and promised at the least to radically alter the conditions of humankind's existence. Introduced into the popular scientific and environmental lexicon in 2000 by the Dutch chemist Paul J. Crutzen, John Bellamy Foster traces the Anthropocene's acceleration to the early 1950s, noting that 'recent scientific evidence suggests that the period from around 1950 on exhibits a major spike, marking a Great Acceleration in human impacts on the environment, with the most dramatic stratigraphic trace of the anthropogenic rift to be found in fallout radionuclides from nuclear weapons testing' (Angus, *Facing the Anthropocene* 15). This later date also has profound relevance for sf, given that the genre's Golden Age in the 1950s was indelibly marked by the possible environmental ramifications of contemporaneous scientific developments, none more so than the atom bomb, as films such as *Rocketship X-M* (Kurt Neumann 1950), *The Day the Earth Stood Still* (Robert Wise 1951), *The Beast From 20,000 Fathoms* (Eugène Lourié 1953), and *On the Beach* (Stanley Kramer 1959) make clear.[6] While human environmental impact can be traced back thousands of years, a great acceleration can be observed from the 1950s on and, as Sayre synopsises: 'can be seen in population, urbanization, dams, transportation, greenhouse gas emissions, surface temperatures, deforestation, fisheries exploitation, nitrogen deposition, and extinctions' (Sayre, 'Politics' 62). Citing the material causes of the great acceleration, Simon Lewis and Mark Andrew Maslin note the impact of 'a major development of novel materials from minerals to plastics to persistent organic pollutants and inorganic compounds' while also tracing the close links between the Anthropocene and European colonial expansion ('Defining the Anthropocene' 176). Without colonialism, they argue, the industrial revolution would have not have been possible on the same scale, for 'the agricultural commodities from the vast new lands of the Americas allowed Europe to transcend its ecological limits and sustain economic growth' ('Defining the Anthropocene' 177). This in turn freed labour sufficiently to pave the way for European industrialisation that would see European nations surge ahead of the rest of the world. Crucially, this '"Great Divergence" of Europe from the rest of the world required access to and exploitation of new lands plus a rich source of easily exploitable energy: coal', meaning that in Lewis and Maslin's own estimation, 'dating the Anthropocene to start about 150 years before the beginning of the Industrial Revolution is consistent with a contemporary understanding of the likely material causes of the Industrial Revolution' ('Defining the Anthropocene' 177).

By any discernible measure, the Anthropocene is a science fictional topic, given that as part of its remit sf promulgates speculative futures, while the Anthropocene, by its very nature, delimits the scope within which such futures can be conceived. Indeed, as Brian Stableford has noted, it has loomed large over the genre to the extent that 'as the twenty-first century began the great majority of science-fiction images of the future were content to take it for granted that the ecocatastrophe was not only under way but already irreversible' ('Science Fiction and Ecology' 140). The aim of this chapter is to survey how European-based sf has engaged with the issue, beginning with two films that present systemic critiques of capitalism's role in the Anthropocene: *The Age of Stupid* (Franny Armstrong 2009), a modified sf documentary framed as a recorded futuristic time capsule, and *Metropia* (Tarik Saleh 2009), a fully animated sf that imagines a future Europe in thrall to a super-corporation and hamstrung by rapidly decreasing oil supplies. I will then move through the scorched earths of the post-apocalyptic landscapes depicted in the German/Swiss release *Hell* (Tim Fehlbaum 2011) and the low-budget British/Irish co-production *The Quiet Hour* (Stéphanie Joalland 2014), both of which relocate the sort of ecological crises familiar elsewhere in the world to continental Europe.

Systemic Failure

In a sense, this chapter builds upon the analysis of sf and the economic crisis put forward in Part Two of this book. The environmentalist George Monbiot gets to the core of the issue: namely, that in the epoch of the Anthropocene, humankind's outsized reach has immediate implications for the continued health of the planet. Monbiot writes:

> The environmental crisis is an inevitable result not just of neoliberalism – the most extreme variety of capitalism—but of capitalism itself. Even the social democratic (Keynesian) kind depends on perpetual growth on a finite planet: a formula for eventual collapse. […] The myth of the self-regulating market accelerates the destruction of the self-regulating Earth. (Monbiot, 'A Lesson from Hurricane Irma: Capitalism Can't Save the Planet–It Can Only Destroy It')

No matter that are our societies are becoming increasingly virtual, their smooth operation is totally contingent upon materiality and the extraction of limited resources from the earth. Richard Maxwell and Toby Miller, Sean Cubitt, and Angelos Koutsourakis have written in detail how cinema and media are complicit in this process,[7] given how, in the words of Koutsourakis, they too are 'part of histories of unsustainable colonial and neo-colonial economic practices that rely on the appropriation of natural wealth and the underpaid labour of indigenous populations' ('Visualising the Anthropocene Dialectically: Jessica Woodworth and Peter Brosens' Eco-Crisis Trilogy' 315). Writing in early 2018, it appears that the worst of the economic crisis in the Eurozone has subsided, for now at least. Recovery has been uneven, however, and the suspicion remains that the toll exacted by the EU's dogged implementation of neoliberal policies will have lasting repercussions for national economies. Invariably, the practice of stockpiling debt, to maintain economic survival, will lead to further problems down the road and ensure that the cycle of boom/bust will continue in perpetuity, an innate failing of capitalism that Karl Marx identified over 150 years ago.[8] Such short-termism is reflected in populist politics as evinced in the current vogue for climate change denial in the United States. We have seen in the previous section of this book how attempts to reboot the European economy after the Second World War differ in character from similar efforts made during the recent economic crisis. Much as the nature of capitalism mutated during the intervening period, so too has our understanding of its direct impact upon the environment. Yet despite knowing what we do, we carry on regardless to the detriment of entire populations as we saw in Chaps. 4 and 5 and, as I argue in this chapter, to the planet itself. The first two films looked at here interpret climate change as the product of systemic failure. *The Age of Stupid*, to begin with, sustains a critique of the neoliberal exploitation of the Global South that will, it makes clear, result in a dystopian post-human future. The film's archivist narrator describes the images onscreen as 'a cautionary tale, not for us, it's too late for us [but] for whoever, or whatever finds this recording'. *Metropia* instead tackles the corporate takeover of political life, imagining a future Europe that is under the sole jurisdiction of a giant multinational conglomerate. With pollution above ground ensuring that the air is no longer safe to breathe, the conglomerate maintains control of a vast interlinked subway network, a state of affairs that essentially grants it dominion over the entire continent's population. Eager for continued growth, however, the company's CEO remains unsatisfied with such a monopoly and makes plans for an even more sinister means of control.

The Age of Stupid

George Monbiot's observation that capitalism is built upon perpetual growth while the planet itself is finite has particular relevance to *The Age of Stupid*, the Franny Armstrong-directed documentary/sf hybrid, in which Monbiot himself makes a brief appearance. Monbiot has been consistent in his contention that to prevent environmental catastrophe, we must free ourselves of the shackles of neoliberalism. For obvious reasons, this is easier said than done. In a European sphere, for example, calls to dismantle, or even reform capitalism, are quickly countered by admonishments invoking the failed policies of the Soviet Union and the dreadful legacy of totalitarianism across the continent. A cursory glance at the EU's neutering of the democratically elected Syriza party in Greece starkly illustrates this trend and demonstrates just how ingrained unquestioning adherence to the principles of the free market is. In Fredric Jameson's terms, 'what is crippling is not the presence of an enemy but rather the universal belief, not only that this tendency is irreversible, but that the historic alternatives to capitalism have been proven unviable and impossible, and that no other socioeconomic system is conceivable, let alone practically available' (*Archaeologies of the Future* xii). In Monbiot's view, this ongoing vetoing of alternatives to untethered capitalism ultimately means abandoning realistic efforts to curb the effects of climate change and therefore accepting the narrative that sustained environmental enervation is all but inevitable. Such thinking backbones Armstrong's *The Age of Stupid*, her third feature-length 'documentary' after *Drowned Out* (2002) and *McLibel* (2005). The novelty of *The Age of Stupid* stems from a formal structure that merges documentary footage of real-life events within a science fictional superstructure, and as such, it is quite different from any other film examined here. The film prominently features the rueful reflections of an unnamed archivist (Pete Postlethwaite) living in the year 2055, by which time the world has been all but destroyed by the effects of climate change. Inverting our expectations of dystopian sf, *The Age of Stupid*, to use Weik von Mossner's description: 'uses contemporary documentary footage to criticize the grave stupidities of the film's "past" from the perspective of a fictional future' ('Troubling Spaces: Ecological Risk, Narrative Framing, and Emotional Engagement in Franny Armstrong's The Age of Stupid' 109). Living alone in an ark-like repository in the Arctic, some 800 km off the coast of Norway, the archivist looks back on what are to us contemporary events in weary disbelief as expressed in his opening monologue: 'We could have saved ourselves, but we didn't. Amazing: what kind of state were we in to face extinction and just shrug it off?'

On board the repository are preserved animal corpses, artworks from national galleries across the globe, and banks of servers preserving the sum totality of human knowledge: every book, film, and piece of music present at this, the last stand of humankind. The repository recalls the real-life Svalbard Global Seed Vault on the Norwegian island of Spitsbergen, which serves as a backup for the world's ever-dwindling seed stock, yet a brief glimpse of Michelangelo's statue of David reminds us that age-old myths concerning our potential to defeat giants, as David did Goliath, hopelessly underestimated our true capabilities as a species. The animal corpses meanwhile serve as a timely reminder that we routinely wipe out entire species and that 'the era of neoliberalism also happens to be the era of the fastest mass extinction of species in the Earth's recent history' (Harvey, *A Brief History* 173). By way of illustration, during *The Age of Stupid*'s production alone, two species—the Caribbean monk seal and the Pyrenean ibex—were declared extinct, with a third: the West African black rhinoceros following in 2011 (Gerken '11 Animals That Are Now Extinct ... And It's Our Fault'). From the vast store of knowledge at his fingertips, the archivist pinpoints instances when we wilfully ignored our capacity for destruction in favour of pursuing short-term gains. On this point *The Age of Stupid* is unequivocal, opening with the title card:

'The future climate events portrayed in this film are based on mainstream scientific projections. Everything from the present day and the past is real news and documentary footage'. We are then transported to various locations around the world as the archivist selects six vignettes from the start of the twenty-first century, in a bid to better understand our apathy. Amongst them we see a would-be airline executive in India, an oil company employee in New Orleans, a windfarm developer in England, two young Iraqi boys whose father has been killed by US forces, a young Nigerian woman selling diesel on the black market to make money for college, and an octogenarian French mountain guide who laments the ruinous damage we have inflicted upon Mont Blanc. Armstrong's activism extended beyond making *The Age of Stupid*, and the same year as the film's release, she launched the '10:10' campaign, encouraging individuals and organisations to reduce their carbon footprint by 10 per cent (von Mossner, 'Troubling Spaces' 115). Additionally, as Rachel A. Howell notes, the film 'garnered a lot of media attention ahead of its release', being 'mentioned in the UK Parliament', while Armstrong herself 'spoke at several events alongside Ed Miliband, then Secretary of State for Energy and Climate Change' ('Lights, Camera … Action? Altered Attitudes and Behaviour in Response to the Climate Change Film The Age of Stupid' 178). Fernand, the French mountaineer, sums up the film's underlying message, when speculating that future generations will blame us for our negligence and deduce that 'we knew how to profit but not to protect'. Profitability, consumption, and exploitation link all six narratives as an illustrated sequence which details Europe's and latterly America's pillaging of African and Middle Eastern resources makes clear. While much has been made of the film's use of documentary footage, ironically, what grants *The Age of Stupid* additional heft is the addition of a modestly rendered sf future. No doubt limited by a production budget of approximately £450,000, Armstrong elects to present brief, computer-rendered images of London under water, Las Vegas subsumed by desert, the Sydney Opera House aflame, and the Taj Mahal in ruins, none of which would pass muster in even a moderately rendered twenty-first-century video game. The future, it suggests, is already over; what residual vestiges of hope remain are to be found in the present where although the hour is urgent, there is still time to do something. *The Age of Stupid*'s unimpressive future visuals and its self-conscious appropriation of the Svalbard Global Seed Vault paradoxically provide more hope and thus utopian potential than its frightening real-life footage, if for no other reason than we can identify them as fake. There is, in other words, still time to avoid such calamities. For the EU, the situation has just become more urgent, with the Chinese government recently informing the World Trade Organization of its intention to ban the import of 24 categories of recyclables and solid waste by the end of 2017. As of now, a whopping 87 per cent of the EU's recycled plastic is exported to China meaning that new accommodations are going to have to be sought (Cole, 'China Bans Foreign Waste–But What Will Happen to the World's Recycling?'). Yet local solutions will not solve planetary issues as the conclusion of *The Age of Stupid* makes clear. As the camera pulls back from the ark, from the Arctic, and eventually from the earth itself, it passes through incalculable fields of abandoned satellites and concentric circles of space trash, which, when set against the pristine vista of the solar system, illustrate just how enormous the problem is and how small and insignificant we are. Failure to countenance the damage being wreaked by capitalist accumulation, Armstrong seems to suggest, is not just short-sighted, it's stupid.

Metropia

Metropia (Tarik Saleh 2009) is a Swedish/Norwegian/Danish animated dystopian sf set in a future Europe that, having near exhausted oil supplies and crashed economically, has effectively ceded political control to a giant multinational conglomerate. Though a Scandinavian production directed by a Swedish filmmaker of Egyptian descent, the film is part-funded by both Eurimages and MEDIA, shot in English, and features the voices of Vincent Gallo, Juliette Lewis, Udo Kier, and Stellan and Alexander Skarsgård. As such, it tallies with the films examined in Chap. 2 in being a European-endorsed film that projects an immensely bleak future for Europe. Saleh and art director Martin Hultman succeed in creating a unique visual style for the film, one notable for dark colours and photo montage inspired by their backgrounds as graffiti artists. Together with lead animator Isak Gjertsen, the pair utilised the advanced 'Animation Cut Out technique' available in the Adobe After Effects editing suite, to create lifelike yet cartoonish characters, built typically according to the film's press book from 'over 80 layers that can be animated and controlled' ('Metropia: Press Book'). Onscreen, the neoliberal takeover of the continent has continued apace to the point that society's main primary source of transportation—an enormous underground railway network that links most of Europe—has been privatised by Trexx, the aforementioned corporation.

When Roger (Gallo), a Stockholm native, starts to hear a stranger's voice in his head, he begins to suspect that Trexx has designs on controlling more than just the continent's rail network.

Metropia's opening scenes are instructive: a title card proclaiming bleakly that 'The end of the millennium marked the end of many things. Natural resources dried up, the global financial markets crashed and the crisis that connected the fate of all people, still left the individual isolated in his ruin'. Roger works in a large, soulless call centre where we view him briefly amongst the multitudes, before a co-worker sidles up to him conspiratorially and asks if he is really 'into biking'. The year is 2024, and when Roger ventures outside, we quickly understand his co-worker's incredulity. Stockholm has been reduced to a post-industrial ruin, with abandoned streets strewn with burnt-out cars and piled high with trash. Smog fills the dark grey skies, as Roger cycles forlornly through empty, dilapidated neighbourhoods like a human version of the eponymous robot in Pixar's *Wall: E* (Andrew Stanton 2008). Human existence has consequently become primarily a subterranean pursuit, for as a following intertitle explains: 'Saying peace and mobility would save us from this collapse, the Trexx Group connected all European subways into one giant system called The Metro'. That the task of rejuvenating a collapsed society falls to a multinational corporation and not a government is telling: by 2024 big business has taken over, and it is no longer necessary to pretend otherwise. There is no need for Trexx to fund electoral campaigns or lobby governments for influence. They *are* the government. The subterranean metro system, which has usurped the decaying cities above as the principal space for human interaction, is thus saturated with advertisements for the company and its various affiliates, much as totalitarian regimes historically plastered public spaces with propaganda. With the planned neglect of cities continuing apace (it is left unsaid, but we can presume that the same pollution was also largely accelerated by corporations), the metro system subsumes the functions of everyday life, with all manner of events held underground, as Roger's stumbling upon the staging of a reality game show makes clear. Crucially, this is facilitated by the metro system's private ownership, resulting in the eradication of public space and the near total commodification of public life. The game show in question is called 'Asylum' and provides contestants with the opportunity to compete for political asylum in Europe. With her first question, the host asks the contestants to 'explain in thirty words or less, why Europe is the place of your dreams', a formulation that seems both ludicrous, given the advanced state of atrophy on display, and terrifying, for it invites us to imagine how terrible things must have become elsewhere. The first contestant's answer that Europeans 'are kind to animals and dogs' leaves unsaid the way humans are treated by contrast.

Roger's suspicions grow with the decibel levels in his head, and soon he uncovers the truth: namely, that Trexx aims to control people's thoughts through mass production of a dandruff shampoo called 'Dangst', advertisements for which are ubiquitous throughout the rail network. With the aid of Nina (Juliette Lewis), a mysterious former spokesperson for the product, he infiltrates the company and inadvertently learns from CEO Ivan Bahn (Udo Kier) that the shampoo seeps into people's brains via their hair, which in turn is transformed into a series of covert antenna capable of intercepting radio messages from Trexx. This breakthrough, the aptly named Bahn reasons, will provide advertisers with direct access to the innermost thoughts of consumers, allowing companies to sell them products that they don't even realise they need. Stressing that his train network is used by over 400 million Europeans, Bahn describes the establishment of Trexx as 'a peace project credited with erasing the final borders between the European people', a cynical co-option of Jean Monnet's famous dictum that 'to create Europe is to create peace'. In his brief yet persuasive analysis of *Metropia*, Pietari Kääpä argues that such homogenisation is made possible by obliteration of distinction. Despite the nominal gains of interconnectedness, what remains is a Europe where 'all regions are the same, all dilapidated lands and inhospitable apartment blocks [and where] nothing distinguishes one place from the other as all forms of culture are now homogeneous corporate culture' (*Ecology and Contemporary Nordic Cinemas: From Nation-building to Ecocosmopolitanism* 144). In this vein, it is instructive that when Roger and Nina pass through a smog-choked Paris while investigating Trexx, they encounter an Eiffel Tower that is covered in advertisements and has essentially been transformed into a giant billboard for Dangst. An earlier, more innocuous episode that takes place within the metro system is equally telling: when Roger is accosted by two burly policemen, they address him as 'passenger', thus signalling the conflation of citizenry with consumerism and, with it, the convergence of rail network and state.[9]

The mass production of Dangst, moreover, is the ultimate execution of biopower: one calculated to commodify all human life. As Kääpä notes, 'the environment has been consumed, but the human body remains the final frontier for chemical exploration and energy production—it is the only resource still to be exploited' (*Ecology* 143). Such a reading has relevance for the current-day EU, and it is instructive that Saleh himself cites Franz Kafka's *The Trial* as his inspiration for *Metropia*. Comparing contemporary democracy as a system analogous to the remote, unintelligible bureaucracy encountered by Josef K, Saleh asks us to 'imagine you're getting crushed by that system, feeling vulnerable to the way it works and runs, and you have to start wondering. If you're trapped in that situation, maybe you start thinking that you are the problem, not the system' ('Metropia: Press Book'). Accordingly, Roger begins to question his sanity, before alighting on the fact that something may in fact be wrong with society. In time, he implicates himself in Nina's plot to overthrow Bahn, detonating a bomb that kills the Trexx CEO. Nevertheless, his actions have limited consequences: Nina, who we learn is Bahn's estranged daughter, has been using him as part of her attempts to stage a corporate takeover. She duly takes control of the company at the film's end, publically lamenting the loss of her father and announcing in a televised speech that at 'moments like these I rely on the guiding principles of Trexx: mobility and openness'. Despite the change of players at the top, the underlying systems will remain intact it seems, even if Nina harbours reservations about the continued use of Dangst by her company. Trexx has moved beyond governmental regulation—it *is* the government and has become the very embodiment of too big to fail.

SCORCHED EARTHS

In contrast to the systemic critiques of *The Age of Stupid* and *Metopria*, the next two films up for discussion—*The Quiet Hour* and *Hell*—plunge us headlong into the aftermath of ecological disasters. Internationally, several notable sf films have recently taken up this theme, salient amongst which are John Hillcoat's 2009 adaptation of Cormac McCarthy's novel *The Road* (2006) and George Miller's *Mad Max: Fury Road* (2015). Europe too has produced such scorched earth films in recent times as we have seen, for example, with *Time of the Wolf* in Chap. 2. Going further back, salient examples include Luc Besson's debut feature *The Last Battle/Le dernier combat* (1983), Piotr Szulkin's *O-Bi, O-Ba-The End of Civilization/O-bi, O-ba - Koniec cywilizacji* (1985), and, of course, Andrei Tarkovsky's *Stalker* (1979). As such these films require us to bear witness to the struggles endured by a handful of survivors, thus replacing the question of how do we avert climate disaster with the more prosaic one of what will it be like after the inevitable disaster occurs. Neither film analysed here dwells unduly upon the causes of their respective apocalypses: *Hell* provides a single title card explaining that rapid increases in the earth's temperatures have led to famine and the end of society as we know it, while *The Quiet Hour* instead attributes its ecological meltdown to parasitical aliens. Both instead share a preoccupation with human survival and extricate politically inflected issues such as border control and migration from the conversation. Consumed by more primordial considerations—the type routinely faced by refugees across the globe on a daily basis—Europe's few remaining people are instead forced to adapt to a world where being European does not confer advantages and where anthropocentric factors have eradicated privileges that were only ever an accident of birth to begin with.

The Quiet Hour

The Quiet Hour is the debut feature of French writer/director Stéphanie Joalland, who had previously directed several short films, including the sf production *Conflation* (2007). Based in Berlin, Joalland is a co-founder of Frenzy Films, a genre-specific production company that she established with British director/producer Sean McConville, a fellow UCLA film school graduate. Inspired by Daphne du Maurier's 1952 novelette *The Birds* (and not the 1963 Hitchcock adaptation), wherein, she noted the likelihood of bird attacks was predicated upon the rising and falling of the tide, Joalland depicts a post-apocalyptic vista where enormous spaceships hover over the earth's surface, killing any human in sight ('The Quiet Hour-Stephanie Joalland, Director & Sean McConville, Producer'). At sunrise and sunset, however, the ships—which double as harvesting machines that strip the planet of minerals—become still, and the earth's remaining humans must instead survive one another. A British/Irish co-production, *The Quiet Hour*'s premise is deceptively straightforward then: a hostile alien invasion wipes out most of the earth's inhabitants, leaving a young woman and her blind sibling to fend for themselves in a remote farmhouse in the British countryside (in reality shot in County Tipperary, Ireland). Part post-apocalyptic sf/part home invasion thriller, the plight of Sarah Connolly (Dakota Blue Richards) and her brother Tom (Jack McMullen) is thus complicated by the dual threat posed by the alien harvesting machines and a marauding gang of humans hell-bent on raiding their supplies.

In a welcome antidote to *The Last Days*, which, as we saw in the previous chapter, denudes its central female protagonist of agency, Sarah is a fierce protector of both her brother and the family home and demonstrates bravery and ingenuity throughout *The Quiet Hour*. Regrettably, such strong female characters are an exception in much European sf, a reality surely not unrelated to the dearth of female sf directors in a European sphere. This is not an insignificant problem for a genre that has long displayed problematic attitudes towards women, and while critics have been quick to praise, for example, the feminist potential of protagonists played by Scarlett Johansson in European co-productions such as *Lucy* (Luc Besson 2014) and *Under the Skin* (Jonathan Glazer 2013), both films, like the overwhelming majority of sf productions, it still seems, were directed by men. Whereas sf literature has benefited immeasurably from the work of writers such as Ursula Le Guin, Margaret Atwood, Octavia Butler, or more recently still, Nnedi Okorafor, sf cinema has proven stubbornly resistant to female directors, certain exceptions notwithstanding.[10] Along with Franny Armstrong who is more renowned as a documentarian, and Kristina Buožytė, whose film *Vanishing Waves* is analysed in Chap. 3, Joalland is one of the few women to buck the trend in contemporary European sf cinema.[11]

The Quiet Hour's engagement with ecological considerations stems from the motives of the alien invaders, who, though never actually seen, spend their days ruthlessly extracting what remains of the earth's resources. Sarah's opening words capture the aliens' remoteness: 'It's been over a year, yet we know nothing about them. Two quiet hours a day is all we have'. Amidst the prevailing scarcity, Sarah's farm is self-sustaining in a limited sense, containing food supplies, hens, and goats, as well as solar panels for both the provision of electricity and their seeming usefulness in preventing alien detection. Unsurprisingly, the house becomes a target for a group of bandits who have been tracking a supposed journalist Jude (Karl Davies) across the countryside. Jude, who gains Sarah's trust after killing one of the bandits, claims that they had earlier raided his own shelter and murdered his wife and child. Cities are now empty, he reports, the aliens having exterminated any opposition foolhardy enough to cross them. The earth's imminent destruction then is divorced from human agency, the destruction wreaked by the Anthropocene subsumed within the aliens' seismic extermination mission. Humankind is thus exculpated from its own disastrous evasion of ecological responsibility, and it is telling that just as Sarah and her brother use solar panels to shield themselves from the aliens, Jude reveals that he successfully reached the farmhouse with the aid of an asbestos-covered fire blanket. They benefit, in other words, from green energy and toxicity alike, with the aliens' struggling to identify either. Nonetheless, the avarice that fuelled centuries of mass overconsumption is present in the form of the scavenger-like gang who lurk in the nearby wilderness. With the aliens now in ultimate control, humans are free to indulge their basest instincts as Anton Bitel's review for the *BFI*'s website makes clear:

> even if it is set in a world—and more specifically in an England – subjugated by aliens bent on mining Earth's natural resources and incinerating anyone who gets in the way, the extraterrestrials themselves are never seen, leaving Joalland to focus instead on the humans below, caught in their own uncivil clash of hope and despair, enlightenment and bestiality. ('Wormholes that Turned: Sci-fi London 2015')

Sure enough, a bloodbath ensues with each of the marauders and eventually Jude himself getting killed. Succumbing to the bleakness, Sarah and Tom contemplate suicide before suddenly and inexplicably the aliens leave in a weak coda that bookends an otherwise solidly constructed narrative. 'They left the same way they came, without warning,' observes Sarah, whose conclusion that 'as we long as we have hope in our hearts, we'll survive' is difficult to square with the preceding 85 minutes. Earlier instead, Jude provides a more compelling interpretation of the alien's indifference to human life, one evidenced both by their ongoing attempts to erase it and their unwillingness to engage in dialogue of any kind. Imagining how earth must look to extraterrestrial eyes: he asks rhetorically: 'What makes us more special than ants, or field mice or dolphins?' This may be *The Quiet Hour*'s most useful contribution to the ecological questions its post-apocalyptic narrative provokes: in relegating humans to semi-nocturnal creatures stripped of all primacy over their environment, the film reminds us that despite our pretensions, we are but inhabitants of a planet that will survive us, even after we make it uninhabitable for human life. Instead of treating humans as equals, or even as sentient beings, the aliens disregard humankind altogether, much as we fail to consider the impact of our actions upon other earthbound species. In refusing to acknowledge humankind's conception of itself, therefore, the unseen aliens undermine the myths, political expediencies, and justifications that we continually put forth to excuse our species' wildly destructive actions.

Hell

Tim Fehlbaum's *Hell* (2011) imagines a 2016 version of Germany reduced to a scorched wasteland where food, water, and gas are in scarce supply. In the film's onscreen world, climate change has radically impacted mainland Europe far sooner than was thought possible, with global temperatures rising by 10° Celsius in the wake of solar flares wreaking havoc upon the Earth's atmosphere. In this nightmarish environment, sisters Marie (Hannah Herzsprung) and Leonie (Lisa Vicari), along with the former's boyfriend Phillip (Lars Eidinger), spend their time scavenging a vast, empty European wasteland for basic supplies. As in *The Quiet Hour*, the trio encounters a lone man, Tom (Stipe Erceg), whom they cannot be certain is trustworthy. As with *The Quiet Hour*, however, Tom proves himself an ally, helping defend the trio from cannibalistic marauders, who as cannibals are wont to do, are intent on imprisoning and eating them. *Hell* is one of a handful of post-apocalyptic German sf films to emerge in recent years, following in the footsteps of *The Cloud/Die Wolke* (Gregor Schnitzler 2006) and *The Coming Days/Die kommenden Tage* (Lars Kraume 2010), which deal with the fallout from a nuclear disaster and the rapid dwindling of the world's oil supplies, respectively. Swiss writer/director Fehlbaum's first and to date only feature-length film, *Hell*, is a notable departure from his previous work in the short films *For Julian/Für Julian* (2003) and *Where Is Freddy?/Wo ist Freddy* (2006), as well as the multiple-director *Not My Wedding/Nicht meine Hochzeit* (2004). Produced by Roland Emmerich, who started out making sf films in Germany in the 1980s before becoming synonymous with Hollywood sf blockbusters that have of late focused heavily upon ecological catastrophes,[12] *Hell* envisions a resource-scarce Germany where water is a rare commodity and stepping out into daylight requires the endurance of extreme heat. The film's title thus works on two levels, 'hell' meaning 'bright' in German and aptly describing in English the burnt-out, barren, and unnaturally hot landscapes of a post-apocalyptic Europe (see Fig. 6.1).

Hell begins with a close-up of an eye opening, calling into question human ontology in a manner that recalls the beginning of *Blade Runner*, a film that is otherwise far removed from *Hell*'s pared back aesthetics. Here, humans can only reflect upon the imprint they have left upon the world with disgust and disbelief. Accompanied by an exhalation of breath, the eye's opening and attendant pupil dilation immediately establishes panic and denies any opportunity for viewers to revel vicariously in the

Fig. 6.1 'Hell'

aesthetics of disaster. Instead we are catapulted straight into the action: the eye belongs to a woman who is frantically attempting to rescue her partner from a crashed car. He admonishes her to run, telling her that they have been caught in a trap, and sure enough, not long after she begins to do so, a large net descends upon her, à la Charlton Heston's George Taylor in *Planet of the Apes* (Franklin J. Schaffner 1968). This brief episode is but an illustration of the way things are now, a point underscored by Fehlbaum's cutting away to the film's title. The shock is in seeing how quickly society has collapsed—it is but 2016 after all—yet ecological catastrophe has swiftly turned mainland Europe into a primordial hunting ground. Unlike *The Quiet Hour*, however, no effort is made to shift the blame for environmental disaster onto aliens: the fault, it is clear, is all ours. Shot in Germany and Corsica, *Hell* in effect imagines a Europe beset by a return of the horrors that it once inflicted upon the rest of the world, with the land stripped bare of resources and human beings enslaved as commodities. Marie, Leonie, and Phillip's desperation sees them search toilets and heating pipes in search of water, while the importance of their car is underscored by the predatory violence that surrounds them: in such a post-apocalypse to stay still is akin to death. Tom's vocation as a mechanic makes him indispensable to the trio, even after they first encounter him attempting to rob their car, an encounter that appropriately enough takes place at an abandoned petrol station. The car's importance can be gleaned by the constant vigilance it requires, with the group highly reluctant to leave it behind for any extended period. Indeed, much of *Hell*'s initial narrative tension stems less from the fear that something may befall its human protagonists per se, as from the omnipresent anxiety that their car might be taken. Given that residing in an actual home is no longer possible, the car doubles as the only comparatively safe communal environment in the film, an occurrence that has historical implications. In *Mobilities*, his study of mass consumption and movement, the British sociologist John Urry argues that as post-war consumer society expanded rapidly during the 1950s, 'the car-driver in the west comes to dwell-*within*-the-car-rather than on the road. Those inhabiting the car can prevent most of the smells and sounds of the road from entering [therefore] the car-driver is surrounded by control systems that allow a simulation of the domestic environment, a home-from-home moving flexibly and riskily through strange and dangerous environments' (*Mobilities* 126). As such, the car is the final link to domesticity, familiarity, and home, yet its presence demands constant vigilance too, so that in Stuart C. Aitken and Christopher Lee Lukinbeal's terms, the car evokes Foucault's conception of panopticism, forcing us to 'simultaneously become jailors and prisoners within a moving panoptic cell' ('Disassociated Masculinities and Geographies of the Road' 357). Cars of course are also a cause of major pollution, and even in 2018, transport inclusive of cars, planes, trains, and shipping remains the largest source of greenhouse gas pollution in America, a trend that is only likely to continue under the current US administration (Milman, 'Vehicles are now America's biggest $CO2$ Source'). The EU instead has shown greater leadership, with individual member states taking it upon themselves to phase out the sale of diesel cars, for instance,[13] yet even so the emission scandal that has enveloped German car manufacturer Volkswagen highlights how corporate greed frequently finds a way around government regulations.[14] Despite the importance of cars in *Hell*, however, there is, in effect, no place to go. The apocalypse is everywhere and denuded of safe zones, Europe becomes less a continent, or a political entity, than an inescapable reality stretching out eternally in all directions.

Where historically Europeans ventured forth into the world and created satellites of Europe from which they could retreat at will—unlike the people they had colonised—here the ecological apocalypse has erased all geographic distinction and denuded Europe of its historically acquired advantages, flattening the inequalities perpetuated by globalisation, which, as Zygmunt Bauman has argued, can largely be distilled to the freedom to move across the planet:

What appears as globalization for some means localization for others; signalling a new freedom for some, upon many others it descends as an uninvited and cruel fate. Mobility climbs to the rank of the uppermost among the coveted values – and the freedom to move, perpetually a scarce and unequally distributed commodity, fast becomes the main stratifying factor of our late-modern or postmodern times. (*Globalization: The Human Consequences* 2)

In *Hell*, everyone is watching for cars, while the quiet stillness of the empty landscape amplifies the rumble of their engines. Before long the group are set upon by car-jackers, who, though unsuccessful in their efforts to steal the car, manage to take Leonie prisoner. After a rescue attempt is unsuccessful, Marie, Phillip, and Tom are captured by a family of farmers who, bereft of animal livestock, have taken to farming and eating humans, who no more than cars have become commodities to exploit. Imprisoned within a barn, Phillip is killed, while Leonie and Marie are told they will become the sexual property of the farmer's sons. The brutal depictions of human bondage that follow are disturbing, yet the only novelty from a historical perspective is that the events occur *within* Europe and not in the colonies it for centuries sought to 'civilise'. *Hell* thus presents a return of history to Europe, a history from which there is no escape. Although the sisters eventually flee with Tom to the presumed sanctuary of the mountains, their joy at procuring fresh water is short-lived: unlike *The Quiet Hour*, there will be no last-minute reprieve. Instead, before them stretches an endless, barren wasteland, and the film concludes with close-ups of the trio's demoralised faces as the realisation dawns that theirs' is a dystopia from which there is no escape.

Notes

1. In his monograph, *Middle Eastern Societies in the 20th Century*, Jerzy Zdanowski reports that 2010 was the hottest year in the region since monitoring began in 1800. Furthermore, in 2011, a record temperature of 53.5 degrees Celsius was recorded in Kuwait (21).
2. In a book chapter entitled 'Putting a Human face on Climate Change', Ashley Dawson draws upon reports from the Intergovernmental Panel on Climate Change and the relief organisation Oxfam to report that there currently exists an estimated 26 million climate refugees, a number that is predicted to rise exponentially, with Dawson writing that by 2050, a whopping '200 million a year will be on the move due to hunger, environmental degradation and loss of land due to climate change' (207–208).

3. Not all European countries were colonial nations of course. Cyprus, Ireland, and Malta, for example, were all colonised by Britain, while numerous Eastern bloc nations, as we have seen, were in turn colonised by the Soviets amongst others.
4. As Richard Youngs notes, the prominent non-profit organisation Germanwatch included Belgium, Denmark, France, Germany, Sweden, and the UK in their list of the top ten most environmentally committed countries (*Climate Change and European Security* 60).
5. Naomi Klein cuts to the heart of such disillusionment in her latest book, *No Is Not Enough: Resisting Trump's Shock Politics and Winning the World We Need*. She writes: 'the most powerful man in the world is a person who says global warming is a hoax invented by the Chinese, and who is feverishly trashing the (already inadequate) restraints on fossil fuels that his country had put in place, encouraging other governments to do the same. And it's all happening at the worst possible time in human history' (113).
6. For a detailed outline of the intersections between 1950s Hollywood sf and ecological concerns, see Chap. 4 ('Conspiracy Thrillers and Science Fiction: 1950s to 1990s') of Pat Brereton's *Hollywood Utopia: Ecology in Contemporary American Cinema*.
7. See Maxwell and Miller's *Greening the Media* (2012), Cubitt's *Finite Media: Environmental Implications of Digital Technologies* (2017), and Koutsourakis' 2017 article 'Visualising the Anthropocene Dialectically: Jessica Woodworth and Peter Brosens' Eco-Crisis Trilogy'.
8. In *Capital, Volume 1*, Marx observes that 'The enormous power, inherent in the factory system, of expanding by jumps, and the dependence of that system on the markets of the world, necessarily beget feverish production, followed by over-filling of the markets, whereupon contraction of the markets brings on crippling of production. The life of modern industry becomes a series of periods of moderate activity, prosperity, over-production, crisis and stagnation. The uncertainty and instability to which machinery subjects the employment, and consequently the conditions of existence, of the operatives become normal, owing to these periodic changes of the industrial cycle' (344–345).
9. Perhaps not coincidentally, Saleh's homeland of Sweden became in 1988 'the first country in the world to vertically separate its railway sector', a practice that sought to stimulate competition and reduce passenger costs, even if in real terms the results have been decidedly mixed (Nilsson 231). For a detailed overview of Sweden's railway policies, see Jan-Eric Nilsson's article: 'Restructuring Sweden's Railways: The Unintentional Deregulation'.
10. Kathryn Bigelow's *Strange Days* (1995) and Mimi Leder's *Deep Impact* (1998) most immediately come to mind in a commercial sense, while

Lizzie Borden's *Born in Flames* (1983), though hardly commercial, has been highly influential in arthouse circles. More recently, and away from Hollywood, Wanuri Kahiu's futuristic Kenyan/South African short film *Pumzi* (2009) has received critical acclaim.
11. We could point to Lucile Hadžihalilović's *Evolution* (2015) as a further example of European sf, even if the film was marketed and conceived of largely as horror. Claire Denis' much-anticipated sf *High Life*, meanwhile, is scheduled to be released in 2018.
12. After directing the West German sf *The Noah's Ark Principle/Das Arche Noah Prinzip* (1984) and co-productions such as *Moon 44* (1990), Emmerich's Hollywood career encompasses the likes of *Universal Soldier* (1992), *Stargate* (1994), *Independence Day* (1996), and *Godzilla* (1998) and more recently the ecological dystopias *The Day After Tomorrow* (2004) and *2012* (2009).
13. In 2017, France and Britain both announced bans on the future manufacture of new diesel and petrol cars and vans which will come into place by 2040, while in early 2018 Ireland announced measures to do likewise but from 2030 onward ('You Won't Be Able to Buy a Petrol or Diesel Car in Ireland After 2030').
14. By early 2018, Volkswagen was facing litigation from up to 60,000 people following findings that its diesel cars did not comply with EU emission legislation. In a scandal that ironically was uncovered in the United States, the *Financial Times* reported that 'the carmaker installed software that artificially lowered nitrogen oxides (NOx) during testing—in 11 m diesel cars sold between 2008 and 2015' (Croft, 'VW faces UK Group Legal Action over Emissions Scandal').

Bibliography

Afionis, Stavros. 2017. *The European Union in International Climate Change Negotiations*. Abingdon: Routledge.

Aitken, Stuart C., and Christopher Lee Lukinbeal. 1997. Disassociated Masculinities and Geographies of the Road. In *The Road Movie Book*, ed. Steven Cohan and Ina Rae Hark, 349–370. London/New York: Routledge.

Angus, Ian. 2016. *Facing the Anthropocene: Fossil Capitalism and the Crisis of the Earth System*. New York: Monthly Review Press.

Bauman, Zygmunt. 1998. *Globalization: The Human Consequences*. Cambridge: Polity.

Bitel, Anton. 2016. Wormholes that Turned: Sci-fi London 2015. *BFI*, November 30. www.bfi.org.uk/news-opinion/sight-sound-magazine/comment/festivals/wormholes-turned-sci-fi-london-2015. Accessed 1 May 2018.

Brereton, Pat. 2005. Conspiracy Thrillers and Science Fiction: 1950s to 1990s. *Hollywood Utopia: Ecology in Contemporary American Cinema*, Intellect, pp. 139–184. Bristol.
Chomsky, Noam. 2017. *Who Rules the World?* London: Penguin.
Cole, Christine. 2017. China Bans Foreign Waste–But What Will Happen to the World's Recycling? *Independent*, October 25.
Croft, Jane and Patrick McGee. 2018. VW Faces UK Group Legal Action Over Emissions Scandal. *Financial Times*, January 28.
Cubitt, Sean. 2017. *Finite Media: Environmental Implications of Digital Technologies*. Durham: Duke University Press.
Davies, Christian. 2017. My Worst Nightmares Are Coming True. *The Guardian*, May 23.
Dawson, Ashley. 2015. Putting a Human Face on Climate Change. In *Climate Change and Museum Futures*, ed. Fiona Cameron and Brett Neilson, 207–218. New York: Routledge.
Euro-Mediterranean Heat—Summer 2017. *World Weather Attribution*, September 2017. wwa.climatecentral.org. Accessed 1 May 2018.
Gerken, James. 2013. 11 Animals That Are Now Extinct … And It's Our Fault. *Huffington Post*, October 22. www.huffingtonpost.com/2013/10/22/11-extinct-animals_n_4078988.html. Accessed 1 May 2018.
Harvey, David. 2005. *A Brief History of Neoliberalism*. Oxford: Oxford University Press.
Hope, Elizabeth Thomas. 2016. *Climate Change and Food Security: Africa and the Caribbean*. New York: Routledge.
Howell, Rachel A. 2011. Lights, Camera … Action? Altered Attitudes and Behaviour in Response to the Climate Change Film The Age of Stupid. *Global Environmental Change* 21 (1): 177–187.
Jameson, Fredric. 2005. *Archaeologies of the Future: A Desire Called Utopia and Other Science Fictions*. London: Verso.
Kääpä, Pietari. 2014. *Ecology and Contemporary Nordic Cinemas: From Nation-building to Ecocosmopolitanism*. London: Bloomsbury.
Klein, Naomi. 2017. *No Is Not Enough: Resisting Trump's Shock Politics and Winning the World We Need*. Chicago: Haymarket.
Koutsourakis, Angelos. 2017. Visualising the Anthropocene Dialectically: Jessica Woodworth and Peter Brosens' Eco-Crisis Trilogy. *Film-Philosophy* 21 (3): 299–325.
Lewis, Simon, and Mark Andrew Maslin. 2015. Defining the Anthropocene. *Nature* 519: 171–180.
Marx, Karl. 1867. *Capital: A Critique of Political Economy. Volume I: The Economist*. Verlag von Otto Meisner.
McCarthy, Cormac. 2006. *The Road*. New York: Alfred A. Knopf.
Metropia: Press Book. *TrustNordisk*. files.trustnordisk.com/files/ftpfiles/movies/Z1413/public/docs/metropia_pressbook.pdf. Accessed 1 May 2018.

Milman, Oliver. 2018. Vehicles Are Now America's Biggest CO2 Source. *The Guardian*, January 1.
Monbiot, George. 2017. A Lesson from Hurricane Irma: Capitalism Can't Save the Planet–It Can Only Destroy It. *The Guardian*, September 13.
Nilsson, Jan-Eric. 2002. Restructuring Sweden's Railways: The Unintentional Deregulation. *Swedish Economic Policy Review* 9: 229–254.
Penley, Constance. 1986. Time Travel, Primal Scene, and the Critical Dystopia. *Camera Obscura* 5 (3): 66–85.
Richard, Maxwell, and Toby Miller. 2012. *Greening the Media*. New York: Oxford University Press.
Sayre, Nathan F. 2012. The Politics of the Anthropogenic. *Annual Review of Anthropology* 41: 57–70.
Sengupta, Somini, Melissa Eddy and Chris Buckley. 2017. As Trump Exits Paris Agreement, Other Nations are Defiant. *New York Times*, June 2.
Squires, Nick. 2017. Lucifer Heatwave Shuts Down Summer Skiing. *The Telegraph*, August 10.
Stableford, Brian. 2005. Science Fiction and Ecology. In *A Companion to Science Fiction*, ed. David Seed, 127–141. Malden: Blackwell.
Tansley, A.G. 1923. *Practical Plant Ecology: A Guide for Beginners in Field Study of Plant Communities*. London: Allen and Unwin.
The Quiet Hour-Stephanie Joalland, Director & Sean McConville, Producer. *TwinCitiesFilmFest*, January 6, 2016. www.youtube.com/watch?v=VJxagZYCPHI. Accessed 1 May 2018.
United Nations Framework Convention on Climate Change. Article 2, 1992. unfccc.int/resource/docs/convkp/conveng.pdf. Accessed 1 May 2018.
Urry, John. 2007. *Mobilities*. Oxford: Polity.
von Mossner, A. Weik. 2013. Ecological Risk, Narrative Framing, and Emotional Engagement in Franny Armstrong's The Age of Stupid. *Emotion, Space and Society* 6: 108–116.
Weston, Del. 2013. *Political Economy of Global Warming: The Terminal Crisis*. New York: Routledge.
Worldometers. www.worldometers.info/world-population/. Accessed 1 May 2018.
You Won't Be Able to Buy a Petrol or Diesel Car in Ireland After 2030. *TheJournal.ie*, February 16, 2018. www.thejournal.ie/electric-cars-ireland-2045-3856261-Feb2018/. Accessed 1 May 2018.
Youngs, Richard. 2014. *Climate Change and European Security*. Abingdon: Routledge.
Zdanowski, Jerzy. 2014. *Middle Eastern Societies in the 20th Century*. Newcastle upon Tyne: Cambridge Scholars.

CHAPTER 7

Multiculturalism and the Changing Face of Europe

> *Under the doctrine of state multiculturalism, we have encouraged different cultures to live separate lives, apart from each other and apart from the mainstream. We've failed to provide a vision of society to which they feel they want to belong.*
> *(David Cameron)*
> *We have been too concerned about the identity of the person who was arriving and not enough about the identity of the country that was receiving him.*
> *(Nicolas Sarkozy)*
> *This [multicultural] approach has failed, utterly failed.*
> *(Angela Merkel)*

Within a period of four months during late 2010/early 2011, the leaders of the EU's three most powerful member states announced the death of multiculturalism in Europe. A project that has its roots in post-1960s' population shifts and social movements as well as early 1970s' responses to the increased diversity of societies concurrent with the spread of globalisation, multiculturalism is an oft-touted and much maligned concept even though its parameters are constantly in flux.[1] Nominally a means of safeguarding the rights of minorities via promotion of tolerance and acceptance of cultural difference, the multicultural project, as distinct from the 'multicultural fact'—described by Ella Shohat and Robert Stam as 'the obvious cultural heterogeneity of most of the world' (*Multiculturalism, Postcoloniality, and Transnational Media* 7)—has met with increasingly stern resistance across the EU in recent times. As commentators were swift to point out,[2] the close timing of David Cameron, Nicolas Sarkozy, and Angela Merkel's pronouncements was hardly coincidental and taken together could be read as an attempt to manufacture and reinforce a nominal Europe-wide consensus on the issue. After all, the three leaders shared largely similar neoliberal economic policies, even if Britain's idiosyncratic relationship with the EU meant that Cameron's impact as a policy shaper in a European context was less pronounced than his French and German counterparts. More plausible, of course, is that like most matters European, the context for their respective remarks was decidedly local. With the fallout from the economic crisis showing little sign of abating, all three leaders found themselves under pressure domestically both from outside their own parties and within. Moreover, as the backlash against austerity measures intensified, the far-right continued to gather momentum meaning that Cameron's Conservative Party, Sarkozy's Union pour un Mouvement Populaire, and Merkel's Christlich Demokratische Union Deutschlands ran the risk of being outflanked by assorted populists and extremists on a myriad of social and domestic issues. The rise of UKIP in Britain, Alternative für Deutschland and PEGIDA in Germany, and Marine Le Pen's reinvigoration of the Front National in France already threatened establishment parties on local and regional levels and now stood to gain further ground nationally.[3] Decrying the tenets of multiculturalism offered a straightforward means of fighting back for the beleaguered leaders and, perhaps just as opportunely, a soft, amorphous target at which to take aim. Yet if their intentions were plain enough to anyone paying even cursory attention to national opinion polls, the issue they sought to address was wilfully unclear, prompting Carlos Alberto Torres to ask in a column for *The Huffington Post*: 'what kind of multiculturalism is dead' ('Is Multiculturalism Dead?'). Noting that 'the discourse about multiculturalism cannot be characterized as homogeneous and coherent', Torres wrote that 'on the contrary, ideas, policies, and practices implemented under the umbrella of multiculturalism are too heterogeneous and diverse to be considered a monolithic model' ('Is Multiculturalism Dead?'). In other words, the three leaders, whom, for shorthand, I will from here on refer to by the neologism 'Mercamsky', were attacking not so much a concrete entity as a multivalent accretion of competing and often contradictory notions, assumptions, and ideals.

The fanfare that accompanied such denouncements at both party level and in right-wing media outlets owed much to an anxiety in such circles and indeed elsewhere that 'something' should be done to fight back against large-scale migration and the threat of Islamic fundamentalism, two largely separate concerns[4] that have nonetheless become increasingly imbricated in popular discourses. Politically motivated disenchantment with multiculturalism is not a new phenomenon,[5] and while the role it plays in diluting the impact of dedicated movements—postcolonial and feminist amongst them—has been noted elsewhere and has perhaps been overstated,[6] multiculturalism's perpetual linkage with an aggregation of multifarious concerns leaves it open to popular disdain. Yet in declaring its failure, Mercamsky were surely duty-bound to suggest an alternative, one that could attend to their constituents' concerns about the effects of large-scale migration upon domestic job markets, as well as the more abstract yet no less troubling balancing act between bolstering national security and safeguarding individual rights. Moreover, it remained unclear what solutions they would offer to tackle pre-existing segregation and imbalances within their respective societies beyond calling for a reinforcement of oblique national values. In the case of France, for example, the issue of how to tackle societal alienation amongst thousands of French citizens—both Muslim and otherwise—left largely to their own devices in sprawling banlieues remains an open question. Sarkozy's contention that France was neglecting its identity by concerning itself overtly with those arriving on its shores is particularly telling, for it gestures toward, but leaves unsaid, the Front National's equation of multiculturalism with the erosion of national identity: an entity that in its most narrow and rigid conceptualisations resists the plurality that multiculturalism implies. Such thinking assumes an inherent fixity of identity that appears especially ill-suited to the realities of a globalised, postcolonial Europe, all the more so when one considers the central role that France plays in the EU, itself an ipso facto multicultural constellation. Besides, the decidedly global ambit of contemporary commerce, one that for better or worse Europe has actively bought into and upon which its native economies are reliant, is itself predicated upon the easing of restrictions related to solely domestic considerations. For Eurosceptics, like Le Pen, such an argument is plainly redundant, yet the reduction of state powers implicit in the signing of the Maastricht Treaty gestures towards a central issue at the heart of multiculturalism itself, namely, the dismantling of European exceptionalism, albeit up to a point.

A Qualified Inclusiveness

Itself a de facto multicultural project, European integration at once enervated the sovereignty of the nation state while simultaneously enforcing the primacy of the EU as a whole, by proxy creating what Naomi Klein has termed a 'fortress continent', that is, 'a bloc of nations that joins forces to extract favourable trade terms from other countries, while patrolling their shared external borders to keep people from those countries out' ('Fortress Continents'). Therefore, while citizens of nations that are signatories to the Schengen Agreement can travel effortlessly throughout the EU, their freedom of movement is counterbalanced by a doubling down on the otherness of those from outside this collective. In other words, the EU embraces a European multiculturalism while buttressing the outer edges of its ever-expanding sphere of influence. Perceived shifts in the collective frequently spike nationalist fervour, a truism that both Brexit and reactions to Merkel's defiant, wholly unexpected, and partially pragmatic[7] response to the Syrian refugee crisis demonstrate, albeit for different reasons. Elsewhere in Europe, refusals on the part of the governing Polish Law and Justice Party to take in refugees on the basis that such people were incompatible with Polish values coincided with the same government calling upon Britain to ensure that its large Polish community would not be effected by Brexit. Such flagrant hypocrisy is by no means exclusive to Poland.[8] The paradoxical nature of such interpretations of European inclusion was addressed by Zygmunt Bauman in *Europe: An Unfinished Adventure* when he observed that, 'inside fortress continents, "a new social hierarchy" has been put in place in an attempt to strike a balance of sorts between blatantly contradictory, yet equally vital postulates [...] of free trade and of the need to pander to popular anti-immigrant sentiments' (21). In such instances the spectre of migration presents both a threat and an opportunity, becoming in many case the *raison d'être* for entire political movements. 'The stranger', Bauman writes in *The Individualized Society*, is 'constantly ante portas—or at the gate; but it is the presumed ill-will of the stranger, of a stranger conspiring to trespass, to break in and invade, that makes the gate tangible' (92). Such anxieties run deep in a continent historically accustomed to dictating terms to the rest of the planet; ergo the decline of European exceptionalism has a role in shaping attitudes to multiculturalism or, as Shohat and Stam would have it, in ensuring that 'contemporary quarrels are but the surface manifestations of a deeper seismological shift: the decolonization of Eurocentric power structures and epistemologies' (*Multiculturalism* 9).

In precarious economic circumstances, the appeal of invoking perceived past glories—nowhere more forcefully or vaguely articulated than in Donald Trump's 2016 electoral slogan: 'Make America Great Again'—[9]is obvious, yet such sentiment all too frequently fails to account for the socio-economic imbalances that have propped up European hegemony for generations. During a speech in Warsaw on his second state visit to Europe in July 2017, Trump gestured towards nationalist subtexts in both Poland and the United States, by speaking obliquely about 'the West' and its values, arguing that 'the fundamental question of our time is whether the west has the will to survive' (Shapiro, 'Donald Trump's Warning About "Western Civilisation" Evokes Holy War'). Whilst the geographical specificity of *what* constitutes the west may be vague, the subtext of *who* counts as 'Western' was far clearer, as embodied by Trump's claim that 'Americans, Poles, and the nations of Europe [...] must work together to counter forces, whether they come from inside or out, from the south or the east, that threaten over time to undermine these values and to erase the bonds of culture, faith and tradition that make us who we are' (Davies, 'Trump Says West is at Risk During Nationalistic Speech in Poland'). A glitch in Eurocentric thinking, as identified by Shohat and Stam, is that it 'bifurcates the world into the "West and the Rest" and organizes everyday language into binaristic hierarchies implicitly flattering to Europe: *our* nations, *their* tribes, *our* religions, *their* superstitions, *our* culture, *their* folklore, *our* defense, *their* terrorism' (*Multiculturalism* 7–8). Trump's appeal to a common culture, faith, and tradition therefore implicitly excludes citizens who, for whatever reason, fail to meet such nebulous criteria and, in the process, intentionally delegitimises much of his own electorate. Yet the idea that building higher walls will somehow keep the enemy out (à la Trump's strategy for the Mexican/US border) is plainly an ill-conceived one. The 2015/2016 terrorist attacks in Paris and Brussels brought perennial questions pertaining to identity into even sharper relief in a European sphere, all the more so because the perpetrators hailed from *within* France and neighbouring Belgium. The far more realistic challenge for Europe, it would seem, is not how to revive the past but rather how best to manage the realities of a postcolonial present.

The films that I will focus on in this chapter explicitly undermine such Eurocentric thinking and foreground instead the spectre of the neglected city space. In the first three films (Luc Besson's *Banlieue 13* 'trilogy'), physical city borders are erected to separate the 'West from the Rest', suggesting in the process bipolar conceptualisations of national consciousness that are frequently in conflict with themselves. In the latter two London-based films instead (*Shank* and *Attack the Block*), the legacy of six decades of real-life divisions is summoned, divisions that indict a multitude of government administrations and call to question the hidden histories that official Britain has frequently sought to bury.[10] The spectre of borders, be they real or socio-economic, is instructive, for as Homi K. Bhabha has argued, the border in and of itself cannot contain one official history, but instead it is only by 'reading between these borderlines of the nation-space that we can see how the concept of the "people" emerges within a range of discourses' (*Location of Culture* 208).[11] Across Europe the ghettoisation of city districts such as Clichy-sous-Bois, where the 2005 Paris riots were most intensely felt, or Molenbeek, a Brussels district that has become a veritable media byword for Islamist radicalisation, has exacerbated a pervasive sense of disconnect and further severed ties between communities and the nation states in which they reside. In real terms this often results in a doubling down on marginalisation for locals in such communities which, like Molenbeek, already struggle with the stigmas attached to social, political, and economic stagnation. Accordingly, as nationalist politicians across Europe strive to fortify borders to keep migrants out, internal divisions are in danger of becoming ever more pronounced. Mercamsky's calculated turn to the right would in turn be repeated by mainstream parties across the EU in subsequent years; witness, for example, Prime Minister Mark Rutte's ramping up of populist rhetoric prior to the 2017 General Election in the historically liberal Netherlands. Merkel's unprecedented welcoming of Syrian refugees showcased a heretofore concealed penchant for the unexpected, however, and, ultimately, she has proved to be an infinitely more durable and skilled politician than her then British and French counterparts, both of whom bowed out amidst turmoil largely of their own making. Yet the anxieties that led to the trio's respective denunciations of multiculturalism remain and have in fact been amplified considerably across Europe in the interim. Based on this premise, when looking at European sf films from the time, we should not be surprised that the spectre of the ghetto, or divided cityscape, has become something of a recurring theme. As I write more about Merkel in my analysis of *The Lobster* in Chap. 5, and German sf in general in Chap. 6, my focus here will be upon France and the UK and in particular Paris and London, two cities that far from being mere national capitals have long been global in reach and thus feature the sort of historic integration issues and socio-economic disparities that characterise an ever-increasing number of cities around the globe.[12] All five films analysed are set in the very near future (which is already our past), thus adding to the immediacy of their visions. Beginning with a brief analysis of *Banlieue 13*—the precursor for *Banlieue 13: Ultimatum*—and a film that establishes the endemic divisions of modern European conurbations in its opening shot, this chapter will set out to interrogate the harsh realities and failed multicultural promises of the European project as experienced by citizens of its two most prominent cities.

PARIS

Films: Banlieue 13 (Pierre Morel 2004) and *Banlieue 13 Ultimatum* (Patrick Alessandrin 2009)

The opening scene of *Banlieue 13*, the Pierre Morel-directed and Luc Besson-produced parkour/dystopian mashup, is in many ways exemplary of sf cinema's ability to crystallise complex contemporary social issues into a neatly packaged snapshot of the future. In an extended 'long-take',[13] the scene presents a searing if none-too-subtle compendium of France's social problems via an omniscient camera moving freely through a near-future banlieue in the outskirts of Paris. Heightening the sense of urgency, the future presented is very near indeed—2013 to be exact—or nine years after the film's release date. In this alternate future, which owes much to simmering racial and economic tensions contemporary to the film's production (tensions that would explode during the 2005 Paris riots), the French authorities seek to resolve social problems in the Parisian banlieues by walling them off, effectively leaving their inhabitants to fend for themselves. When a local gang steal a nuclear-enabled missile, the government spot an opportunity to rid themselves of their obligations once and for all by detonating it within Banlieue 13—the most troublesome ghetto in Paris, leaving two outsiders in a race against time to save the day. Beginning with a close-up of a rat emerging through a crack in a wall that bears the legend—'Date de Securisation: Oct 20 2010'—cinematographer Manuel Teran's camera tilts gradually upward revealing both the forbidding height of the wall and the barbed wire that tops it. Once above the wall, the camera moves swiftly downward and inward towards the banlieue, passing through a burned-out car and settling momentarily on a drug dealer conducting business, before moving restlessly onward past baseball bat-wielding youths, a homeless man, and a junkie in the process of shooting up. Recalling both *The Matrix* (Lana and Lily Wachowski 1999) and the title sequence of David Fincher's *Seven* (1995)—two films that share with *Banlieue 13* a preoccupation with urban dystopia—the viewer is then transported through an intercom system into a flat, where men and women smoke weed, and out again as we follow a joint flicked through a waste disposal chute into a corridor strewn with heroin addicts in various states of consciousness. Out we move to street level again where an elderly woman pushes a shopping trolley out of a graffiti-strewn supermarket, above which—and alongside shotgun-toting neighbours—resides Leïto (David Belle): the embattled protagonist and moral centre of the film. In portraying the banlieue in such a fashion, Morel walks a tightrope between indicting French authorities for decades of neglect towards the peripheries of their major cities and tacitly suggesting that inhabitants of such areas are responsible for their own downfall. For Lisa Purse, who has written on *Banlieue 13* in her monograph *Contemporary Action Cinema*, the scene is indicative of the film's wider representational issues and philosophically of a piece with some of Hollywood's less challenging fare:

> the overt stylisation of the opening, which privileges an idealised flight through the environment over a pedestrian, restricted existence within it, and which elides over more banal realities of the banlieue in order to characterise it as a place where criminality and weapons are ever-present, suggests that the film is less interested in bringing to attention the socio-economic disenfranchisement experienced in the real banlieues [...] In fact, like many US films set in environments that are the site of real social or economic disenfranchisement or political tensions (such as the urban 'ghetto', or the Middle East), here the location is emptied of its controversial real-world socio-political resonances, so that the banlieue we are offered becomes a fictional, exoticised space, a depoliticised pretext for its violent narrative. (179)

The free-floating camera offers viewers omnipotence over the marginalised space, allowing for a vicarious yet safely removed experience of the banlieue, especially as the camera in this sequence is not aligned with any inhabitant's point of view. It does not pause until it rests upon the figure of Leïto staring into a split mirror that offers two angles of his face and, with it, two approaches he can take: passivity or action. Like Purse, Isabelle Vanderschelden emphasises the depoliticised space of the banlieue arguing that *Banlieue 13* blends 'together different nationalities and genre conventions to the extent that national characteristics become virtually imperceptible' ('Strategies for a Transnational/French Popular Cinema' 47). While I agree for the most part with both analyses, it is noteworthy that in such a heavily 'exoticised' space, our principle guide and onscreen surrogate happens to be white, an initially innocuous detail perhaps, but one that nevertheless becomes somewhat jarring when we consider the franchise in its totality and take into account its unofficial third film, *Brick Mansions* (Camille Delamarre 2014), a US-Canadian remake of *Banlieue 13*, the screenplay for which was written by Luc Besson and co-produced by his EuropaCorp production company.

From Paris to Detroit and Back Again

It should be stressed from the outset that Besson's devotion to the Parisian peripheries appears genuine and is exemplified in production terms by EuropaCorp, a production company he founded and that is based in the custom-built 'Cité du Cinéma' campus in the suburb of Seine-Saint-Denis, a facility that supports local film education in addition to large-scale film production (Petterson, 'American Genre Film in the French Banlieue: Luc Besson and Parkour' 26). Besson's unique position in the interstices between French and Hollywood film culture and the role that EuropCorp plays is taken up by David Petterson who argues that, ultimately, 'in the same way the cultural diversity of the French banlieue contests narrow conceptions of what it is to be French, Besson, through his companies and his films, harnesses this space to expand what French cinema is or should be' ('American Genre Film' 51). *Brick Mansions* was released after Petterson's article, yet its repetition of a central trope of both *Banlieue 13* and *Banlieue 13: Ultimatum* highlights a problematic aspect of all three films. In transposing a film shot in the French capital to US soil, it is curious to note that Besson and Delamarre elected to shoot not in Washington, nor in the largest US cities of New York, Los Angeles, and Chicago—all four of which have significant socio-economic and racial divisions—but in Detroit, a comparatively economically depressed city that has suffered more than its own share of racial tension. In a sense, the decision to greenlight an American-based remake is apt, for *Banlieue 13*'s debt to Los Angeles and New York is considerable.[14] Nonetheless, Delamarre and Besson opted for Detroit, with on-location shooting alternating between there and Montreal, which functions as an onscreen stand-in for the Motor City. Home to the three main US car manufacturers in General Motors, Ford, and Chrysler, Detroit suffered greatly from the financial crisis, becoming the largest American city to file for bankruptcy in 2013, the year before *Brick Mansions* was released (the film, incidentally, is set in 2018). Reprising his *Banlieue 13* role, albeit with a new name (Lino), David Belle stars alongside Paul Walker who, in his second last onscreen performance, plays undercover policeman Damien Collier. As in the original, Lino and Damien put aside their differences to join forces: this time with the intention of taking down Tremaine Alexander, a ghetto kingpin played by Wu-Tang Clan rapper RZA. The central casting of two white leads in this scenario is curious, even as it reprises a formula central to both *Banlieue 13* and *Banlieue 13: Ultimatum*, where Belle is joined by fellow parkour practitioner Cyril Raffaelli who plays the policeman Damien Tomaso. In Paris, the idea of two white saviours rescuing the banlieue is at the very least awkward, especially in a film that purports to rail against government-imposed inequality. Transposing the same formula to Detroit instead seems reckless and endorses Purse's linkage of *Banlieue 13*'s emptying the banlieue 'of controversial real-world socio-political resonances' with Hollywood mores, chief amongst them in this case being the ever-durable spectre of the white saviour.[15] Furthermore, it crystallises an obvious problem with both Paris-based films, namely, that the voyeuristic portrayal of an othered banlieue cannot hope to escape a multifaceted white supremacist past, if the only solution proffered is the intervention of more white men. Detroit's troubled record of racial tensions, as exemplified historically by the 1967 Detroit riot, is still very much in evidence today, with the historian Thomas J. Sugrue noting that the city has been 'ranked among the 10 most segregated metropolitan areas in the United States since the mid-20th century' ('A Dream Still Deferred'). Moreover, in a city where 79.7 per cent of the population is black, the idea of white saviours not only undercuts black agency but also feeds upon the idea of an exoticised and othered urban space, one where white characters serve as chaperones for white audiences ('Quick Facts: Detroit City, Michigan'). Such is the case in *Banlieue 13* and *Banlieue 13: Ultimatum*, and while Petterson is correct in his assertion that 'the banlieue residents here will turn out to be better defenders of French Republican values than those who live on the other side of the wall' ('American Genre Film' 43)—they do after all bond together to overthrow corrupt politicians—they are reliant upon the strategic and physical exertions of Damien and Leïto to achieve their aims. Thus, while *Banlieue 13*, the first film of the three, has been described by James F. Austin as 'a curious mix, radically dystopian at the film's beginning and radically utopian at film's end' ('Destroying the Banlieue: Reconfigurations of Suburban Space in French Film' 89), its sequel *Banlieue 13: Ultimatum* bears out the reality that without Damien and Leïto's intervention, the banlieue will be destroyed by an indifferent French government.

As characters, they represent two variations on a theme: Damien, an undercover policeman, embodies the benign side of law enforcement, while Leïto, a big-hearted vigilante, is intent on eliminating drug trafficking from his neighbourhood. The former's credentials provide access, the latter's ingenuity a plan, whilst their individual parkour talents and athleticism grant them mastery of their physical terrain. The 'exoticised space' identified by Purse in *Banlieue 13* is ramped up in *Banlieue 13: Ultimatum*, where, three years after the end of the first film, the neighbourhood is hopelessly divided into five racially segregated gangs (African, Arab, Caucasian, Hispanic, and Chinese) while again facing an external threat, this time from the State Security Chief Walter Gassmann (Daniel Duval), a stooge for a multinational corporation that plans to bomb, redevelop, and gentrify the area. After a brief overture, which reprises the conclusion of *Banlieue 13*—where Damien, Leïto, and his sister Lola (Dany Verissimo) stand triumphantly outside the banlieue—director Patrick Alessandrin cuts to three years in the future (2016) where we are again confronted by rats outside a ghetto wall. Again, the camera tilts vertically up before floating above the wall and through the banlieue as an omnipotent observer, albeit this time frenetic editing is used to both deny a sense of cohesion and visually separate the racial factions. Detailing street life, this opening scene presents the various gangs in reductive fashion—at one point we witness an Arab woman smuggling dynamite under her burqa, at another we see skinheads adorned with white power and SS tattoos fight one another. The gang-enforced divisions essentially ensure that in place of one banlieue, there are five, with the death of the district's overlord leaving the various factions fighting one another for supremacy. Leïto's task, therefore, is to unite the gangs and thwart Gassmann. Petterson sees utopian potential in the film's conclusion when, after foiling the plot, Leïto convinces the gang leaders and the French president that they should destroy the area anyway and rebuild it from scratch. 'Banlieue residents', Petterson suggests, 'want change as much as everyone else, but only when they are included in the political process' ('American Genre Film' 43): a reading he links directly to Nicolas Sarkozy's aborted plans to revitalise the Parisian banlieues in 2008.[16] Petterson locates this optimistic denouement within Hollywood traditions and states that 'the extent to which the film repeatedly emphasizes an idealistic, optimistic narrative reveals the way it engages social problems through the language of American genre cinema' ('American Genre Film' 38). His argument is persuasive, yet I would suggest an addendum that in some ways the film is *too* faithful to American genre cinema, for it blindly adheres to an unwritten, time-worn requirement that a white hero must emerge to save the day. As with its antecedent, *Banlieue 13: Ultimatum* is propelled entirely by Damien and Leïto's agency, and whilst a rainbow coalition of gangs emerges by the end of the film, the fact remains that they are powerless without Leïto to unite them.

Rehabilitating Whiteness

Unlike other denizens of the district in *Banlieue 13: Ultimatum*, who are hemmed in physically and psychologically by the giant concrete wall, Leïto roams free and is granted access to areas of the city that his neighbours are routinely denied. Tellingly, we first encounter him *outside* of the banlieue, attempting to blow up sections of the wall and then effortlessly evading a score of policemen. He assumes a unique physical primacy over the city, succeeds in integrating himself into the favour of all the gangs, and serves as a counterpoint to white police and governmental excess. He also provides a segue into the 'otherness' of the banlieue, acting as a white surrogate for white audiences and assuaging any guilt they may harbour about their own societies, by being both a response and a solution to discriminatory governmental policies. Despite his attempts to rid the banlieue of drugs, Leïto enjoys an easy rapport with the gang leaders, and so, while the African kingpin Molko (MC Jean Gab'1) responds with incredulity to Leïto's attempts to destroy the banlieue walls, claiming that they protect 'his culture and society' from the outside world, he is content to simply issue a warning to his would-be antagonist. Outside the banlieue, Leïto also demonstrates effortless mastery over law enforcement, most obviously when Damien is falsely arrested for drug possession and he deliberately gets himself arrested to rescue his friend. His subsequent experience in prison contrasts sharply with an earlier scene in the film when a black inmate pleads for his rights before being brutally executed by the police. For Leïto, instead, getting arrested is merely a game that provides him with a fresh environment in which to exert his physical dominance. During an extended set piece at the police station, Leïto and Damien seem barely encumbered by the laws of physics, as they overpower dozens of guards, bounce off walls, and, at one point, jump clean through a ceiling. If on the one hand such scenes can be dismissed as knowing appropriations of some of the dumber aspects of action cinema, on the other, to retort that Besson's trilogy of banlieue films is simply played for fun is to excuse the blinkered racial politics that underpins the series, a claim I wish to back up with a closing example from *Banlieue 13: Ultimatum*. While Alessandrin's film may, on the surface, present a critique of France's indifference towards its own citizens, in reality it disregards institutional racism sufficiently for the French president to appoint Leïto overseer of the banlieue's rejuvenation at the film's end, assuring him that Damien will grant the necessary permission to undertake his task. Despite being confronted with a multicultural group of community leaders, all of whom risked their lives to save both him and the banlieue, the president immediately favours a white saviour. Concurrent with Shohat and Stam's contestation that 'Eurocentric discourse embeds, takes for granted, and normalizes, in a kind of buried epistemology, the hierarchical power relations generated by colonialism and imperialism' (*Multiculturalism* 8), Leïto's elevation is of a piece with an even more jarring normalisation of white supremacy evident in the film, namely, the passive representation of the banlieue's skinhead leader Karl le Skin (James Deano). Despite being festooned with swastika tattoos, Karl slots quietly into the film's diegesis and is presented as little more than a willing, if taciturn, member of Leïto's coalition to save the banlieue from Gassmann. In the process of doing so, the group are accosted by a hulking, shaven-headed white policeman who Damien overpowers. With French and EU flags prominent in the background, Damien kicks the man in the groin, before the gang leaders show common purpose by verbally abusing and assaulting him, a sequence which climaxes with Karl calmly administering a textbook head-butt to the prone goon's face. The sequence is repeated soon afterwards in the film's penultimate scene when the group dispose of Gassmann. In fact, as *Banlieue 13: Ultimatum* closes, we see Karl laughing and smoking cigars in a boardroom with his fellow gang leaders, with EU and French flags again prominent on the table (see Fig. 7.1). In light of the trilogy's existing problems then, this seemingly unquestioning inclusion of a Nazi as a smiling member of a plucky coalition of the downtrodden is more than a little problematic, all the more so in a country that suffered under Nazi occupation during the Second World War and that continues to flirt with the prospect of elevating a Le Pen to the Élysée Palace.

Fig. 7.1 'Banlieue 13: Ultimatum'

LONDON

Films: Shank (Mo Ali 2010) and *Attack the Block* (Joe Cornish 2011)

A debut feature of the Somali-British director Mo Ali, *Shank* follows in the footsteps of the *Banlieue 13* films in its scattergun appropriation of tenets of the hood film, the action film, and dystopian sf. Like its Paris-based counterparts, *Shank* is also set in a major metropolis in the very near future—in this case 2015 London—that at the time of writing is already past tense. In both instances, we can see the temporal proximity of the onscreen futures as being indictments of the bleakness of the present, for they suggest that near catastrophe is not just likely but imminent. Any possibility of remedial action in such a scenario is thus affectively foreclosed as the future's proximity bears down upon the present. Ali wastes little time in establishing *Shank* as a hood film/sf hybrid and showcases his influences from the outset. Channelling Mathieu Kassovitz's *Hate/La Haine* (1995),[17] *Shank* opens with a credit sequence featuring grainy black-and-white riot footage that suggests a historical continuum of oppression that intensifies the claustrophobia of a foreclosed present. The riot footage gives way to animated images of tower blocks, CCTV cameras, and razor wire, respective symbols of societal neglect, surveillance, and fear. As such, the film unapologetically follows in the footsteps of British urban films that themselves took inspiration from *La Haine*, chief amongst them *Bullet Boy* (Saul Dibb 2004) and *Kidulthood* (Menhaj Huda

2006). *Shank*'s debt to the latter is especially pronounced: in addition to casting *Kidulthood*'s Adam Deacon in the central role of Kickz, a poster of the film features prominently in a local gym where brothers Junior (Kedar Williams-Stirling) and Rager (Ashley Thomas) spar with one another. Kickz, Junior, and Rager are part of a south London gang called 'the Paper Chaserz' who become embroiled in a feud with 'the Souljahz', a violent and sadistic rival gang. Full of rapid-fire editing, chase scenes, and street fights, *Shank*—which takes its title from the prison slang for improvised knife attacks—is highly derivative on a formal level, yet its novelty, as a contemporaneous *Guardian* review noted, lies in its futuristic setting.[18] Shot on location at the Heygate Estate in south London, *Shank* received the backing of the Damilola Taylor Trust, a foundation set up in memory of the ten-year old Nigerian schoolboy who bled to death after being attacked in a Peckham estate in 2000. In its own words, the Trust is 'committed to providing inner-city youths with opportunities to play, learn and live their lives free of fear and violence, and with optimism for a future where opportunities flourish', and its support of *Shank* is presumably linked to the possibilities that the shooting of a feature film in the neighbourhood would afford local youths ('Damilola Taylor Trust'). While the Trust's endorsement linked the film to a real-life tragedy, it is highly debatable whether *Shank* actually succeeds in critiquing the conditions that beget urban violence, and it met with largely negative reviews as critics decried its seemingly ambivalent attitude to violence.[19] As in Joe Cornish's *Attack the Block*, which I will turn to in due course, the centre of London is absent as Ali focuses upon life within his south London estate, a decision no doubt partially informed by budget restraints (*Shank* was shot for an estimated £385,000) but one that nevertheless accentuates the divide that exists between the locals and the global centre of commerce that surrounds them.

THIRD WORLD LONDON

By setting *Shank* in the nominal future, Ali could afford to rebuff complaints that his film depicts the area in a poor light and instead paint the production as a warning about the consequences of continued governmental neglect. His version of London is squalid as the opening scenes take pains to illustrate: one especially striking scene shows a drunken man defecating on the street, while beside him a topless prostitute solicits for business. 'This', Junior informs us in the first of his many voice-overs, 'is how we live'. Junior explains that the area's decay is due to a combination of privatisation and governmental indifference: 'the government doesn't direct funds anymore so we have to take things for ourselves'. Through Junior we learn that the rich seal themselves off in 'safe zones', while he and his friends steal and resell food to survive in what one of his customers refers to as 'third world London'. Illustrated onscreen graphics detail a familiar list of dystopian leitmotifs to have assailed the community in recent times: the economy has collapsed, crime and murder rates are way up, the population is soaring, and food supplies have grown scarce, while we also learn that schools in the neighbourhood have been shut down by the government. The neighbourhood's social and economic isolation from its surrounds is accentuated by a near total absence of recognisable landmarks, so that unlike say *28 Weeks Later*, which I cover in Chap. 8, the film openly rejects tourist-friendly depictions of London. Instead, the confines of the Heygate Estate represent the totality of the world on display and, by proxy, the geographical and social restrictions imposed upon its residents. In Chap. 5, we have seen how estrangement of the familiar in sf finds its roots in Brechtian attempts to expose overarching social structures, and as Vivian Sobchack reminded us in a memorable analysis of Richard Fleischer's *Soylent Green* (1973), it does not require a large budget to execute since it relies on the 'visual subversion' of everyday items (*Screening Space* 131). Similarly to *Shank*, *Soylent Green* also portrays a dystopian metropolis and is a film that, in Sobchack's words, 'is at its best when visually convincing us that the staples of life we take for granted today are completely unknown to all but the most influential and wealthy inhabitants of New York City in the year 2022' (*Screening Space* 131). Like *Shank*, this is principally achieved by emphasising a scarcity of and resultant demand for food, allowing Fleischer to present a world where 'a tomato and a wilted stalk of celery are as strange and wondrous as any alien plant life designed in the studio' (*Screening Space* 87). *Shank* is similarly reliant upon what Sobchack identified as a commonality amongst low-budget sf films, namely, a rigorous dependence upon their 'visual use of a familiar world' (*Screening Space* 132). When the Paper Chaserz highjack an armoured van, therefore, the gang jubilantly rifle through its cargo of tinned and vacuum-packed foods as if they were gold. Food has become a precious commodity that people will risk their lives to obtain, a point made brutally clear when, in the very next scene, Junior and his friends are ambushed by the Souljahz, who seize their rival's bounty and stab and kill Rager in the process.

As with sf's visual retooling of the familiar, however, context is everything when applying real-world analysis to onscreen depictions of the future. After all, people dying due to lack of food is an everyday occurrence throughout the globe. The novelty of *Shank*, thus, lies in its transposition of daily crises from elsewhere in the world into the heart of London while challenging preconceptions about the supposed sophistication of Western Europe. By concentrating upon life within a neglected estate and moving away from ubiquitous cinematic images of Westminster, the Gherkin or the Shard, *Shank* brings us closer to a city where, by 2013, the *BBC* was reporting that a staggering 28 per cent of Londoners were categorised as living in poverty ('More Than a Quarter of Londoners "In Poverty"'). While much of the discourse in the run-up to David Cameron's Brexit referendum centred around the economic disparity between London and the rest of the UK, such narratives ran the risk of equating the centre of a global financial powerhouse with the city at large, blurring in the process the latent inequalities that assail the lives of potentially millions of Londoners. Appropriately enough, *Shank* closes with its first shot of the City of London skyline, framed from the vantage point of Junior and his friends who peer out across the financial district from the roof of a decrepit tower block. In a voice-over that closes out the film, Junior asserts that he knows two things about life: the importance of money ('keep strong and get on that paper chase') and the need to 'find where the beauty is hiding when you're living in squalor'. The proximity of the skyscrapers is striking and a stark reminder of the ever-increasing co-existence of extreme poverty and wealth in Europe's major cities.

One District, Two Worlds

Restrictions and neglect affect every element of daily life within Junior's Heygate Estate community, and although *Shank* is set in a possible future, it continuously gestures towards deeply ingrained imbalances that have long assailed British life. A sign at the entrance to Junior's abandoned school, 'Feton School Co-educational', has the 'f' spray-painted over so that it reads 'Eton', sardonically referencing one of the most prestigious and expensive private schools in Britain. In 2010, the year of *Shank*'s release, David Cameron became the 19th British Prime Minister to be educated at the Berkshire School. Just as attendees of Eton can point to such a lineage and justifiably expect life to provide them with opportunity, residents of the Heygate Estate could be forgiven for expecting the worse from a society that has continually neglected them. As Loretta Lees and Mara Ferreri outline in their article 'Resisting Gentrification on its Final Frontiers: Learning from the Heygate Estate in London (1974–2013)', the Southwark council estate 'was built on "slum" cleared land and completed in 1974. Only 30 years later, in the 2004 masterplan for regenerating the area, it was slated as a "slum" for demolition' ('Resisting Gentrification' 15). A three-decade interval, in other words, had done nothing to improve the area or to elevate its status above that of a slum. Nevertheless, the estate is centrally located, situated just over a mile from London Bridge to the north and the same distance from Westminster Bridge to the west. As Lees and Ferreri make clear, this land is immensely valuable, being located 'in an area immediately adjacent to the much prized "zone 1" of London, as understood by the underground map as well as by real estate investors' ('Resisting Gentrification' 15). Unlike Paris, where banlieues were largely built on the outskirts of the city, in London it is not uncommon to find large public housing estates close to the city centre and adjoining affluent private developments. Such proximity of wealth and poverty should not surprise anyone familiar with the city, especially in the aftermath of the 2017 Grenfell Tower fire: a horrific occurrence that took the lives of 71 people in North Kensington, an area that is home to numerous upmarket developments as well as to David Cameron himself. Like Heygate, Grenfell was also built in 1974 and suffered badly from governmental neglect in the interim decades. That efforts to maintain the building were scuppered by financial restrictions is all the more galling given the affluence of Grenfell's surrounds, yet the feeling persists that such neglect is commonplace across London.[20] Lees and Ferreri add that Heygate was 'slated for "regeneration" in the late 1990s', with its demolition proposed as the ultimate long-term solution ('Resisting Gentrification' 17). From thereon in, the local council 'deferred all but minimal maintenance of the estate' in advance of the 'decant' of residents who were promised accommodation on the redeveloped site, yet, as time passed and some residents left, the council used part of the estate as 'short-term, insecure, emergency "temporary accommodation"', while other units were left empty and boarded up', thus exacerbating the area's decline ('Resisting Gentrification' 17). Unlike their London neighbours who inhabit gated communities, residents of British council estates who have purchased their homes via the 'Right to Buy' scheme[21] are disenfranchised in such a scenario, for they are at once property owners *and* tenants of the local authority who own the land upon which their homes are built

('Resisting Gentrification' 15). Typically, such residents are the last to leave failing tower blocks as they have an active financial stake in their homes. Such was the case with Heygate where, 'towards the end of the displacements of both secure and insecure tenants, [...] resistance in and around the estate mainly focused on helping property owners (leaseholders) to gain fair compensation, while also raising awareness of the process of displacement' ('Resisting Gentrification' 15). In its depiction of nebulous aliens attacking Heygate, Joe Cornish's *Attack the Block* directly draws upon such concerns as well as interrelated fears of gentrification. A much larger production than *Shank*,[22] *Attack the Block* again follows the adventures of a young multicultural street gang in a neglected London estate, this time a fictional neighbourhood in Brixton.

GENTRIFY THE BLOCK

Shot in the Heygate Estate, as well as Bemerton Estate in Islington and Myatt's Field in Brixton—both of which were also 1970s-era developments—,*Attack the Block* features John Boyega and Jodie Whittaker in key roles as gang leader Moses and trainee nurse Samantha, respectively. Together with his friends Pest (Alex Esmail), Dennis (Franz Drameh), Biggz (Simon Howard), and Jerome (Leeon Jones), Moses is forced to fight for his neighbourhood against murderous gorilla-like aliens with luminescent fangs, who have mysteriously dropped out of the sky. Lighter in tone than *Shank* and infinitely more self-aware, *Attack the Block* knowingly plays upon Hollywood sf tropes[23] while reworking the spectre of the alien invasion, a recurrent staple of the genre. Defying a long-established sf trend, where aliens land in or hover over the political and economic centres of major US cities—as seen, for example, in *The Day the Earth Stood Still*, *Independence Day*, or *War of the Worlds*—*Attack the Block* presents an alien invasion occurring in a politically and economically marginalised community. Doing so frustrates the establishment of facile dichotomies between alien others, on the one hand, and humankind on the other while undercutting racial subtexts detectable in alien invasion narratives since the Golden Age of sf in the 1950s. Although alien invasion films such as *Invasion of the Body Snatchers* (Don Siegel 1956) and *It Came from Outer Space* (Jack Arnold 1953) are more commonly linked with fears over the spread of communism, Eric Avila has persuasively linked their enduring appeal to white anxieties about the incursion of ethnic minorities into America's cities. In many such films, aliens were coded as 'other' and thus threatening to the dominant white hegemony yet nebulous enough to defy easy categorisation. Moreover, such nebulousness ensured that the typical alien other was sufficiently malleable in construction to demonise any number of non-white minorities. The 1950s notably saw many white Americans migrate to the suburbs of major cities as increasing numbers of black Americans were drawn to urban areas in search of employment. As Avila observes, 'the rise of Hollywood science fiction paralleled the acceleration of white flight in postwar America and [...] also captured white preoccupations with the increasing visibility of the alien Other' ('Dark City: White Flight and the Urban Science Fiction Film in Postwar America' 88). 'The popularity of films about alien invasions', Avila thus posits, 'suggests that mainstream white audiences may have viewed the movement of blacks and other racialized minorities into the cities as not so much a migration, but rather an invasion of what had previously been white space' ('Dark City' 89). In the UK, the 1950s also saw large-scale inward migration from Britain's former colonies in the wake of the enactment of the 1948 British Nationality Act, which theoretically allowed for anybody born within the British Commonwealth to live and work within Britain. Hundreds of thousands of people migrated to Britain in the wake of British India's independence in 1947, while many more moved from the Caribbean and Africa. In the case of the Caribbean, by way of illustration, the National Archive estimates that half a million people from the West Indies alone migrated to Britain between 1948 and 1970 ('Bound for Britain: Experiences of Immigration to the UK'). As in the United States, the resultant shift in urban demographics did not go unchallenged, as, for example, the 1958 Notting Hill race riots, the 1967 founding of the National Front, and Enoch Powell's infamous 1968 'Rivers of Blood' speech bear grim testimony to. In the intervening decades, London grew to become increasingly racially diverse with large concentrations of migrants settling in communities such as Newham, Brixton, and Bethnal Green to name but three high-profile examples. Against this historical backdrop, *Attack the Block*'s playful attitude to genre is both deliberate and instructive, for as I will now seek to illustrate it repurposes heavily allegorised staples of 1950s' sf for a twenty-first-century, postcolonial British audience.

Noting how *Attack the Block* 'not only echoes Hollywood tropes in general, but also alludes to scenes in well-known films', Sherryl Vint suggests that the film's interaction with sf history is telling, as it 'deploys these allusions to critical effect, asking us to question our image of the hero in such films and—

much more significantly—our image of hoodie-wearing, generally nonwhite teenagers' ('Visualizing the British Boom; British Science Fiction and Television' 174). If the multicultural heroes of *Attack the Block* are recalibrated to allow for the postcolonial realities of modern-day Britain, then so too are the aliens, whose invasion of the community can be read in tandem with efforts to repopulate inner city London through ongoing processes of gentrification. Lees and Ferreri observe that 'the state-led gentrification and social cleansing of the final gentrification frontiers in inner London—both council estates and low income tenants—have been on-going since the late 1990s', a pattern that typically involves the exposure of low-income housing to private investors, which in turn 'legitimates the application of market logic' to social housing ('Resisting Gentrification' 14). What begins as regeneration swiftly degenerates into gentrification, particularly in geographically lucrative areas. In Heygate, these developments met with considerable local resistance during a period contemporaneous with *Attack the Block*'s release. With plans to raze the estate to the ground at an advanced stage, the community's remaining leaseholders formed the Heygate Leaseholders Group (HLG) in 2010, in a last ditch bid to resist their removal from the area. Within two years, however, the local council issued a compulsory purchase order for the remaining residences in advance of the demolition of the estate to make way for a new development called Elephant Park, which, the HLG noted in a press release, would price many locals out of the area:

> The 1200 homes here on the Heygate were truly affordable to local people. The 2500 luxury new homes set to replace them will cost upwards of £500,000 to buy, and if there are any new 'affordable' homes provided then the most affordable of these will likely cost around £275 per week to rent. This regeneration scheme was conceived on the premise of creating a more 'mixed community'. In reality what we are seeing is state-sponsored segregation: the large-scale displacement of those on lower incomes by high earners and overseas buy-to let investors. ('Resisting Gentrification' 20)

In *Attack the Block*, the link between the aliens and such clinical gentrification processes is made explicit when Moses suggests to Pest that the alien invasion was a racially motivated government plot: 'Government probably bred those things to kill black boys. First they sent in drugs, then they sent guns and now they're sending monsters in to kill us. They don't care man. We ain't killing each other fast enough. So they decided to speed up the process'. The initially reluctant Moses plays a pivotal role in rallying his friends against the invasion, a cause that will in time see him emerge as an unlikely community leader. When we first encounter him and his gang, they are in the process of mugging the entirely blameless Samantha, while we later learn that Moses doubles as a dealer for local drug czar Hi-Hatz (Jumayn Hunter). As such, the alien invasion serves as a rallying cry for Moses and his friends who will find common cause with Samantha and an assortment of other locals in the battle for control of the estate. Like his biblical namesake leading the Israelites across the Red Sea, Moses fights to save a displaced community, while his place in the pantheon of historical British insurrectionists is underscored by Cornish's setting the film on Guy Fawkes Night, an annual celebration of the failed 1605 attempt to blow up the House of Lords. In positioning the multicultural locals as defenders of British terrain, Cornish explicitly frames the alien invasion within government-endorsed gentrification processes that would see them replaced with higher-income residents. Sarah Ilott points out that Cornish therefore 'portrays black characters as inherently British rather than Britain's Other, challenging the way that racist rhetoric attempts to position those of non-white ethnicity' ('"We Are the Martyrs: You're Just Squashed Tomatoes!" Laughing through the Fears in Postcolonial British Comedy: Chris Morris's *Four Lions* and Joe Cornish's *Attack the Block*' 3), just as I would add here that *Attack the Block* challenges historically embedded white supremacist undertones in sf itself. Doing so allows Cornish to portray the neoliberal actions of successive British governments as being unpatriotic, especially if we consider that a salient result of intensified gentrification across London has been a huge upsurge in luxury second homes left vacant by wealthy and often foreign owners.[24] Both Ilott and Vint note the latent symbolism of Moses' ultimate moment of triumph, wherein he leads the aliens into his apartment before setting them ablaze and leaping out of a vertiginous balcony clasping a Union Jack. Moses has become an exemplary British hero, yet tellingly, official Britain remains hostile, and the police arrest him on his return to terra firma for his involvement in the mugging of Samantha. She demurs that Moses was in fact 'protecting her' as the assembled crowd chant passionately for his release. The resistance, it appears, has just begun.

Notes

1. In their edited collection *Multiculturalism, Postcoloniality, and Transnational Media*, Ella Shohat and Robert Stam write that 'the concept of multiculturalism is polysemically open to various interpretations and subject to diverse political force fields; it has become a contested and in some ways empty signifier onto which diverse groups project their hopes and fears' (6).

2. Writing for *Reuters*, for example, religion correspondent Tom Heneghan detected a clear Muslim-specific undercurrent in the pronouncements of Cameron, Sarkozy, and Merkel, noting that 'despite their differences, all three say they have a problem with the integration of Muslims and their statements on multiculturalism clearly focus on those minorities' ('Sarkozy Joins Allies Burying Multiculturalism').
3. In the 2015 French regional elections, for example, the Front National topped the polls, attaining almost 28 per cent of the popular vote. In the UK, meanwhile, UKIP did likewise in the 2014 European Parliament election, an event not without irony given the party's voluble opposition to continued UK membership of the EU. The AfD's electoral impact in Germany had for a time been more modest—falling short of the required 5 per cent threshold in the 2013 Federal Election, for example—but grew exponentially by the 2017 General Election, when it attracted almost 13 per cent of the popular vote, making it the country's third largest party.
4. While terrorists were almost certainly smuggled into Europe via the refugee trail from Syria, the same trail exists because an overwhelming majority of Syrians were fleeing persecution *from* terrorism, be it the state-sanctioned variety practised by Bashar Assad's brutal regime or the medieval acts of barbarism perpetrated across Syria and northern Iraq by ISIS.
5. Stam and Shohat continue: 'The various attacks on multiculturalism, from both *left* and *right*, have made us forget that the term does have certain advantages. The *multi* in multiculturalism brings with it the idea of a constructive heterogeneity, while *culture*-an integral part of the economy in the postmodern epoch-foregrounds an area of practice and analysis sometimes neglected by Marxist approaches. Putting the two words together enacts a coalitionary strategy that implicitly goes beyond binarism of race relations or black studies or Asian studies or whiteness studies' (*Multiculturalism* 8).
6. Chandra Mohanty, for instance, has argued that Western feminist movements have often been complicit in perpetuating an ideal of global struggle that nevertheless downplays historical imbalances in place of assuming 'an ahistorical, universal unity between women', one guilty of 'completely bypassing social class and ethnic identities' (*Feminism Without Borders: Decolonizing Theory, Practicing Solidarity* 31).
7. For all the acclaim (and for that matter vitriol) that Merkel has received for her actions in certain quarters, it must also be acknowledged that with an ageing population and one of the world's lowest birth rates, the decision to import a young and cost-effective workforce was not without its advantages in a German context.
8. Poland was certainly not alone in expecting unique treatment for its own citizens; for instance, Ireland's questionable follow-through on its promise to accept 4,000 Syrian refugees did little to dilute its government's annual St. Patrick's Day pleas that special exemptions be provided for unregistered Irish nationals living in the United States.

9. The most obvious rejoinder to Trump's bellicose sentiment is to ask *when* was America great and *for whom*. For Europe, the cradle of colonial expansion, such questions have especial relevance.
10. As I write this, the breaking Windrush scandal threatens to bring down the Theresa May-led Conservative government and has, to date, led to the resignation of the British Home Secretary Amber Rudd.
11. These discourses, Bhabha continues, form a 'double narrative movement' that complicates the nation's (and by proxy the continent's) ability to define itself, begetting a liminal space wherein the claims of people to be 'representative provokes a crisis within the process of signification and discursive address' (*Location of Culture* 208).
12. In *The Making of a World City: London 1991–2021*, Greg Clark categorises London and Paris as being, along with Tokyo and New York, two of 'the historic big four' global cities. Since 2012, Clarke notes, London 'has extended its lead in the *Global Power City Index* and achieved top spot for the first time in the *Cities of Opportunity* study, while Paris, 'Western Europe's other urban powerhouse', has also performed strongly 'despite its deeper immersion in the Eurozone slump' (126).
13. The 'long-take' here comprises several shots in a disguised manner akin to the effect achieved by Alfonso Cuarón and his cinematographer Emmanuel Lubezki during the extended 'long-take' sequences in *Children of Men* (2006).
14. Not only does *Banlieue 13* borrow freely from John Carpenter's dystopian productions *Escape from New York* and *Escape from LA*, it also owes much to American 'hood' films such as *Boyz n the Hood* (John Singleton 1991), *Menace II Society* (Albert and Allen Hughes 1993), *New Jack City* (Mario Van Peebles 1991), and *Do the Right Thing* (Spike Lee 1989).
15. The white saviour is a time-honoured feature of Hollywood films that shows little sign of abating. Recent examples include Tom Cruise saving nineteenth-century Japan in *The Last Samurai* (Edward Zwick 2003), Matt Damon saving eleventh-century China in *The Great Wall* (Zhang Yimou 2016), and Sandra Bullock turning an impoverished black youth into a star professional footballer in *The Blind Side* (John Lee Hancock 2009). For a detailed history of the white saviour complex, see Matthew Hughey's 2014 monograph *The White Saviour Film: Context, Critics and Consumption*.
16. Petterson elucidates: 'In the final scene, Damien, Leïto, the president, and the gang leaders sit around a table smoking cigars. The president asks them if they know Jean Nouvel, the famous French architect. They do not, but the reference inserts the film into the context of Nicolas Sarkozy's failed plans to remake and modernize Paris and its banlieue on a mass scale, the so-called Grand Paris project announced in 2008. Sarkozy got as far as soliciting and publicly debating proposals from architects all over the world, including Jean Nouvel, but the project stalled because Sarkozy refused to work with local political authorities, preferring instead to impose changes from on high' ('American Genre Film' 43).

17. A prime example of the banlieue film, a subgenre that has its origins in the *policier* films of the 1980s and early 1990s and was primarily concerned with the experiences of migrants on the outskirts of French cities, *La Haine* depicts a Parisian landscape rife with racial tension, inequality, and social disenchantment. In addition to portraying the corrosive reality of life on the margins of French society in 1995, the film operates as an almost eerie premonition of coming events, most saliently the 2005 Paris riots.
18. In a review of *Shank*, *The Guardian*'s Cath Clarke writes that 'just when you thought grimy gang drama had run out of steam, along comes this dystopian variation, set in a recession-ravaged London 2015' ('Shank').
19. Writing for *Total Film*, for example, Matt Glasby noted 'that the entire narrative can be easily compressed into a 90-second dream sequence says much more than the garbled anti-violence messages', while Michael Leader of *Film4* decried an emphasis upon style over substance, lamenting that 'the film becomes a pummelling succession of indulgent flourishes that serve no narrative purpose' (https://www.rottentomatoes.com/m/shank/).
20. Ahead of a public enquiry into the fire, Michael Mansfield QC, who spoke on behalf of many of the bereaved Grenfell families, focused on this very imbalance asking: 'How on earth, in the 21st century, in one of the richest boroughs of the United Kingdom, can a block like this just go up in flames with so many casualties involved?' (Boycott and Gentleman, 'Grenfell Labelled a "National Atrocity" as Lawyers Begin Giving Evidence').
21. In its simplest terms, the 'Right to Buy' scheme entitles residents of British council estates to purchase their homes for a nominally discounted fee.
22. *Attack the Block*, which was produced by StudioCanal, Film4, Big Talk Pictures, and the UK Film Council, benefited from an estimated production budget of $13 million (*Box Office Mojo*).
23. Noting its debt to sf films such as John Carpenter's *Escape from New York* (1981) and *The Thing* (1982), Sherryl Vint locates *Attack the Block* alongside contemporary 'British films that humorously recontextualize well-known Hollywood conventions in inappropriate British contexts, such as Edgar Wright's *Shaun of the Dead* (2004) and *Hot Fuzz* (2007)' ('Visualizing the British Boom' 174). The casting of Nick Frost as local drug dealer Ron strengthens this link further, given that he had a central role in both of Wright's films, as does the involvement of Big Talk Pictures which co-produced them.
24. This trend is unlikely to abate any time soon. In January 2018, *The Guardian* reported that 'More than half of the 1,900 ultra-luxury apartments built in London last year failed to sell […] The total number of unsold luxury new-build homes, which are rarely advertised at less than £1m, has now hit a record high of 3,000 units' (Neate, 'Ghost Towers: Half of New-Build Luxury London Flats Fail to Sell').

BIBLIOGRAPHY

Austin, James. 2009. Destroying the Banlieue: Reconfigurations of Suburban Space in French Film. *Yale French Studies* 115: 80–92.
Avila, Eric. 2001. Dark City: White Flight and the Urban Science Fiction Film in Postwar America. In *Classic Hollywood: Classic Whiteness*, ed. Daniel Bernardi, 52–71. Minneapolis: University of Minnesota Press.
Bauman, Zygmunt. 2001. *The Individualized Society*. Cambridge/Malden: Polity.
———. 2004. *Europe: An Unfinished Adventure*. Cambridge/Malden: Polity.
Bhabha, Homi K. 1994. *The Location of Culture*. London/New York: Routledge.
Bound for Britain: Experiences of Immigration to the UK. *The National Archives*. www.nationalarchives.gov.uk/education/resources/bound-for-britain/. Accessed 1 May 2018.
Boycott, Owen, and Amelia Gentleman. 2017. Grenfell Labelled a "National Atrocity" as Lawyers Begin Giving Evidence. *Guardian*, December 11.
Clark, Greg. 2015. *The Making of a World City: London 1991–2021*. Chichester: Wiley.
Clarke, Cath. 2010. Shank. *Guardian*, March 25.
Damilola Taylor Trust. damilolataylortrust.co.uk. Accessed 1 May 2018.
Davies, Christian. 2017. Trump Says West Is at Risk During Nationalistic Speech in Poland. *The Guardian*, July 6.
Glasby, Matt. 2010. Shank. *Total Film*, March 25.
Heneghan, Tom. 2011. Sarkozy Joins Allies Burying Multiculturalism. *Reuters*, February 11.
Hughey, Matthew. 2014. *The White Saviour Film: Context, Critics and Consumption*. Philadelphia: Temple University Press.
Ilott, Sarah. 2013. "We Are the Martyrs: You're Just Squashed Tomatoes!" Laughing Through the Fears in Postcolonial British Comedy: Chris Morris's *Four Lions* and Joe Cornish's *Attack the Block*. *Postcolonial Text* 8 (2): 1–17.
Klein, Naomi. 2003. Fortress Continents. *The Guardian*, January 16.
Lees, Loretta, and Mara Ferreri. 2016. Resisting Gentrification on Its Final Frontiers: Learning from the Heygate Estate in London (1974–2013). *Cities* 57: 14–24.
Mohanty, Chandra. 2003. *Feminism Without Borders: Decolonizing Theory, Practicing Solidarity*. Duke University Press. More Than a Quarter of Londoners "In Poverty". *BBC*, 15 October 2013. www.bbc.co.uk/news/uk-england-london-24517391. Accessed 1 May 2018.
Neate, Rupert. 2018. Ghost Towers: Half of New-Build Luxury London Flats Fail to Sell. *The Guardian*, January 26.
Petterson, David. 2014. American Genre Film in the French Banlieue: Luc Besson and Parkour. *Cinema Journal* 53 (3): 26–51.
Purse, Lisa. 2011. *Contemporary Action Cinema*. Edinburgh: Edinburgh University Press.

Quick Facts: Detroit City, Michigan. *United States Census.* www.census.gov/programs-surveys/decennial-census/decade.2010.html.

Shapiro, Walter. 2017. Donald Trump's Warning About "Western Civilisation" Evokes Holy War. *The Guardian*, July 7.

Shohat, Ella, and Robert Stam. 2003. *Multiculturalism, Postcoloniality, and Transnational Media.* New Brunswick: Rutgers.

Sobchack, Vivian. 2004. *Screening Space: The American Science Fiction Film.* 2nd ed. New Brunswick: Rutgers University Press.

Sugrue, Thomas J. 2011. A Dream Still Deferred. *New York Times*, March 26.

Torres, Carlos Alberto. 2013. Is Multiculturalism Dead? *The Huffington Post*, August 2.www.huffingtonpost.com/carlos-alberto-torres/is-multiculturalism-dead_b_2641808.html. Accessed 1 May 2018.

Vanderschelden, Isabelle. 2007. Strategies for a Transnational/French Popular Cinema. *Modern and Contemporary France* 15 (1): 37–50.

Vint, Sherryl. 2013. Visualizing the British Boom: British Science Fiction and Television. *The New Centennial Review* 13 (2): 155–178.

PART IV

Another Planet: Hollywood SF Production in Europe

CHAPTER 8

European SF and Hollywood

In this chapter I wish to address what has long been the elephant in the room when it comes to European cinema, even more so when engaging with genre in a European sphere: namely, the spectre of Hollywood. Counterintuitive as it may seem, it would appear obvious that no study of European genre film can hope to claim any sort of authority without engaging with that same cinema's relationship with Hollywood. At the outset of this book, I sought to outline the uneasy relationship that has existed between genre and European cinema and have hinted at various intervals at how an oft-dichotomous mode of interpretation has emerged, one that historically placed the work of prominent European auteurs in opposition to the supposedly mechanical tendencies of genre cinema. Such binaries hold little sway for me, for even a cursory glance at European film history provides ample evidence that many of its greatest practitioners made genre pictures of a sort: Antonioni, Bergman, and Rossellini shot road movies in the respective shapes of *The Adventure/L'Avventura* (1960), *Wild Strawberries/Smultronstället* (1957), and *Journey to Italy/ Viaggio in Italia* (1954), while as we have seen, Lang, Resnais, Godard, Truffaut, Marker, Fassbinder, and many others, besides, directed seminal sf films. In Chaps. 1 and 4, moreover, we have seen how doyens of contemporary European arthouse cinema such as Michael Haneke, Lars von Trier, and Yorgos Lanthimos have in recent years turned to sf at various intervals. Elsewhere we have observed examples of straight-up genre films

© The Author(s) 2018
A. Power, *Contemporary European Science Fiction Cinemas*,
Palgrave European Film and Media Studies,
https://doi.org/10.1007/978-3-319-89827-8_8

from Europe that, although lacking the commercial clout of most Hollywood productions, adhere to classical sf conventions, even if in the case of *Grabbers* or *Iron Sky* they are able to do little more than lampoon them. Yet, while a vogue for the genre has historically been in evidence amongst the continent's more high-brow directors (and it is certainly curious how many of them elected make sf films at one point or another), the market leader in Europe remains Hollywood by an almost comical distance. European filmgoers flock to see Hollywood blockbusters, and even leaving aside commercial behemoths such as *Avatar* (which attracted over 75 million cinema admissions in the EU alone) and *Star Wars: The Force Awakens* (over 36 million admissions) (*'Database on Admissions of Film Released in Europe'*), any rational commercial analysis of European viewing trends shows that, even in its own backyard, European sf is but a minor consideration as far as the wider public are concerned. This should not be construed as an attempt to denigrate European sf films or to downplay their influence rather as a simple illustration of how the commercial imperatives that drive the respective industries differ enormously. A 2014 editorial in the 'Supporting European Cinema' issue of *Studies in European Cinema* neatly underscored this reality by comparing the annual budget of Eurimages (approximately €25 million p/a) with that of Steven Spielberg's 2008 Hollywood release *Indiana Jones and the Kingdom of the Crystal Skull* (a film that incidentally updated the franchise's wry embodiment of 1940s' b-movie tropes to instead engage with 1950s' sf) (1–2). At the time of writing, the editorial noted that *Kingdom of the Crystal Skull*'s budget of $185 million was akin to 'not that much under 50% of the figure for all the movies given Eurimages support since 1989' ('Supporting' 2). Such figures are sobering, not least for those who have been subjected to *Indiana Jones and the Kingdom of the Crystal Skull*.

A statistical report into sf films released in Europe from 2000 to 2014, undertaken by Huw Jones for the University of York-based project 'Mediating Cultural Encounters through European Screens', starkly illustrates just how dominant Hollywood sf is in Europe. Tracking cinema attendance statistics from the European Audiovisual Observatory's 'LUMIERE Pro database' (a useful and freely accessible online resource),[1] Jones provides an illuminating, if somewhat restrictive, overview of sf viewing figures across the EU's 28 member states, as well as Iceland, Liechtenstein, Norway, and Switzerland, the four members of the European Free Trade Association ('Statistical Report: Science Fiction Films in Europe'). The report makes for interesting reading with several observations standing out. Amongst assorted reflections, Jones notes that sf films are most popular in Slovakia, Britain, and Hungary and least popular in Italy, Greece, and the Netherlands; while 22 per cent of all European sf productions are British, a trend that shouldn't really astound us when we consider linguistic factors. Noting that the number of sf productions screened in European cinemas had been steadily increasing since the turn of the millennium, Jones calculated that there were 134 sf films produced in Europe during the stated time period, representing less than 1 per cent of overall European productions, a paltry figure redeemed somewhat by the fact that sf films account for 9 per cent of the concurrent European box office receipts ('Statistical Report'). This discrepancy speaks of an overriding truth, however, insofar as it can be explained by the prominence of North American sf (of which Hollywood is the overwhelming contributor), which accounts for a staggering 93 per cent of cinema admissions for sf films in Europe. Indeed, the report states that, of the top 25 most lucrative sf films released in European cinemas since 2000, only one, Luc Besson's *Lucy* (2014), is not an American production—and even at that, it was shot in English and features Scarlett Johansson in the titular role. British director Christopher Nolan's *Inception* (2010) and *Interstellar* (2014), as well as Alfonso Cuarón's *Gravity* (2013), are counted as US/UK co-productions in the study, as is *Terminator 3: Rise of the Machines* (Jonathan Mostow 2003) which also includes Germany as a co-producing nation, yet the vast bulk of funding for all four films was provided by Hollywood studios. Hence, to count them as European in this context strikes me as more than a little problematic.[2] No such ambiguity exists elsewhere, however, for all 20 of the remaining listed films are solely US productions. By Jones' own admission, the report is not entirely ironclad for a variety of reasons that I will briefly outline below. Yet, I would first add that any statistical anomaly in evidence is likely to *downplay* the impact of Hollywood sf on European screens, for, amongst other things, the report does not include *Avatar* in its calculations. Moreover, two of the top four highest-grossing films of all time,[3] *Star Wars: The Force Awakens* and *Jurassic World* (Colin Trevorrow), were released in 2015, and so their final viewing figures were not yet available at the time of the report's publication. As Jones acknowledges, a difficulty with the MeCETES survey is that it relies upon genre designations provided by the Internet Movie Database (IMDb) to attain a consistent definition of sf, while some of the Lumiere admissions data from the early 2000s can be somewhat sketchy.[4] To illustrate the first caveat, IMDb designates *Avatar* as action, adventure, fantasy—and not sf—despite the film's preoccupation with ten-foot-tall, blue aliens who inhabit the planet Pandora in the twenty-second century. If I were to follow suit and adhere to IMDb designations when selecting films to analyse for this book, then neither *The Lobster*, which is listed by the site as being a comedy, a drama, and a romance, nor *Time of the Wolf* (a drama, and—in a first for Haneke—a romance) would be eligible for consideration. Splitting hairs over genre definitions could take us back as far as Mary Shelley's *Frankenstein* at least and, as I have argued in Chap. 1, may ultimately prove self-defeating. Jones' decision to follow IMDb designations in his report must be seen within the wider context of the MeCETES project, which uniformly utilises IMDb in its methodological approach, and as such, his logic for doing so is sound. While not prescriptive, the report is helpful in providing an indicative overview of the dominance that Hollywood sf enjoys on European screens: a dominance in accordance with trends across European cinema that have been apparent for generations and one that was factored into the Maastricht Treaty and the General Agreement on Tariffs and Trade (GATT) negotiations of 1993—and by proxy hardwired into the very frameworks of the drive towards greater European integration.[5] In short, there is no escaping Hollywood: a commercial behemoth that dwarfs the revenues enjoyed by indigenous European fare. The relationship between Hollywood and European cinema is ever mutable, however, and we should be careful to avoid applying facile aesthetic dichotomies to either, or to succumb to making of Hollywood a straw man, in opposition to what Thomas Elsaesser describes as the 'self-ascription' of European cinema as 'a good other' ('European Cinema' 17). What I propose here, instead, is illustrating how the success of *28 Days Later*, one of the breakout films of twenty-first-century European sf, begat a sequel that illustrates how prominent US constructions of Europe—of the type that in another era led to the Marshall Plan—steadfastly endure to this day.

9/11 AND THE DECLINE OF US HEGEMONY

As I have sought to illustrate throughout this study, sf in Europe has experienced a significant revival since the turn of the millennium, an upturn that coincided with a host of developments ranging from Y2K, animal diseases, terrorism, financial crises, large-scale migration, rapid technological innovation, and human-caused climate change, all of which provided a wealth of material for screenwriters. Y2K fears over global computer networks crashing appear quaint at this remove, and few films were made about a craze rendered instantly obsolescent by the passing of the twentieth century. By contrast, 9/11 shook US conceptualisations of itself to the core and radically altered the global political landscape in the decade and a half to come. As Aaron Derosa writes, by 'the mid-twentieth century, it was hard for Americans not to imagine their communities as exempt from history' given that 'America was unscathed from two world wars that decimated Europe' ('Nostalgia for the Future: Temporality and Exceptionalism in Twenty-First Century American Fiction' 100). 9/11 irrevocably shattered this delusion and in its savage brutality suggested that the United States was in fact 'no longer exempt from history and no longer a Virgin Land' ('Nostalgia for the Future' 101). Accordingly, 9/11 became the dominant cultural referent for sf in the years following the atrocity, especially as the genre's capacity for the fantastic provided space for representation of the otherwise unpresentable.[6] Consequently, popular sf became increasingly wedded to apocalyptic narratives, and it remains the case that 'in a post-Fordist, post 9/11 reality, the imaginary of imperial ruin and ruination has become pervasive' (Hell and Schönle, *Ruins of Modernity* 4). The catastrophic 'War on Terror' that ensued has had horrific implications for stability across the globe, and in a sense, America has been rethreading the ontological ramifications of what George W. Bush labelled 'the decisive ideological struggle of the twenty-first century' ever since ('Bush: Iraq a "Decisive Ideological Struggle"'). 9/11 exposed a heretofore concealed vulnerability that irreparably altered America's conception of itself, and consequently, onscreen representations of America were themselves subject to change.

My decision to focus initially upon *28 Days Later* (Danny Boyle 2002) can be traced to both the film's opportune production cycle that took in the periods before, during, and immediately after 9/11, and to the subsequent commercial and critical acclaim it enjoyed. A British production, its success in time resulted in a Hollywood-backed sequel, which shifted the focus from a British cultural frame of reference to an American conceptualisation of the UK. Released in 2007, *28 Weeks Later* (Juan Carlos Fresnadillo) reflects upon the legacy of US foreign policy in the interim half decade since the original and critiques how an absence of advance planning led to turmoil in Afghanistan and Iraq. In many respects, we are still living in a post-9/11 world, as the emergence of ISIS, the Syrian refugee crisis, and Donald Trump's executive order banning entry to the United States from seven Muslim countries attest to. While it may be premature to announce the terminal decline of the United States as the pre-eminent global superpower, the nation's international influence has shrunk visibly under a Trump presidency more concerned with domestic matters in keeping with its 'America first' mandate. Following on from Bush's two failed wars and Barack Obama's disastrous 'red line' in Syria—not to mention his sadistic embrace of drone warfare[7]—the prospect of American hegemony continuing in perpetuity no longer looks assured. Indeed, the fact that it is even open to question exposes a dramatic decline for a nation that, at its post-war highpoint, was able to reshape large tracts of continental Europe. In her article 'Abject Times: Temporality and the Science Fiction Film in Post-9/11 America', wherein she links 9/11 to the demise of postmodernism as the dominant cultural logic, Vivian Sobchack argues that the attacks on the World Trade Center signalled a spiral of decline from which there is no obvious recovery. She writes:

> … in the aftermath of that collective trauma, there began a non-stop—and televised—plague of domestic and global disasters that seem never-ending: wars that, instead of 'shocking and awing', could not be won, and reminded everyone of America's defeat in Vietnam; devastating hurricanes at home and tsunamis abroad; a Great Recession that still hasn't ended for 99 percent of Americans, and financial corruption and collapse that robbed people of their homes and retirement accounts; and, of course, an exponential increase in domestic and global terrorism. (21)

Despite record highs being reported on Wall Street in 2017, familiar fault lines within the US economy remain[8] and, when coupled with a pronounced rupturing of US-European political consensus, threaten to expose underlying instabilities at any moment. Uniform European opposition to the US withdrawal from the Paris Agreement illustrates such discord, as does the European reaction to the relocation of the US's Israeli embassy from Tel Aviv to Jerusalem. Again, it is near impossible to divorce such foreign policy decisions from domestic American politics since they are principally calculated to appeal to Trump's political base. Nevertheless, such actions have global implications and do little to quell opposition to US imperialism, to the point where we have become almost inured to US embassies warning Americans to practise vigilance when travelling abroad. Insofar as it is both pre- and post-9/11, *28 Days Later* occupies a unique moment of transition: for although it elliptically captures something of the immediate zeitgeist of 9/11, its principal focus I would argue is upon deconstructing an inward British tourist trail. Its sequel, instead, is unable to avoid the pervasive aftereffects of a post-9/11 world, and so, while it is again set solely within Britain, it is coded almost exclusively within an American frame of reference. In its depiction of a US-led NATO force restoring stability to a devastated London, *28 Weeks Later* neatly captures the paranoia of a post 9/11 world, particularly as the inadequacy of the restoration efforts is exposed by a resurgence of a deadly virus. In restoring London only to see it collapse once more, *28 Weeks Later* speaks to US cultural domination while anticipating its demise, all the while returning us to our jumping-off point for this book: a bygone post-war era where an ailing Europe was reliant upon and wholly receptive to a multifaceted US intervention.

In the immediate aftermath of 9/11, George W. Bush urged Americans to continue flying and spending, appealing for citizens to 'do your business around the country. Fly and enjoy America's great destination spots. Get down to Disney World in Florida. Take your families and enjoy life the way we want it to be enjoyed' ('A Nation Challenged; Excerpts from Bush Speech on Travel'). As we will see in due course, Bush's equation of Disney World with American life has particular relevance to *28 Weeks Later*, which essentially makes a theme park out of London and, thus, enacts a logical progression of American cultural imperialism. For Britain, meanwhile, the need to restore 'normality' was exacerbated by a reliance on American capital, with US tourists contributing more per capita to the UK exchequer than visitors from any other nation ('Headline Trends in Inbound Tourism to the UK'). British Prime Minister Tony Blair also emphasised travel and commerce as key responses to 9/11, expressing his belief that people 'should go about their daily lives: to work, to live, to travel and to shop—to do things in the same way as they did before September 11' (Jones and Smith, 'Britain Needs You to Shop, Says Blair').

Unlike *Shank* and *Attack the Block*, which, as we have seen in Chap. 7, focus on neglected margins of the city, both *28 Days Later* and *28 Weeks Later* prominently feature the historic and touristic centre of London, making extensive use of recognisable landmarks. The opening of the former film, for example, features an extensive set piece wherein central protagonist Jim (Cillian Murphy) wanders freely along an empty Westminster Bridge and onwards through an abandoned city centre. Danny Boyle's principal frame of reference throughout the film is British, with a curious debt owed to conceptions of nationhood that can be traced to eighteenth-century romanticism. In *28 Weeks Later*, instead, Juan Carlos Fresnadillo's London is at once modern and in thrall to yuppie culture of the 1980s, media imagery of the wars in Iraq and Afghanistan, and Hollywood conceptualisations of Europe. It is, in other words, an entirely American version of London, albeit a knowing one as we shall see in due course. A brief examination of the production history of both films may help clarify the reasons behind this shift in narrative impetus. A locally realised production, *28 Days Later* was shot on a comparatively modest budget of $8 million and was partly financed by the now defunct UK Film Council. Distributed worldwide by 20th Century Fox, the film grossed over $80 million in total and, crucially, over $45 million (or five and a half times its budget) in the US market alone ('28 Days Later'). Receiving largely positive reviews on both sides of the Atlantic, the film's critical and commercial success paved the way for other productions to follow, and notably the other examples listed here all benefited from the financial backing of Hollywood studios. Where Fox's input into *28 Days Later* was largely limited to marketing (coming on board at the distribution phase), the studio financed its sequel, *28 Weeks Later*, from the outset through its short-lived, genre-specific subsidiary, Fox Atomic. Andrew MacDonald, *28 Weeks Later*'s producer, signalled the film's intentions from an early juncture, declaring: 'we were quite taken aback by the phenomenal success of the first film, particularly in America. We saw an opportunity to make a second film that already had a built-in audience' (Hawkins, '28 Weeks Later: Synopsis'). Appealing to American audiences would be achieved, in part, by appropriating US politics—a method deployed in equal measure by contemporaneous dystopias *V for Vendetta* (James McTeigue 2005) and *Children of Men* (Alfonso Cuarón 2006)— and relocating the war on terror to the land of the US's erstwhile colonial rulers. In so doing, *28 Weeks Later* perpetuates 'the global viability of an imaginary wherein New Europe, a ruptured continent rife with terrorism, mafias and unstable nuclear technology, is no longer the inspirational Old World, but rather a demonized repository for Hollywood's fears' (Archer, 'Paris je t'aime (plus) Europhobia as Europeanness' 186). Though less successful than its predecessor (grossing $64 million against an estimated outlay of $15 million), *28 Weeks Later* was not an immodest success. *V for Vendetta* (Warner Bros) and *Children of Men* (Universal) meanwhile, with their thinly veiled critiques of the Bush administration, benefited from major studio backing and enjoyed contrasting fortunes. The former was a resounding success, grossing over $152 million from an original outlay of $54 million; the latter, though favourably reviewed, failed to make a box office profit, despite a robust $76 million budget (*Box Office Mojo*).

Like *28 Weeks Later*, both films were adaptations of British texts, with *V for Vendetta*, a 1980s-based graphic novel by Alan Moore, and *The Children of Men*, a 1992 novel by P.D. James, serving as source material. In both instances, the films deviated considerably from their sources, eschewing critiques of specifically British political concerns in favour of a broader, more contemporary, and indubitably American frame of reference. *V for Vendetta* demolishes Alan Moore's critique of Thatcherism, to instead focus upon the rise of a right-wing Christian leadership that seeks to eradicate Muslim extremists from British life. Moore's view that the film is merely 'a Bush-era parable by people too timid to set a political satire in their own country' is, accordingly, difficult to dismiss (Vineyard, 'Alan Moore: The Last Angry Man'). Similarly, *Children of Men* is heavy with references to Islamic fundamentalism and Abu Ghraib, despite James' source novel being published in 1992, some three years before George W. Bush was so much as Governor of Texas. By contrast Neil Marshall's *Doomsday* (2008), which also prominently features a deadly virus, evokes historical regional divides in the UK—most notably the polarising policies of the Thatcher regime and issues surrounding Scottish sovereignty— failed dismally both critically and commercially.[9] Its preoccupation with the Conservative Party's policies of the 1980s (as evinced by the rebuilding of Hadrian's Wall as a metaphor for Scotland's ambivalence towards the Tories, in addition to its unflattering portrayal of a Prime Minister none too subtly named John Hatcher) did little to win over US audiences, while its b-movie sensibilities jarred with the polished aesthetics of *V for Vendetta* and *Children of Men*. Where *Doomsday* locates key scenes in and around Glasgow, *28 Days Later* and *28 Weeks Later* benefit from shooting in London, a global tourist destination. What changes from *28 Days Later* to its sequel is the cultural mode of reference: the first film plays upon tropes common to domestic British film and tourism, while the second is framed within an almost exclusively American context, which loops us back to our point of departure, namely, the continued dominance enjoyed by Hollywood sf productions on EU screens.

GOING ON HOLIDAY BY MISTAKE: *28 DAYS LATER*

Channelling influences from novels such as John Wyndham's *The Day of the Triffids* (1951) and Richard Matheson's *I Am Legend* (1954), *28 Days Later* focuses upon the plight of a handful of post-apocalyptic survivors as they journey from central London to the Lake District. Awakening from a coma in an abandoned London hospital, bicycle courier Jim must traverse a landscape devoid of locals but ravaged by the outbreak of the 'rage virus', a malady that transforms its victims into unusually hyperactive zombies. Together with fellow survivors, Selena (Naomie Harris), as well as father and daughter Frank (Brendan Gleeson) and Hannah (Megan Burns), Jim must journey to the countryside outside Manchester, where the last vestiges of law and order are upheld by an isolated and increasingly desperate army regiment. Following several near-fatal skirmishes with the infected in London, Jim, Selena, Frank, and Hannah escape the city in a black taxicab: an instantly recognisable staple of London life and a vehicle that will become a literal site for the act of tourism as the film progresses. Traversing the English landscape within such a vehicle, the group become surrogate tourists, sole if unwitting benefactors of a sector rendered obsolete by the collapse of British society. The black taxicab offers viewers the opportunity to experience the devastation wreaked upon English country life while wryly drawing attention to itself as a tourist vehicle. Boyle's use of handheld cameras, naturalistic lighting, and location shooting furthermore suggests the aesthetics of reportage, granting a patina of 'authenticity' to the mise en scène and enacting what Vivian Sobchack identified as a 'major visual impulse of all sf films', that of visualising 'the unfamiliar [...] with a verisimilitude which is, at times, documentary in flavor and style' (*Screening Space* 88). The offshoot of such a visual style is that the extraordinary is suffused with sufficient layers of mundanity to grant a certain credence to onscreen events. Consequently, the film's engagement with contemporaneous pre-9/11 anxieties, such as the 'mad cow' epidemics that assailed British livestock in the 1990s and early 2000s, assumes a matter-of-fact air, with images of animal carcasses piled high in fields appearing both contemporarily and imminently plausible. Judicious use of prominent English locations is key to this effect. On their first evening in the countryside, by way of illustration, the group pass flowing rivers and a lush forest, before parking up and spending the night beside the ruins of the twelfth-century-Waverley Abbey in Surrey. Here they partake in a picnic, happily eating fresh fruit, while in the background wild horses roam the fields. The contrast with city living is epitomised by a sudden absence of chaos, violence, and squalor, and even allows room for a nascent relationship between Jim and Selena to grow.

The taxi then drives on towards the Lake District, traversing a tourist trail that has attracted visitors to Britain for generations and has featured in such iconic British films as *Brief Encounter* (David Lean 1945) and *Withnail and I* (Bruce Robinson 1987). Indeed, the latter film's depiction of two Londoners who have 'gone on holiday by mistake' appears especially relevant, particularly as they, like the protagonists of *28 Days Later*, at one point barricade themselves into a Lake District cottage to ward off the threat of hostile locals. In a volatile environment, the taxi provides a welcome sense of familiarity, a communal space that recalls John Urry's equation of cars with domesticity quoted in Chap. 6: namely, that automobiles provide their drivers with 'a home-from-home moving flexibly and riskily through strange and dangerous environments' (*Mobilities* 126). Yet, dangerous as Boyle's Britain may be, it self-consciously deconstructs the traditional British family excursion to the countryside and, in so doing, signifies the need to start over again. In this light, we can note that Jim's flight from London occurs only after he discovers that his parents have committed suicide to avoid succumbing to the rage virus; while Frank contracts the virus during the journey, leaving Hannah also parentless. In Frank's absence, Jim assumes the role of proxy-patriarch of the group, his budding romance with Selena the next step towards a surrogate family unit that will be united together in an idyllic cottage at the film's end.

Fittingly, it is at that bucolic region celebrated by Wordsworth—one that relies heavily on the tourist industry—where the three survivors cement their bond. The appropriation of the Lake District itself here is intriguing for, although a world-famous tourist resort, it is nonetheless a deliberate cultural construction, a point Urry argues together with Carol Crawshaw in 'Tourism and the Photographic Eye':

> The Romantic imagery of the Lake District, which is widely accepted as natural, was in fact culturally constructed from the middle of the Eighteenth Century onwards. Before 1750 or thereabouts the region was described in the journals of notable travellers as wild, barren, frightful. (185)

Shooting on location, Boyle films a space that is inherently romantic, resonant to the spectator, yet underpinned by a level of superficiality that the visual gaze merely serves to propagate. This is fitting when one considers that 'following the "invention" of the camera in 1839, photography played a dominant part in the emergence of a tourist industry in the Lakes', allowing the visual arts to democratise the 'Lakeland experience' ('Tourism' 185). Boyle, one could argue, is merely replicating a derivative photographic discourse by similarly exploiting the region's undoubted beauty and guiding his viewers through a heavily codified, inauthentic landmark. By reintroducing less-welcoming elements of its history through the threat of impending violence, *28 Days Later* juxtaposes the region's 'wild, barren, frightful' past with a mollified present and in so doing reconciles both elements of its actuality. It is at once tranquil and frightening, familiar and alien, reassuring and exciting, and therefore plays both upon tourism dynamics and conceptualisations of sf as a genre. Cinematographer Anthony Dod Mantle's camera can thus be said to mimic past representations of a region that long appeared 'to demonstrate the power of a visual discourse organised around a romantic conception of the visual which is undertaken by professional photographers' ('Tourism' 185), making possible a time-space vacuum through which viewers can witness past and present collide in a post-apocalyptic future.

The region thereby consumed and captured, *28 Days Later* returns us to the familiar: restoring the comforts of home in the film's conclusion with a scene depicting the survivors recovering in a rural Lake District cottage. Inside, a genteel sequence worthy of Jane Austin unfolds. Selena sews in the kitchen and Jim sleeps upstairs, while Hannah, playing outdoors, hails the imminent arrival of a rescue team with unbridled joy. Filmed in 35-mm widescreen, the ending jars with the overall aesthetic of a film shot with handheld digital video cameras: a visual demarcation that separates the journey from its conclusion and codes the horrors witnessed as past tense. The thrill-filled vacation is captured in a stylistic form akin to holiday footage assembled together into a home movie. This aesthetic and technical shift serves to wipe the slate clean and put distance between the horrors of global terrorism and the lives of those watching. This cleansing pattern will continue in *28 Weeks Later*, where the East End of London will be reimagined, regenerated, and homogenised, before being dismantled again: a trial run of sorts for the area's hosting of the 2012 London Olympic Games, the opening ceremony of which was directed, coincidentally, by Danny Boyle.

WELCOME TO LONDON: *28 WEEKS LATER*

With the threat of the rage virus seemingly diminished, a US-led military operation sets out to rebuild Britain in Juan Carlos Fresnadillo's *28 Weeks Later*. Restoring staples of British life such as shops and bars, and closely monitoring public spaces, the mission plants the seeds for a broader regeneration of British society. When a young family return to London, they see first-hand the improvements that have been made, before being forced to flee again when the virus returns, imperilling their lives and provoking a disastrous response from the unprepared army. A key reversal of the plot of *28 Days Later* is in evidence within the opening five minutes of its sequel. Where the protagonists of *28 Days Later* fled London for the presumed sanctuary of the English countryside, here, Don Harris (Robert Carlyle) abandons his wife Alice (Catherine McCormack) and takes to the river to evade the oncoming quasi-zombie hordes and return to London. The tourist trail has been inverted, and in place of pastoral English tranquillity as a counterpart to the stresses of urban chaos, we now have a reverse voyage: one where all roads lead to the capital, and safety in numbers is decreed to be the most desirable state of affairs.

Following Don's escape from the countryside, *28 Weeks Later* cuts to London, eyeing the city through a gaze that is at once introductory and familiar. A camera mounted on a helicopter surveys the city from above, espying any number of noted landmarks before cutting to ground level. Following several establishing shots of the city, Fresnadillo cuts to the sight of an overhead aircraft passing behind two tower blocks, followed by a brief title card proclaiming '28 Weeks Later'. We next see a shot of an American soldier eyeing the city through the scope of his rifle. Immediately, then, the film establishes an American tourist gaze the very moment after it directly references 9/11: the legacy of the event by now seared into the national consciousness. Crucially, the early shots of the city reinforce the feeling that a specific version of London is on display. As Fred Botting points out:

> A new London is framed in a sequence of aerial establishing shots, transformed, rebuilt, and relocated in the economic upheavals of the 1980s. Shots of Docklands, Canary Wharf, and the Millennium Dome offer recognisable architectural emblems of Thatcherite economic and social transformation and Blairite "Cool Britannia". ('Zombie London: Unexceptionalities of the New World Order' 159)

This version of London is a city pliable to US political and economic interests and is carefully calibrated to speak to US exceptionalism. The shots of the financial district symbolise an era when the relationship between London and Washington was particularly cordial: the spectres of Canary Wharf and the Docklands recalling a Britain whose government's policies chimed with the model of big business put forward by Reaganomics and, above all, with the sort of neoliberal deregulation so aggressively pursued by Ronald Reagan and Margaret Thatcher. Botting's reference to Blair is well founded, given the ultimate economic direction of his new Labour movement's much vaunted 'third way', which grew out of an explicit rejection of Labour's socialist principles beginning with the revision of clause IV of the party's constitution in 1995.[10] Unwilling or unable to untangle himself from economic models put in place by his Tory predecessors Thatcher and John Major, Blair's stewardship was noteworthy for its progression of the neoliberal project, while his unwavering endorsement of American foreign policy after 9/11 led to the two countries going to war together, despite not having a mandate to do so from the UN Security Council.[11] In its framing and use of locations, *28 Weeks Later* speaks to both occurrences. Five years before New York was left reeling from 9/11, the Docklands' status as the financial heart of the British Empire led to its being targeted by the Provisional IRA in a 1996 bombing campaign. Ending a 17-month ceasefire, the IRA's targeting of Canary Wharf was thus laden with symbolic intent. Keen to shore up security while minimising the impact upon the tourism industry—England was hosting that summer's European football championships, the final of which was to be held in London—the British government responded by implementing heightened security measures across the Docklands. The Metropolitan Police erected a veritable ring of steel around the financial district, with 'the whole Dockland peninsula comprising four entry points which at times of high-risk assessment would have armed guards' (Coaffee, 'Rings of Steel, Rings of Concrete and Rings of Confidence' 205). Through its depiction of US soldiers re-enacting this fortification of the Docklands, *28 Weeks Later* implicitly links US and British trauma and, in the process, consigns terrorist attacks on both nations to the same bank of collective memory.

Tellingly, Tammy (Imogen Poots) and Andy (Mackintosh Muggleton), Don Harris' children, and the surrogate tourists of *28 Weeks Later*, arrive in this new London via airplane. The siblings are processed along with other survivors in a terminal at Heathrow Airport where, a stringent medical examination notwithstanding, they have a mundane tourist experience: strolling through moving walkways, following clearly marked pathways, and waiting in queues. Stripped of tension and the threat of terror, the airport is a sanctuary, albeit an artificial one. In his 1995 evaluation of the defining features of supermodernity, Marc Augé notably argued that airports are a prime example of the 'non-place' (*Non-places: Introduction to an Anthology of Supermodernity* 93), a space where people co-exist for sustained periods of time without living together.[12] For Augé, such non-places constitute a salient characteristic of the supermodern: homogeneous spaces where people come together out of necessity rather than out of a desire for interaction and commonality. Homogeneity, Augé felt, stripped airports of individuality or defining characteristics. In this regard, the Harris children's repatriation is eerily uncanny: that they are returning to a country recently ravaged by hordes of zombies feels almost incidental. It is a sense of unlikely normality that calls to mind John Berger's suggestion that 'reality is always at one remove in an airport' as people make a conscious attempt to conform to security regulations (*And Our Faces, My Heart, Brief as Photos* 229). Therefore, the military's efforts to restore normality in *28 Weeks Later* are first road-tested in the microcosmic space of the airport, before being rolled out to the city at large. Steps to extend a 9/11 analogy to account for this heightened security have notably been taken elsewhere. Anirban Kapil Baishya, for example, notes that the airport scenes are 'reminiscent of heightened, often extreme screening and security procedures that followed the 9/11 attacks': an observation lent additional credence by the prominence afforded two symbolic high-rise towers in the film's opening scenes ('Trauma, Post-Apocalyptic Science Fiction and the Post-Human' 14). Yet, in an age of rampant globalisation where one can find an endless succession of Starbucks or McDonald's in most cities (and airports) on earth, it is also the case that airports frequently serve as a wider model for society at large to emulate. As distinct from Augé, John Urry has suggested that the idea of airports as non-places is too reliant upon 'a sedentarist notion of place', noting instead 'how places are increasingly like airports' (*Mobilities* 147). For Urry, it is necessary to consider the experiences of people who staff airports while also being aware of the increased drive towards making airports 'seem more like destinations' replete with shops, bars, hotels, and restaurants (*Mobilities* 148). As airports grow to resemble microcosms of urban destinations (laden with city centre conveniences and facilities), while simultaneously providing a space where 'each passenger is transformed through a series of planned and timed steps' (*Mobilities* 147), it stands to reason to suggest that they, in turn, provide a blueprint for sprawling cities to follow, particularly given the need for airports to be especially vigilant towards terrorism. The more cosmopolitan the place, Urry continues, the more likely it is to be 'produced and consumed through multiple mobilities very much akin to the multiple ways that airports function and are organized' (*Mobilities* 149). There are few cities more cosmopolitan than London, and it is instructive to note how *28 Weeks Later* directly interacts with this idea of the extended airport—or tourist zone—and the mobilities that enable people to traverse it. This notion is propagated by Fresnadillo's ensuing depiction of London as a largely sealed-off terrain: one where the repatriated are located in a 'Green Zone' colony on the Isle of Dogs, near the city's east end. As Baishya points out, the use of the term 'Green Zone' is a loaded one, referring as it does to the International Zone of Baghdad taken over by US troops in 2003 during the invasion of Iraq ('Trauma' 15). Passengers arrive there by way of a shuttle train coming to and from the airport—an enclosed moving vehicle akin to a taxi from which they can view a once-great metropolis. The shuttle is an extension of the airport and provides a haven for tourists to view 'authentic' English life, albeit at an appropriate and deliberate remove à la the taxi in *28 Days Later*. Just as 'regular and safe air travel is centrally implicated in producing global ordering' (*Mobilities* 149), here the airport is extended to convince the tourist (and consumer) that this is a society stable enough to reinvest their confidence in it. Yet as we will see, Fresnadillo establishes such frameworks only to symbolically tear them down, when a reappearance of the rage virus causes the army's resistance to crumble.

THE RETURN OF THE LOCAL

US support in rebuilding post-war Europe did not come cheap, as Charles S. Maier outlines in 'Alliance and Autotomy: European Identity and US Foreign Policy Objectives in the Truman Years'. For Maier, the fiscal inequality that existed between the United States and Europe after 1945 lent itself to exploitation, ensuring that 'it would have been very difficult for any system of economic linkages or military alliance not to have generated an international structure analogous to empire' (275). Happily, warding off communism went hand in hand with the expansion of US markets, ensuring that in Maier's words 'hegemony was in the cards, which is not to say that Americans did not enjoy exercising it (once they had resolved to pay for it)' ('Alliance and Autotomy' 275). Beginning in earnest in 1948, American interests in Europe were propelled economically via the Marshall Plan, which allotted $13 billion in economic aid, and militarily through the Truman Doctrine, which led to the formation of NATO in 1949. Monetarily, Britain was the primary beneficiary of the former as

American goods flooded into the European market.[13] Yet, while the Second World War established the United States as the pre-eminent power on the planet, the years after confirmed Britain's diminishing influence on a world stage it once dominated. Nevertheless, this process was far from immediate, with Britain remaining the world's third largest economy by 1950, and 'although now dwarfed by the USSR and the US as a military power, it still possessed many of the attributes for its period of global hegemony in the nineteenth century' including 'the largest colonial empire [...] and the City of London, the most important financial and commercial centre in the world economy' (Vickers, *Manipulating Hegemony* xi). Since then the dissolution of the British empire has happened gradually, if not yet entirely, while Britain's military and economic clout no longer bear comparison with the world's most powerful states. Instead, the myth of American exceptionalism prevails in some quarters—making liberal reference to 'the greatest nation on earth' still appears to be a mandatory requirement in American political life—despite the immense damage inflicted by US interventions across the globe in the interim decades. The notion gained unassailable traction during the Second World War, when the nation's intervention helped turn the tide against the Axis powers. Ever since, the United States has retained a strong influence over European affairs, to the point that Europe doubled as America's back yard and a shining endorsement of American values. As Victoria de Grazia writes, the 'Marshall Plan was advertised to Americans as bringing a high standard of living to Europeans. At home, propaganda films documented that tax dollars were being well spent on remaking Europe in America's image, helping consolidate the Consumer Republic in the 1950s and to making many Americans believe that their way of life was the most virtuous on the planet' ('The Marshall Plan and Consumerism'). It is altogether appropriate, then, that the carefully controlled, Americanised London of *28 Weeks Later* is introduced with a reference to 1950s Hollywood, just as its demise will later be prefigured with a nod to the same era.

Having navigated their way through the city, Tammy and Andy Harris arrive in the Isle of Dogs where they are greeted by their father who has procured a job as caretaker of a block of luxury apartments (as well as an opulent flat for his family). In a controlled and conspicuously patrolled environment, the family is presented with a simulacrum of reality not unlike arriving at a package holiday destination via a pre-booked bus ride from the nearest airport. They have their every whim catered for (their military liaison proudly announces the erection of a supermarket and 'even a pub' for their benefit), while each step of their journey back to London is facilitated by NATO forces.[14] However, such assistance comes at a cost, and overhead shots of sprawling city landscapes reinforce the theme of intense surveillance. Street corners are conspicuously marked by security cameras, while soldiers patrol the rooftops. In this regard, Urry remarks that 'all cities are increasingly like airports in how forms of surveillance, monitoring and regulation are being surreptitiously implemented as part of the global "war on terror"' (*Mobilities* 149). Penetration of the Green Zone by unwanted locals (rage virus victims), it is clear, would shatter any pretence of security. It is notable then that Fresnadillo frames the Green Zone sequences within references to 1950s Hollywood. This is achieved at the beginning of the film, via the motif of the rifle scope, which recalls the opening of Alfred Hitchcock's *Rear Window* (1954), in which photographer L.B. Jeffries (James Stewart) spies clandestinely on his neighbours, an activity that the bored soldiers also undertake to pass the time (Figs. 8.1 and 8.2). The nod to Hitchcock is hardly incidental, given his extraordinary success in Hollywood and the huge popularity he enjoyed amongst US audiences, while, on a more practical level still, it immediately establishes an American gaze and contextualises London within a Hollywood framework (Doyle (Jeremy Renner), the soldier in question, eyes the camera (and by proxy the viewer) through the rifle scope and mutters 'welcome to London'). The second filmic reference signals the collapse of the Green Zone and the failure of the US-led mission in London, when Tammy and Andy leave the designated zone to pay a visit to their former home. Commandeering a pizza delivery scooter as they do so, the

Fig. 8.1 'Welcome to London'

Fig. 8.2 'Rear Window'

Fig. 8.3 '28 Weeks Later'

scene provides an unexpected light note in the film and is incongruously reminiscent of Audrey Hepburn and Gregory Peck's iconic scooter trip around Rome in *Roman Holiday* (William Wyler 1953) (Figs. 8.3 and 8.4). *28 Weeks Later*'s recalling of a film that at first glance appears little more than a Hollywood take on the Cinderella story—a frothy distraction for a nation stepping up its conflict with the USSR and coming off the back of the Korean War—appears odd at first glance. In the context of post-war

Fig. 8.4 'Roman Holiday'

US aid, however, it is apposite, given that it packages the children's adventure within the American cultural tradition (and US conceptions of Europe). Even the title of Wyler's film suggests a pleasurable and, by nomenclature, touristic excursion, while its narrative agency is granted not by Italian characters, as one might expect, but by an industrious and ultimately good-natured American journalist, played by that great paragon of US virtuosity Gregory Peck. Here, events take a sinister turn, as the children's contaminated mother emerges from the family home and triggers the return of the rage virus to London. Soon the city resembles a war zone as hordes of rage victims attack its inhabitants. Overhead, US snipers make little distinction as they shoot down both the infected and noninfected alike. It is only when they return to the skies via a US helicopter that the children's safety is restored. Yet, by now we have come full circle with the evacuation evoking images of the 1975 Fall of Saigon and with it America's defeat in Vietnam which, as Vivian Sobchack reminded us at the outset, represented the first major body blow to the late capitalist myth of American exceptionalism and set in place a spiral' war that, instead of "shocking and awing," could not be won' ('Abject Times' 21).

CONCLUSION

Where in *28 Days Later* protagonists flee to the Lake District, a region that despite a rich history owes its origins to a deliberate construction, their counterparts in *28 Weeks Later* return to an artificial London that cannot conceal its past. Unlike Danny Boyle, whose culturally significant Lake District is a curious amalgamation of Britain's past, present, and future heritage, Juan Carlos Fresnadillo's London is visibly an American creation, framed within the contexts of US cultural memory (*Rear Window*, *Roman Holiday*), economic past (Marshall Plan, Thatcher, and Reagan alliance), and political present (Iraq, Afghanistan). Therefore, just as the Marshall Plan was sold to Americans as proof of the virtuosity of American life, *28 Weeks Later* highlights how damaging the myth of American exceptionalism became in real terms. The immediacy here comes from relocating events in Fallujah and Baghdad to the streets of London. Where *28 Days Later*'s hopeful ending is compounded by an aesthetic leap from digital to 35 mm footage that relegates the journey undertaken to the posterity of home movies—a term that implies a home from which to safely view such footage—*28 Weeks Later* seeks to regenerate its narrative by relocating the action to Paris via the Channel Tunnel. Concluding with images of rage victims emerging onto French soil, it is clear that the military's policy of containment has failed. Perhaps sensing the staleness of exposing London to yet another attack, Fresnadillo leaves open the possibility of a sequel (the mooted but as-of-yet unrealised *28 Months Later*), one presumably shot at least partly in France. Dwindling financial returns appear likely to sideline any such project in the medium to long term, even if one cannot help feeling that in light of Brexit this represents a lost opportunity. While the US may well be in decline, it was telling that Theresa May took pains to be the first foreign leader to meet with Donald Trump after his inauguration as president, with the two leaders underlining the 'special relationship' that existed between Britain and America and May extending an invitation to Trump for an official state visit (Kanter, 'May and Trump reaffirm the "great bond" between Britain and America'). Trump, who has been an enthusiastic backer of Brexit and a fervent critic of the EU, has persistently taken aim at Britain in the interim, reserving special opprobrium for the London Mayor Sadiq Khan.[15] Nonetheless, May and her colleagues in government have been notably slow to criticise him, given that the UK's traditional reliance upon America as a trading partner is likely to become even more pronounced once the former leaves the EU.

Indeed, as the global obsession with Trump proves, America, even in decline, retains the fascination of the world, and its dominance on European cinema screens is, therefore, highly unlikely to abate anytime soon. This is especially true for the sf industry, which, as the spate of sf films to emerge during the George W. Bush era illustrates, is likely to become even more prolific in response to Trump's historically erratic stewardship. In Europe, as ever, these films have an inbuilt following, and the dominance outlined by Huw Jones at the outset of this chapter should only increase in the years ahead.

Notes

1. See: http://lumiere.obs.coe.int/web/search/.
2. *Interstellar*, for example, was co-produced by Paramount and Warner Bros. as well as by Legendary Entertainment, a California-based media company that was acquired by the Chinese-owned conglomerate Wanda in 2016. It achieves its British co-production status by dint of the involvement of Nolan's own company Syncopy Inc. *Inception* followed a similar arrangement, albeit without the presence of Paramount. Like *Terminator 3: Rise of the Machines* (Arnold Schwarzenegger) and *Gravity* (Sandra Bullock, George Clooney), both films feature American stars Leonardo DiCaprio and Matthew McConaughey in starring roles and were marketed as Hollywood productions.
3. As mentioned in Chap. 1, the list of all-time highest-grossing films changes significantly when adjusted for inflation, yet between them *Avatar*, *Star Wars: The Force Awakens*, and *Jurassic World* are estimated to have grossed close to $7 billion (*Box Office Mojo*).
4. In general, I have found the Lumiere database to be a useful tool that provides a valuable, free public service. A disclaimer on its homepage, however, should serve as a large enough caveat emptor to caution users from adopting its findings verbatim: 'the sources of information it has selected are generally considered trustworthy by experts in the respective countries. However, the Observatory, whose tasks do not include monitoring ticket sales in its member states, is unable to verify or vouch fully for the accuracy of the information provided by the various sources used' ('*Database on Admissions of Film Released in Europe*').
5. During the General Agreement on Tariffs and Trade (GATT) negotiations of 1993, the French government sought out measures to counteract the dominance of American film and television on European screens, by arguing that culture should be exempt from free trade agreements. Specifically, it introduced the idea of a 'cultural exception' (essentially protectionism

for Europe's audio-visual industries) in a bid to restore some balance to a market where, by 1992, 'the U.S. share in the top five European markets (France, Germany, Italy, Spain, Great Britain) had risen to 83 per cent' (Buchsbaum, *Exception Taken: How France Has Defied Hollywood's New World Order* 91). Today, Article 207 of the 'Treaty on the Functioning of the European Union' states that 'The Council shall also act unanimously for the negotiation and conclusion of agreements [in] in the field of trade in cultural and audiovisual services, where these agreements risk prejudicing the Union's cultural and linguistic diversity' ('Consolidated Version of the Treaty').

6. A number of films were released which restaged the attack on New York, albeit through surrogates such as monsters, aliens, or zombies. In many instances, taglines in the films' advertising gives a clear indication of the subtext: *Cloverfield* ('Some Thing has Found Us'), *War of the Worlds* ('They're Already Here'), and *I Am Legend* ('The Last Man on Earth is not Alone') being some of the more obvious examples.

7. Writing in the *New York Times*, Micah Zenko, a senior fellow at the Council on Foreign Relations, points out 'Whereas President George W. Bush authorized approximately 50 drone strikes that killed 296 terrorists and 195 civilians in Yemen, Pakistan and Somalia, Obama has authorized 506 strikes that have killed 3,040 terrorists and 391 civilians […] A technology developed and matured shortly before 9/11 to kill one individual, Osama bin Laden, became the default tactic for a range of counterinsurgency and counterterrorism missions outside of traditional battlefields' ('Obama's Embrace of Drone Strikes Will Be a Lasting Legacy').

8. Amidst rising inequality in American society at large, *Reuters* reported in November 2017 that 'U.S. stocks climbed to record highs on Monday, helped by optimism about merger activity and as investors bet that a Republican plan to cut corporate taxes would bolster earnings' (Randewich, 'Wall Street Hits Record High as Investors Eye Mergers').

9. Backed by Rogue Pictures, then a subsidiary of Universal, *Doomsday*, despite opening in 1936 screens across the United States (as opposed to *28 Days Later*'s 1260), recouped just $11 million of its $30 million budget in an indifferent US market (*Box Office Mojo*).

10. Clause IV, which was written into the Labour Party's constitution in 1918, pledged support for 'common ownership of the means of production, distribution and exchange, and the best obtainable system of popular administration and control of each industry or service'. Influenced by Professor Anthony Giddens, who argued that class-based divisions of left and right had become redundant in a globalised world, Blair's revision of the clause was calculated to avoid marginalising the party in the eyes of the right and to appeal to the political centre.

11. Weighing up the influence of Thatcher and Reagan's economic policies, David Harvey writes that 'the alliance of forces they helped consolidate and the majorities they led became a legacy that a subsequent generation of political leaders found hard to dislodge. Perhaps the greatest testimony to their success lies in the fact that both Clinton and Blair found themselves in a situation where their room for manoeuvre was so limited that they could not help but sustain the process of restoration of class power even against their own better instincts' (*A Brief History of Neoliberalism* 63).
12. Building upon Jean Starobinski's 1990 article, 'Les cheminées et les clochers', which sought to locate modernity at the site where the past exists in a present that, nonetheless, simultaneously lays claim to it, Augé argues that if places can thus be defined as 'relational, historical and concerned with identity', then a space which cannot be defined in these ways must thus be a 'non-place'. Such non-places, Augé suggests, are by-products of supermodernity, a state of being that seeks to reconcile the transience of contemporary society: one defined by time spent in places in flux, such as supermarkets, road networks, and hospitals, a world 'surrendered to solitary individuality' (*Non-places: Introduction to an Anthology of Supermodernity* 78). Hotel chains, theme parks, and airports constitute for Augé examples of non-places, locations where people pass through without engaging in meaningful interaction.
13. Britain received $3176 million in aid, considerably more than the next highest recipient France, which received $2706 (Vickers, *Manipulating Hegemony* 44).
14. In *Who Rules the World?*, Noam Chomsky describes NATO as a 'US intervention force' arguing that as the United States contributes up to 75 per cent of NATO's annual budget, the distinction between US and NATO forces is negligible (45).
15. Since his inauguration, Trump has persistently sought to portray Britain as crime-ridden and overrun by migrants, most saliently in his retweeting of spurious anti-Muslim videos posted by the far-right group Britain First in November 2017 (one of the few occasions that May has saw fit to demur with her US counterpart, a reaction that in turn earned her a stern rebuke from Trump) ('Trump Hits Out at UK PM Theresa May after Far-right Video Tweets'). Following the 3 June 2017 terrorist attacks on London Bridge and Borough Market which led to seven deaths and up to fifty injuries, Trump—wilfully misrepresenting Khan's appeal for calm amidst an intensified police presence—criticised the London mayor for perceived timidity in the face of terror and labelled his response to the attacks as 'pathetic' (Krever, 'Timeline: How Trump's Relationship with the London Mayor Grew so Heated'). In May 2018, to give a final example, Trump claimed that knife crime had become an epidemic in Britain, describing an unnamed London hospital as a 'war zone' (Smith, 'Donald Trump says London Hospital is Like "War zone"').

Bibliography

A Nation Challenged; Excerpts from Bush Speech on Travel. *New York Times*, September 28, 2001.
Archer, Neil. 2015. Paris je t'aime (plus) Europhobia as Europeanness in Luc Besson and Pierre Morel's Dystopian Trilogy. In *The Europeanness of European Cinema: Identity, Meaning, Globalization*, ed. Mary Harrod, Mariana Liz, and Alissa Timoshkina, 185–198. London: I.B. Tauris.
Augé, Marc. 1995. *Non-places: Introduction to an Anthology of Supermodernity*. London/New York: Verso.
Baishya, Anirban Kapil. 2011. Trauma, Post-Apocalyptic Science Fiction and the Post-Human. *Wide Screen* 3 (1): 1–25.
Berger, John. 1984. *And Our Faces, My Heart, Brief as Photos*. New York: Pantheon.
Botting, Fred. 2010. Zombie London: Unexceptionalities of the New World Order. In *London Gothic: Place, Space and the Gothic Imagination*, ed. Lawrence Phillips and Anne Witchard, 153–171. London: Continuum.
Buchsbaum, Jonathan. 2017. *Exception Taken: How France Has Defied Hollywood's New World Order*. New York: Columbia University Press.
Bush: Iraq a "Decisive Ideological Struggle". *NBC*, August 31, 2006. www.nbcnews.com/id/14599961/ns/politics/t/bush-iraq-decisive-ideological-struggle/#.WvIKdi_MzOQ. Accessed 1 May 2018.
Chomsky, Noah. 2017. *Who Rules the World?* London: Penguin.
Coaffee, Jon. 2004. Rings of Steel, Rings of Concrete and Rings of Confidence: Designing Out Terrorism in Central London Pre and Post September 11th. *International Journal of Urban and Regional Research* 28 (1): 201–211.
Consolidated Version of the Treaty on the Functioning of the European Union-Part Five: Common Commercial Policy-Article 207. *Official Journal*, May 9, 2008.
Crawshaw, Carol, and John Urry. 1997. Tourism and the Photographic Eye. In *Touring Cultures: Transformations of Travel and Theory*, ed. Chris Rojek and John Urry, 176–195. London: Routledge.
Database on Admissions of Film Released in Europe. *Lumiere*. lumiere.obs.coe.int/web/search/. Accessed 1 May 2018.
de Grazia, Victoria. 2006. *Irresistible Empire, America's Advance Through Twentieth-Century Europe*. Cambridge, MA: Harvard University Press.
Derosa, Aaron. 2015. Nostalgia for the Future: Temporality and Exceptionalism in Twenty-First Century American Fiction. In *Narrating 9/11: Fantasies of State, Security, and Terrorism*, ed. John N. Duvall and Robert P. Marzec. Baltimore: Johns Hopkins University Press.
Elsaesser, Thomas. 2015. European Cinema into the Twenty-First Century. In *The Europeanness of European Cinema: Identity, Meaning, Globalization*, ed. Mary Harrod, Mariana Liz, and Alissa Timoshkina, 17–33. London: I.B. Tauris.

Evans, Owen. 2014. Supporting European Cinema. *Studies in European Cinema* 11 (1): 1–2.
Harvey, David. 2005. *A Brief History of Neoliberalism*. Oxford: Oxford University Press.
Hawkins, Richard. 2007. 28 Weeks Later: Synopsis. Cast, Crew, Danny Boyle, Robert Carlyle Interviews and The Destruction of London. *SciFiUK Review*, April 30. scifi.uk.com/2007/04/30/28-weeks-later-synopsis-cast-crew-danny-boyle-robert-carlyle-interviews-and-the-destruction-of-london/. Accessed 1 May 2018.
Headline Trends in Inbound Tourism to the UK. *Visit Britain*. www.visitbritain.org/insightsandstatistics/inboundtourismfacts/index.aspx. Accessed 1 May 2018.
Hell, Julia, and Andreas Schönle, eds. 2010. *Ruins of Modernity*. Durham: Duke University Press.
Jones, Huw. 2016. Statistical Report: Science Fiction Films in Europe. *Mediating Cultural Encounters Through European Screens*, January 18. mecetes.co.uk/statistical-report-sci-fi-films-in-europe/. Accessed 1 May 2018.
Jones, George, and Michael Smith. 2001. Britain Needs You to Shop, Says Blair. *The Telegraph*, September 28.
Kanter, Jake. 2017. May and Trump Reaffirm the 'Great Bond' Between Britain and America. *Business Insider*, January 27.
Krever, Mick, and Theodore Schleifer. 2017. Timeline: How Trump's Relationship with the London Mayor Grew so Heated. *CNN*, June 6. edition.cnn.com/2017/06/05/politics/donald-trump-sadiq-khan-timeline/index.html. Accessed 1 May 2018.
Leggott, James. 2008. *Contemporary British Cinema: From Heritage to Horror*. London/New York: Wallflower.
Levine, Paul, and Harry Papasotiriou. 2010. *America Since 1945: The American Moment*. 2nd ed. Basingstoke/New York: Palgrave.
Maier, Charles S. 1989. Alliance and Autonomy: European Identity and US Foreign Policy Objectives in the Truman Years. In *The Truman Presidency*, ed. M.J. Lacey, 273–298. Washington, DC/Cambridge: Woodrow Wilson International Center for Scholars and Cambridge University Press.
Pollard, Tom. 2011. *Hollywood 9/11: Superheroes, Supervillains, and Super Disasters*. Boulder: Paradigm.
Randewich, Noel. 2017. Wall Street Hits Record High as Investors Eye Mergers. *Reuters*, November 6.
Smith, David, and Jamie Grierson. 2018. Donald Trump Says London Hospital Is Like "War Zone" Because of Knife Crime. *The Guardian*, May 5.
Sobchack, Vivian. 2004. *Screening Space: The American Science Fiction Film*. 2nd ed. New Brunswick: Rutgers University Press.
———. 2017. Abject Times: Temporality and the Science Fiction Film in Post-9/11 America. In *Reality Unbound: New Departures in Science Fiction Cinema*, ed. Aidan Power, Delia González de Reufels, Rasmus Greiner, and Winfried Pauleit, 12–33. Berlin: Bertz+Fischer.

Starobinski, Jean. 1990. Les Cheminées et les clochers. *Magazine littéraire* 280: 26–27.
Treaty on the Functioning of the European Union. *Official Journal*, 115, 2008. eur-lex.europa.eu/legal-content/EN/TXT/?uri=CELEX:12008E207.
Trump Hits Out at UK PM Theresa May After Far-right Video Tweets. *BBC*, November 30, 2017, '28 Days Later.' *Box Office Mojo*. www.boxofficemojo.com/movies/?id=28dayslater.htm. Accessed 1 May 2018.
Unemployment Statistics. *Eurostat*. ec.europa.eu/eurostat/statistics-explained/index.php?title=Unemployment_statistics. Accessed 1 May 2018.
Urry, John. 2007. *Mobilities*. Oxford: Polity.
Vickers, Rhiannon. 2018. The Marshall Plan and Consumerism. *The Vienna Review*, June 1. www.viennareview.net/news/front-page/the-marshall-plan-and-consumerism. Accessed 1 May 2018.
Vineyard, Jennifer. 2006. Alan Moore: The Last Angry Man. *MTV*, August 30. www.bbc.com/news/world-us-canada-42176507. Accessed 1 May 2018.
Zenko, Micah. 2016. Obama's Embrace of Drone Strikes Will Be a Lasting Legacy. *New York Times*, January 12.

PART V

Beyond Europe?

CHAPTER 9

Conclusions and Roads Ahead

A fundamental difficulty with writing about the EU in the twenty-first century is the omnipresent risk of instant obsolescence. When I first outlined the contours of this project in 2013, Europe was a much different place, as was the world at large. For one thing Britain was still a fully functioning, if occasionally cantankerous, member of the EU, while further East—and with Croatia on the cusp of full EU membership—the nascent Euromaidan movement in Ukraine hinted that deeper European integration (and expansion) might soon be afoot. Outside of Europe, Barack Obama held the US presidency and had declared that further use of chemical weapons by Bashar al-Assad in Syria would constitute 'a red line', a threat that had yet to be proved empty (Hunt, 'Obama's Red Line Comes Back to Haunt Him'). Concurrently, Jama'at al-Tawhid wal-Jihad had yet to spawn ISIS and attempt to establish a caliphate across Syria and northern Iraq. In other news, a television personality named Donald Trump followed luminaries such as The Bushwhackers and Sgt. Slaughter in being inducted into World Wrestling Entertainment Incorporated's Hall of Fame in Madison Square Garden. It is tempting, albeit futile, to imagine the ramifications for Europe and the world at large had even one of these situations evolved differently: yet, all serve too to highlight the ephemeral nature of much that we hold to be self-evident. In his seminal text *Mobilities*, the sociologist John Urry cautioned against what he described as 'an epochal hubris that presumes that one's own moment is somehow a special moment in transition and hence that decisions taken in the moment of the now are more fateful than those that have been taken at other times' (277). While he is of course right, one cannot but be taken by the sheer weirdness of the world right now, or the swiftness with which we have come to accept chaos as an everyday component of our lives. As the examples of Britain and Croatia show, the cartographic composition of the EU remains in flux, perhaps now more so than ever, while Russia's annexation of Crimea—an event that seems to have been largely forgotten by a media dazzled by the Kremlin's efforts to influence foreign elections—exposes the deceit that Europe at large has been becalmed by the supposed triumph of Western democracy. Suffice to say that writing on and attempting to keep up to date with contemporary crises in the European context is akin to holding water in one's hands. Sf films have thankfully provided me with an anchor to try to make sense of things, even if some of their narratives look almost pallid when set against a timeline of real-life events. Perhaps because of this, sf appears to me more vital than ever, signifying somehow a vanguard of resistance against forces that would seek to push back against the tides of change and seek refuge in blinkered notions of tradition. Or, to return to a quotation of Isaac Asimov relayed in this book's introductory chapter, sf is important because it 'fights the natural notion that there's something permanent about things the way they are right now' (Freedman, *Conversations with Isaac Asimov* 135). Novels such as *Nineteen Eighty-Four* or the *Handmaid's Tale* were meant to serve as warnings to society after all, not as prospective manuals for governance.

Omissions and Partial Histories

It is my hope that in providing a survey of twenty-first-century European sf, this book also delivers a snapshot of a particular moment in time or a counter history if you will. That said, any claim to historicity on my part is of course at best partial. Much can be gleaned from this book's omissions, just as I hope something worthwhile can be taken from the case studies that have been included. A stated goal was to identify some of the greatest crises to have beset the EU in recent times and chart the ways in which sf films have engaged with them. Essaying the fallout from the economic and migration crises was therefore imperative, but I freely allow that both occurrences impacted upon individuals in a multitude of ways. In relation to the economic crisis, for example, I have endeavoured to show how neoliberal policies have reinforced underlying fault lines in European society, amongst them the enduring blight of patriarchy. As I wrote in Chap. 3, however, European sf cinema is itself guilty of gender discrimination, particularly given that, even now, the overwhelming bulk of its directors are male. Therefore, while films such as *Womb* (Benedek Fliegauf 2010), *Ex Machina* (Alex Garland 2015), and *Under the Skin* (Jonathan Glazer 2013) tackle questions of female bodily autonomy, they do little, as male-directed productions, to tackle industrial biases against women: biases that as we have seen extend to European society at large.[1] Directors such as Stéphanie Joalland, Kristina Buožytė, and Franny Armstrong buck this trend, but there is clearly some distance to travel before anything approaching equality can be glimpsed, as the wave of sexual assault scandals that rocked Hollywood and the wider world throughout 2017 makes clear.

A separate complication is that a definitive view of the EU cannot be provided from within the EU itself. With this book, I have attempted to provide a survey of twenty-first-century European sf films, linking my findings to wider socio-economic and political happenings during this time. Insofar as this has not been attempted before, I remain hopeful that such an approach has merit. Nevertheless, for a more complete picture to eventually emerge, I contend that ultimately a decentring of Europe itself needs to be undertaken in order to attend to outside sf visions of the EU. After all, the outlook from Paris, Brussels, London, or Berlin is hardly paradigmatic of views from the rest of the world, vast tracts of which were colonised and plundered by European nations. Indeed, the crises faced by the politicians who preside over Europe's comparatively wealthy economies must appear tame to denizens of the 'developing nations' of the Global South—a description we apply liberally to conceal the fact that their development has been systematically stymied by centuries of European subjugation. I have tackled these issues in Chaps. 4 and 7, albeit from the standpoint of European cinema: a standpoint that in this regard will always be partial.

Cinema does not exist in a vacuum. By mixing examinations of film industries with aesthetic analysis, I have attempted to make clear the material connections between often fantastical or esoteric films and the economic environments from which they have emerged. In the case of Bulgaria, for instance, this meant analysing an industry without any 'native' sf films: a reality attributable to US capital certainly, yet one that was facilitated by an opening up of the Bulgarian economy that EU membership necessitated. Globalisation remains at the heart of European policy, an aspect reflected in film production and distribution as well as one that the acceptance of Canada—as the 38th and first non-European member of Eurimages in March 2017—makes clear. While it would be churlish to suggest that globalisation has had an entirely negative impact on Europe—if anything it has doubled down on Europe's historical privileges—the suspicion remains that the advantages proffered by the free market are coming with an increasingly exorbitant price tag. Within five kilometres of the office in which I write this resides the European headquarters of Apple, as well as major branches of Dell EMC and Amazon, amongst a host of other multinational corporations that are major employers in what is but a small, regional city. None of this would be possible without access to the EU market, yet history teaches us that relying upon the benevolence of multinational corporations is hardly a sustainable long-term economic plan. As we saw in Chap. 6, Tarik Saleh's *Metropia* envisions the consequences for the EU when corporations begin to subsume the social functions of states, and if its vision of the EU in 2024 seems unduly alarmist, we have already seen in Chaps. 4 and 5 how the commodification of European social life was greatly extended during the economic crisis in the Eurozone.

Moving Forward

Having looked in depth at onscreen portrayals of European futures—a great deal of which are negative and, thus, seemingly endorsing the Jamesonian perspective that we have lost the ability to imagine brighter futures—some obvious questions remain about the future of the EU. All such films are products of the European environment from whence they came, and it should depress us slightly to learn that even sf funded by the Council of Europe essentially suggests that we are doomed. Let's consider some of these films momentarily. *Time of the Wolf* envisions a European no-man's land/continental refugee camp where the strong prey on the weak and death trains rattle by but never stop. *Melancholia* imagines not just the death of enlightenment values and centuries of European artistic practices but also the instantaneous eradication of the planet itself. *Iron Sky* meanwhile restages the defeat of the Nazis only for the Allies to swiftly turn on one another and effect a nuclear war—if the plot sounds ludicrous, we should remember that, moon Nazis aside, this almost happened during the Cold War. Meanwhile for all its absurdity, *The Lobster* arguably comes closest to engaging with the stark realities of the EU's policies, in that it presents its blameless protagonists with two terrible choices, both of which presuppose the infallibility of those doing the asking. Moreover, they foreclose the possibility that a third way may be possible. Again, there is a solid historical precedent at play, particularly if we consider the ideological surrender of the European left to the interests of big business since the late 1970s, a process described thusly by Zygmunt Bauman:

> The abrupt surrender of state control over capital's undertakings did not happen without resistance. There was a time following the Reaganite/ Thatcherite coup d'etat when Europeans voted social democrats back into power in thirteen out of fifteen member states of the European Union. It proved to be a short-lived episode, though. All over the place, though with varying degrees of conviction and zeal, the parties once identified with the project of the social state presided, once in government, over its further dismantling. Instead of reasserting public control over public resources, they ceded more national assets to the free play of market forces and made more resources once excluded from commodification amenable to profit-making and capital accumulation. (*Europe: An Unfinished Adventure* 78)

Unsettling as the continental upsurge of the far-right in recent years may be, it is an occurrence made possible, in large part, by the paralysis of the left in the face of the free market: a collapse analogous to the European left's abandoning of nationalism to the right and a trend that stands in stark contrast to leftist politics in other areas of the globe, such as South America. Citing Europe's experiences, Bauman decrees that 'there are no local solutions to global problems', for 'the globalization of capital and trade, the removal of capital's local restraints and obligations, and the resulting extraterritoriality of major economic forces have made a "social state in one country" all but a contradiction in terms' (*Europe* 78). The EU's treatment of Greece bears this out, illustrating a truth that Ulrike Guérot describes as 'self-evident in today's EU: that a people can be governed by a single market, that deregulation is the goal and that anyone who proposes social controls of markets is a dangerous Marxist radical' ('Millions of Voters Didn't Want Brexit: Why Should They Lose EU Citizenship'). In this vein, one of the more brutal consequences of *The Lobster*'s seemingly inalienable decree—one that I neglected to mention in my analysis of the film—is how it leads characters to turn on one another: indeed it actively encourages it. In the finest traditions of divide-and-conquer tactics, single people in *The Lobster* can prolong the time allocated to them to find a companion, by hunting down other fugitive singles.

Amidst a highly fraught situation, pitting people against one another serves the purpose of reinforcing the overarching system, while occluding from vision and public discourse its underlying callousness. 'What is crippling', to invoke Jameson, 'is not the presence of an enemy but rather the universal belief, not only that this tendency is irreversible, but that the historic alternatives to capitalism have been proven unviable and impossible, and that no other socioeconomic system is conceivable, let alone practically available' (*Archaeologies* xii). Nationally, we see such division in the demonisation of welfare recipients or minorities, while on an EU-wide scale, fault is routinely ascribed to 'lazy' Greeks, even if job security is increasingly becoming a thing of the past and statistics show that Greek workers in fact work the longest hours in the EU.[2] Accordingly, let's consider my home country of Ireland for a moment, a nation that has undoubtedly been one of the major historical beneficiaries of the European project. Light on large-scale native industry, the nation's future is almost entirely contingent on the presence of multinational corporations on its shores, corporations that in turn thrive upon deregulation and indeterminate loopholes in the free market. At the height of the economic crisis in 2011 and with the nation's major export once more its own people, the then Prime Minister Enda Kenny expressed his belief that, within five years, Ireland would 'become the best small country in the world in which to do business' (O' Dwyer, 'Doing Business in Ireland: Not Quite the Best Small Country for Businesses'). Remaining loyal Europeans and dutifully swallowing the economic medicines prescribed by the EU would be a non-negotiable step in this process, and by the end of Kenny's tenure, Ireland did indeed emerge blinking into the sunlight, newly prosperous and a shining example to its errant Southern European neighbours. Yet, somewhere along the well-trodden path from bust to boom, it had been forgotten that central to Kenny's election strategy was a pledge to secure a write-down on Ireland's mountainous debt—an initiative that was summarily quashed by the European Central Bank ('Kenny's big gaffe was in the Dáil, not in Davos'). The taxpayer, instead, shouldered the entire cost of Ireland's collapsed banking sector, while bondholders of those same banks had their investments protected. Meanwhile, Apple, which by 2017 was worth in excess of $750 billion[3] and has operated in Ireland since 1980, was ordered by the European Commission to pay €13 billion in unpaid taxes to the Irish State, a ruling that in a tragi-comic turn of events the Irish government set out to appeal ('Ireland Forced to Collect €13bn in Tax from Apple That it Doesn't Want').[4] Even though by any metric, social inequality has worsened considerably in the interim—as exemplified by interlinked homeless and housing crises—or that the nation now possesses a crippling level of debt, which will be felt for generations to come, Ireland had 'bounced back' and was to become, in the words of Kenny's successor Leo Varadkar, 'a light unto the world' (Duggan, 'Q&A: Ireland's Leo Varadkar on Brexit, Trump and Keeping Ireland "At the Center of the World"'). Under the subheading 'Globalism has been good to Ireland', Varadkar adorned the cover of *Time* magazine within weeks of his becoming (unelected) Taoiseach in June 2017, burnishing the island's image as a champion of the free market and, by proxy, as a shining example of the ultimate rectitude of the EU's austerity policies. No matter that Greece remained floundering or that two weeks earlier the Italian government was forced to bail out two prominent banks, again relieving bondholders and saddling an additional €17 billion of debt on Italian taxpayers.[5] In fact, as early as 2015, Ireland was already arguing against any write-down of Greek debt, showcasing an attitude which has long held traction in Germany[6] and that we can sum up here as 'we ate shit, so they should too'. As we have seen in Chap. 3 with regard to the refugee crisis, notions of solidarity in a EU sphere are all too frequently aspired to up until the point that they collide with national interests.

And so, despite the announced point of departure of how we might imagine a better future for the EU, not surprisingly we arrive crippled by existing practices at an impasse. The problem with the EU, though it may not appear revelatory, *is* the EU itself: and until we can think beyond its current architecture and imagine something genuinely new, we will remain in crisis. For all that non-believers may laugh at the notion, sf can play a role in doing just that. If nothing else, the resurgence of the genre in a European sphere—one that this book has set out to track—shows a willingness on the part of filmmakers to respond to their circumstances and at least try to imagine alternatives. And so what if their plots seem far-fetched? Does anybody seriously look at the state of the world right now and deduce that things are somehow normal? Sf is a call to action, a testing ground and a point of departure for a society 'where one cannot imagine any fundamental change in our social existence which has not first thrown off Utopian visions like so many sparks from a comet' (Jameson, *Archaeologies* xii). European integration started out as an experiment and a radical one at that. And because of this, some faith in the EU remains, if only because the prospect of a Europe-wide retreat into toxic nationalism is almost too depressing to countenance. There remains a sense, however ill-founded, that for most Europeans the continuation of the European project remains in their best interests and that, in the words of the late British MP Jo Cox, that 'we are far more united than the things that divide us'. With the United States increasingly intent to abdicate responsibility, moreover, the EU's role as a peace broker and advocate for scientific advancement suddenly seems more urgent than ever. Whether a relentless pursuance of market appeasement and austerity measures has fatally undermined it, however, remains to be seen. Utopia, as Lyman Tower Sargent wrote, advocated change catering 'to our ability to dream, to recognize that things are not quite what they should be, and to assert that improvement is possible' ('The Three Faces of Utopianism Revisited' 26). It can be a destination in other words that even if it remains out of reach can at least point us in the right direction, just as the EU, as I have argued throughout this book, can best be described as a pragmatic utopia, one that for all its compromises has helped bring a general, if not total, peace to Europe. In the current climate, it would be dangerous to take such a noble accomplishment for granted. Read this way, the sf films analysed in this book, though perhaps overwhelmingly dystopian in theme, are a diagnosis of sorts, for even if bleak in places and fantastical in others, they all ask us to consider fundamental questions about the EU and the value that we place in it, questions that must be answered, if we wish to proceed with the ongoing project that is Europe.

Notes

1. The struggle for European women to maintain autonomy over their own bodies remains a pressing concern, as recent attempts at suppressing women's rights in Poland make clear—to say nothing of the draconian abortion laws that long persisted in the Republic of Ireland prior to the landmark 2018 referendum on the removal of the Eighth Amendment from the country's constitution.
2. Findings from a 2015 Organisation for Economic Co-operation and Development report show that the average Greek worker worked 42 hours a week, as distinct from Germans, for example, who on average work 35.5 hours a week (*Forbes*, 13 March 2015).
3. In May 2017, Forbes listed Apple as the largest public company in America as well as the world's most valuable brand. Apple's market cap (or total market value of all of its shares) was listed by the same publication at $752 billion ('America's Largest Public Companies').

4. The fear persists for the Irish government that accepting the EC's findings would be tantamount to admitting that Ireland's corporate tax rules provide it with an unfair advantage over other EU nations, which, as we saw in Chap. 4, is essentially what the EC was suggesting ('State Aid: Ireland Gave Illegal Tax Benefits to Apple Worth up to €13 Billion'). Given the high number of multinationals based in Ireland (and the large numbers of voters that they employ), Irish politicians have long demonstrated a marked reluctance to say anything that could be construed as critical of this arrangement.
5. After an emergency cabinet meeting on 25 June 2017, the Italian government announced its intention to wind up the failing banks Veneto Banca and Banca Popolare di Vicenza. As reported in *The Guardian*, the government then intended to liquidate both lenders, a plan 'which leaves the state footing the bill for bad loans on both banks' books, plus restructuring costs' (Wearden, 'Italy to wind up two failing banks at potential cost of €17bn').
6. In an interview with the *New Federalist*, Ulrike Guérot points to a discrepancy between German academic and public attitudes towards the crisis, noting that while scientific publications frequently sought to address 'the central institutional deficiencies of the Euro governance [...] in the political discourse we had a different discussion going on. [...] This discussion was dominated by the idea, that we in Germany "pay for everybody", that we are the victim' ('An Invitation to Bravely Think About the Future of Europe').

Bibliography

America's Largest Public Companies. 2017. *Forbes*, May. www.forbes.com/companies/apple/. Accessed 1 May 2018.

Bauman, Zygmunt. 2004. *Europe: An Unfinished Adventure*. Malden: Polity.

Bergfelder, Tim. 2005. The Nation Vanishes: European Co-productions and Popular Genre Formula in the 1950s and 1960s. In *Cinema and Nation*, ed. Mette Hjort and Scott Mackenzie, 139–152. London: Routledge.

Browne, Vincent. 2012. Kenny's Big Gaffe Was in the Dáil, Not in Davos. *The Business Post*, January 29.

Duggan, Jennifer. 2017. Duggan, 'Q&A: Ireland's Leo Varadkar on Brexit, Trump and Keeping Ireland "At the Center of the World". *Time*, July 13.

Freedman, Carl. 2005. *Conversations with Isaac Asimov*. Jackson: University of Mississippi Press.

Guérot, Ulrike. 2016a. An Invitation to Bravely Think About the Future of Europe. *The New Federalist*, August 12.

———. 2016b. Millions of Voters Didn't Want Brexit: Why Should They Lose EU Citizenship? *The Guardian*, July 1.

Hunt, Albert R. 2013. Obama's Red Line Comes Back to Haunt Him. *New York Times*, September 2.
Ireland Forced to Collect €13bn in Tax from Apple That it Doesn't Want. 2017. *The Guardian*, December 5.
Jameson, Fredric. 2005. *Archaeologies of the Future: A Desire Called Utopia and Other Science Fictions*. New York: Verso.
Marx, Karl. 1867. *Capital: A Critique of Political Economy. Volume I: The Economist*. Hamburg: Verlag von Otto Meisner.
O' Dwyer, Peter. 2016. Doing Business in Ireland: Not Quite the Best Small Country for Businesses. *Irish Examiner*, July 18.
Peet, John. 2014. The Luck of the Irish. *The Economist*, October 14.
Power, Aidan. 2017. Modern Inclinations: Locating European Science Fiction Cinema of the 1960s and 1970s. In *Future Imperfect: Science, Fiction, Film*, ed. Rainer Rother and Annika Schaefer, 29–41. Berlin: Bertz & Fischer.
Rohac, Dalibor. 2015. Europe Returns to the 1930s. *Politico*, September 9. www.politico.eu/article/europe-returns-to-the-1930s-revolt-leadeship-nazi/. Accessed 1 May 2018.
Roth, Philip. 2004. *The Plot Against America*. Boston: Houghton Mifflin.
Sargent, Lyman Tower. 1994. The Three Faces of Utopianism Revisited. *Utopian Studies* 5 (1): 1–37.
State Aid: Ireland Gave Illegal Tax Benefits to Apple Worth up to €13 Billion. 2016. *European Commission*, August 30. europa.eu/rapid/press-release_IP-16-2923_en.htm. Accessed 1 May 2018.
Thurman, Judith. 2017. Phillip Roth E-mails on Trump. *The New Yorker*, January 30.
Urry, John. 2007. *Mobilities*. Cambridge: Polity.
Wearden, Graeme. 2017. Italy to Wind Up Two Failing Banks at Potential Cost of €17bn. *The Guardian*, June 25.

Index[1]

NUMBERS AND SYMBOLS
28 Days Later, 16, 224–233, 236, 241, 243n9
28 Weeks Later, 21, 206, 225, 227–229, 232–237, 239, 241

A
Adventure, The/L'Avventura, 133n26, 221
Age of Stupid, The, 20, 170, 172–175, 178
Alessandrin, Patrick, 197, 201, 203
Ali, Mo, 204, 205
Alphaville/Alphaville: une étrange aventure de Lemmy Caution, 14, 18
Alps/Alpeis, 139, 140, 143, 163
Alternative für Deutschland, 192
Amour, 36, 79
Angus, Ian, 166, 169
Anthropocene, 21, 163–185
Antonioni, Michelangelo, 77, 133n26, 221
Apple Inc., 121, 132n25, 254, 256, 258n3
Armstrong, Franny, 20, 170, 172–175, 180, 253
Asimov, Isaac, 13, 16, 252
Assad, Bashar-al, 213n4, 251
Attack the Block, 120, 196, 204, 205, 209–212, 215n22, 215n23, 227
Atwood, Margaret, 180
Augé, Marc, 234, 235, 244n12
Avatar, 13, 23n14, 106, 222, 223, 242n3

B
Baccolini, Raffaella, 121, 122
Baishya, Anirban Kapil, 235, 236
Balkan War, 65, 66
Banlieue 13, 195, 197–201, 204, 214n14

---

[1] Note: Page numbers followed by 'n' refer to notes.

Banlieue 13: Ultimatum, 197, 199–204
Baudrillard, Jean, 64, 65
Bauman, Zygmunt, 8, 184, 194, 255
Bergman, Ingmar, 43, 221
Berlusconi, Silvio, 123, 125, 128, 133n29
Besson, Luc, 178, 180, 195, 197, 199, 203, 223
Blade Runner, 131n18, 182
Blair, Tony, 98, 150, 227, 234, 243n10, 244n11
Bould, Mark, 9, 18
Boyle, Danny, 17, 225, 227, 230–232, 241
Brazys, Samuel, 95, 96, 129n5, 130n8
Brecht, Bertolt, 16, 144, 145, 156n5
Brenner, Neil, 99, 111
Brexit, 5, 8, 11, 12, 23n13, 53, 55, 83n15, 121, 194, 207, 241, 257
Brick Mansions, 199, 200
Brief Encounter, 231
Brody, Richard, 142, 155n2
Brunette, Peter, 43
Buñuel, Luis, 77, 79
Buožytė, Kristina, 19, 34, 74–77, 79, 86n32, 180, 253
Bush, George W., 150, 225–229, 242, 243n7
Butler, Octavia, 180

C

Cabinet of Dr. Caligari, The/Das Cabinet des Dr. Caligari, 77, 78, 86n31
Cabral, Ricardo, 104–106, 110
Cameron, David, 3, 192, 207, 208, 213n2
Campbell, Bruce, 60
Canary Wharf, 233, 234
Cannes Film Festival, 42, 46, 67

Carnation Revolution, 110, 111
Carney, John, 112, 115–117
Carney, Kieran, 112, 115
Carriers, 148, 149
Catalan independence movement, 20
Celtic Tiger, 114, 116, 120, 121
Children of Men, 154, 214n13, 228, 229
Chomsky, Noam, 7, 23n8, 164, 165, 167, 244n14
Churchill, Winston, 3–6, 22n4, 22n7
Clarke, Arthur C., 16
Climate change, 4, 20, 21, 163–185, 224
Code Unknown/Code inconnu, 35, 39
Coelho, Pedro Passos, 101
Cold War, 9, 54, 55, 156n6, 254
Collins, Richard, 6, 7, 22n7
Cornish, Joe, 120, 204, 205, 209, 212
Council of Europe (CoE), 19, 29, 30, 33, 35, 36, 40, 41, 47, 48, 49n10, 141, 254
Council of the European Union, 73
Cowen, Brian, v
Cox, Jo, 60, 258
Crimea, 54, 252
Csicsery-Ronay, Istvan, 109
Cuarón, Alfonso, 154, 214n13, 223, 228
Cubitt, Sean, 17, 171

D

Dalí, Salvador, 79
Dancer in the Dark, 35, 42
Dawn of the Dead, 150
Day the Earth Stood Still, The, 116, 128, 169, 209
Delamarre, Camille, 199
Detroit Riots, 200
Dogme 95, 43

Dogtooth/Kynodontas, 139, 140, 143–145, 147
Doomsday, 229, 243n9
Dr. Strangelove, 47
Dumb and Dumber, 163

E
Eleftheriotis, Dimitris, 18
Element Pictures, 117, 141
Elsaesser, Thomas, 18, 32, 34, 35, 56, 224
Emmerich, Roland, 182, 187n12
Erdoğan, Recep, 54
Eurimages, 19, 29–48, 58, 59, 75, 85n24, 113, 140–142, 149, 152, 175, 222, 254
Euromaidan movement, 251
European Central Bank, 10, 44, 94, 96, 147, 256
European Coal and Steel Community (ECSC), 5, 7, 29
European Commission, 10, 11, 74, 76, 85n28, 94, 96, 121, 132n25, 153, 167, 256
European Economic Community (EEC), 5, 6, 8, 29, 30, 104, 110, 146, 156n6
European Free Trade Association, 222
European Union (EU), vii, 3–12, 17, 19–21, 22n7, 23n9, 23n13, 29–33, 36, 39, 40, 44, 45, 48, 50n13, 53–81, 83n14, 84n18, 93–95, 97, 98, 100–105, 115, 120, 121, 128, 129n1, 131n12, 132n25, 143, 147, 149–153, 156n7, 163, 167, 168, 171, 172, 175, 178, 184, 187n14, 191–194, 196, 203, 213n3, 222, 229, 241, 251–258, 259n4
Eurozone, v, vii, 10, 11, 20, 36, 40, 44, 93–95, 99, 100, 102, 103, 105, 114, 129n1, 129n3, 129n4, 131n13, 143, 149, 153, 171, 254

F
Fahrenheit 451, 14
Fassbinder, Rainer Werner, 14, 77, 221
Fehlbaum, Tim, 21, 170, 182, 183
Fekete, Liz, 70, 84n17
Ferreri, Mara, 208, 211
Fianna Fáil, v, 103
Fidesz, 69, 71, 72, 83n14, 83n15, 84n16, 84n18
Fine Gael, 103
Fisher, Mark, 98, 100, 103, 124, 155n3
Flassbeck, Heiner, 100
Foucault, Michel, 109, 184
Fresnadillo, Juan Carlos, 21, 225, 227, 232, 233, 236, 238, 241
Freud, Sigmund, 78, 80, 81
Friedman, Milton, 98, 102, 131n13
Fritzsche, Sonja, 17, 18
Fukuyama, Francis, 10, 99

G
Galt, Rosalind, 34, 37, 49n3, 130n9
Garland, Alex, 253
Gender pay gap, 153
General Agreement on Tariffs and Trade (GATT), 224, 242n5
Gentrification, 120, 209, 211, 212
German Expressionism, 15, 77
Globalization, 33, 56, 82n5, 94, 184, 185, 191, 253–255
Global South, 10, 165, 166, 168, 172, 253
Godard, Jean-Luc, 14, 35, 37, 221
Golden Age, The/L'Âge d'or, 77, 79
Grabbers, 113, 115, 117–121, 222

Grenfell Tower fire, 208
Grundmann, Roy, 41
Guérot, Ulrike, 97, 255, 259n6
Guess Who's Coming to Dinner?, 71

H
Habermas, Jürgen, 7
Halle, Randall, 31
Haneke, Michael, 14, 19, 30, 32, 35–37, 39–42, 48, 49n3, 49n8, 49n9, 141, 221, 224
Hardiman, Niamh, 95, 96, 129n5, 130n8
Harvey, David, 56, 130n11, 173, 244n11
Hate/La Haine, 204
Hayek, Friedrich, 98
Hell, 21, 170, 178, 179, 182–185
Heygate Estate, 205–209
Heygate Leaseholder's Group (HLG), 211
Hitchcock, Alfred, 77, 179, 238
Hunter, I.Q., 17

I
I Love You, I Love You/Je t'aime, je t'aime, 14
Indiana Jones and the Kingdom of the Crystal Skull, 222
International Monetary Fund (IMF), v, vi, 10, 44, 96, 99, 100, 125, 128
Internet Movie Database, 223
Invasion of the Body Snatchers, 209
Iordanova, Dina, 58, 59, 82n6
Irish Film Board (IFB), 112–118, 142
Iron Sky, 19, 30, 32, 34–37, 45–48, 222, 254
Islamic State of Iraq and the Levant, 10, 213n4, 225, 251
Italian Neorealism, 14

J
Jameson, Fredric, 9, 12, 98, 120, 172, 256, 257
Jetty, The/La Jetée, 14
Joalland, Stéphanie, 21, 113, 170, 179–181, 253
Jupiter's Moon/Jupiter holdja, 19, 34, 57, 67–74
Jurassic World, 13, 223, 242n3

K
Kääpä, Pietari, 46, 47, 177
Kafka, Franzd, 178
Kenny, Enda, 256, 257
Kershaw, Ian, 6, 22n6, 23n11
Khan, Sadiq, 241, 244n15
Klein, Naomi, 101, 102, 131n13, 131n14, 156n7, 186n5, 194
Koutsourakis, Angelos, 144, 145, 156n5, 171, 186n7
Krasteva, Yonka, 55, 56
Kristeva, Julia, 80, 81
Kubrick, Stanley, 47, 112

L
Lake District, 229–232, 241
Lang, Fritz, 14, 221
Lanthimos, Yorgos, 14, 20, 34, 35, 113, 117, 139–148, 155n1, 155n2, 221
Lapavitsas, Costas, 100
Last Days, The/Los Últimos Días, 20, 104, 148–154, 180
Last Man on Earth, The/ L'ultimo terrestre, 20, 121–124, 126–129
Law and Justice Party/Prawo i Sprawiedliwość, 69, 168
Le Guin, Ursula, 180
Le Pen, Marine, 11, 81n1, 192, 193, 203
Lean, David, 231
Lees, Loretta, 208, 211

Lehman Brothers, 9, 93
Lisbon Treaty, 23n9, 44
Liz, Mariana, 30, 31, 48n1, 93, 132n19
Lobster, The, 20, 34, 104, 113, 115, 139–145, 147, 148, 155n2, 156n9, 196, 224, 254, 255
Lochery, Neill, 105
Lucy, 180, 223
LUMIERE Pro database, 222
Lykidis, Alex, 40

M
Maastricht Treaty, 81n2, 93, 94, 99, 104, 193, 224
Maček, Ivana, 63, 65
Macron, Emmanuel, 11
'Mad Cow' disease, 113, 230
Mad Max: Fury Road, 178
Maier, Charles, S., 236
Marasović, Nevio, 19, 62, 65, 83n11
Marker, Chris, 14, 221
Marques, Viriato Soromenho, 104–106, 110
Marshall Plan, 5, 7, 102, 224, 236, 237, 241
Marx, Karl, vi, viiin1, 171, 186n8
Matrix, The, 85n27, 198
May, Theresa, 214n10, 241, 244n15
Mazierska, Ewa, 18, 56
MEDIA (Mesures pour l'encouragement et le developpement de l'industrie audiovisuelle), 31, 48n1, 85n24, 149, 175
Mediating Cultural Encounters through European Screens, 222
Melancholia, 30, 32, 34–36, 38, 41–46, 48, 49n6, 50n12, 254
Méliès d'Or, 75, 85n25, 109
Méliès, Georges, 4, 22n2

Merkel, Angela, 146, 147, 192, 194, 196, 213n2, 213n7
Meštrović, Stjepan, 65, 66
Metropia, 21, 34, 35, 170, 172, 175–178, 254
Mises, Ludwig von, 98
Molenbeek, 196
Monbiot, George, 98, 99, 171, 172
Monnet, Jean, 7, 177
Morel, Pierre, 197, 198
More, Thomas, 9
Mount Blanc, 163, 174
Movimento Cinque Stelle, 103
Moylan, Tom, 13
Mr. Nobody, 34, 49n7
Multiculturalism, 21, 191–212
Mundruczó, Kornél, 19, 34, 57, 67, 68, 70–72, 83n12

N
Navarro, Tino, 20, 104, 106, 109
Neoliberalism, 98, 99, 103, 111, 124, 130n11, 153, 171–173
Neo-Nazis, 72, 83n15, 148
9/11, 150, 224–229, 233–235, 243n7
North Atlantic Treaty Organization (NATO), 54, 62, 227, 236, 238, 244n14
Nu Boyana Film Studios, 19, 61, 83n10

O
Obama, Barack, 226, 243n7, 251
Okorafor, Nnedi, 180
Orbán, Viktor, 68–71, 74, 83n13, 83n14, 84n18, 84n20
Orwell, George, 83n11
Oxfam, 105, 130n10, 131n15, 153, 185n2

P

Pacinotti, Gianni, 20, 121–123, 125, 126
Papandreou, George, 128, 147, 156n8
Paris Agreement, 167, 168, 226
Paris riots, 196, 197, 215n17
Pastor Àlex, 20, 148
Pastor, David, 20
Peck, Jamie, 99
Penley, Constance, 12, 169
Petri, Elio, 106, 121
Petterson, David, 199–201, 214n16
Phillips, Tony, 97, 99
Piano Teacher, The/La pianist, 39, 49n9
PIIGS (Portugal, Ireland, Italy, Greece, and Spain), 10, 20, 93–129, 139–155
Pinochet, Augusto, 102, 131n13
Planet of the Apes, 183
Plot Against America, The, 4
Precarity, 3, 9, 20, 98, 101, 103, 104, 121–127, 134n36, 150, 168, 195
Pueyo, Víctor, 150
Purse, Lisa, 198, 200, 201
Putin, Vladimir, 54

Q

Quiet Hour, The, 21, 113, 115, 170, 178–183, 185

R

Reagan, Ronald, 98, 99, 131n13, 234, 241, 244n11
Real Playing Game, 20, 104, 106–111, 131n17
Rear Window, 238, 239, 241
Rebordão, David, 20, 104, 106, 109
Resnais, Alain, 14, 43, 221
Rivi, Luisa, 22n3, 29, 55, 130n9
Roman Holiday, 239–241
Rossellini, Roberto, 221

Roth, Philip, 4, 21–22n1
Ryner, Magnus, 101, 102, 129n2

S

Saleh, Tarik, 20, 34, 35, 170, 175, 178, 186n9, 254
Sardar, Ziauddin, 17
Sarkozy, Nicolas, 192, 193, 201, 213n2, 214n16
Sayre, Nathan F., 168–170
Schengen Area, 55, 94
Seconds, 106
Shank, 196, 204–207, 209, 215n18, 227
Sharpe, Kenan Behzat, 143
Shelley, Mary, 17, 224
Shklovsky, Viktor, 16
Shohat, Ella, 191, 194, 195, 203, 212n1, 213n5
Show Must Go On, The, 19, 57, 62–67, 83n11
Siege of Sarajevo, 63
Simpsons, The, vi
Sinnerbrink, Robert, 42, 43
Sobchack, Vivian, vi, 37, 206, 226, 230, 240
Sorrentino, Paolo, 117, 142
Soviet Union, 5, 7, 9, 53, 56, 68, 72, 74, 76, 81, 99, 172
Spielberg, Steven, 23n14, 50n15, 85n27, 118, 128, 222
Springer, Claudia, 4
Srebrenica Massacre, 41, 63
Stam, Robert, 191, 194, 195, 203, 212n1, 213n5
Star Wars: The Force Awakens, 13, 114, 222, 223, 242n3
Suvin, Darko, 16, 144
Svalbard Global Seed Vault, 173, 174
Syfy Channel, 61
Syrian Civil War, 72
Syriza, 100, 103, 147, 172

T
Tansley, A.G., 168
Tarkovsky, Andrei, 14, 43, 178
Taylor, Damilola, 205
Tenth Victim, The/La decima vittima, 106, 121
Thatcher, Margaret, 98, 99, 131n13, 229, 234, 241, 244n11
Theodore, Nik, 99, 111
Third Reich, 6, 9, 45
This Must be the Place, 142
Time of the Wolf/Le temps du loup, 30
Todorov, Tzvetan, 16
Torner, Evan, 18, 39, 40
Torrano, Gallardo, 149, 151, 152
Treaty of Rome, 3, 5, 7, 9, 11, 22n3, 29, 96
Trial, The, 178
Troika, The, 96, 97, 99–101, 105, 111, 114, 119, 146
Truffaut, François, 14, 221
Truman Doctrine, 236
Trump, Donald, 4, 21–22n1, 69, 164, 168, 186n5, 195, 214n9, 225, 226, 241, 242, 244n15, 251, 257

U
UKIP, 83n15, 192, 213n3
Under the Skin, 180, 253
Unemployment, vi, viiin2, 9, 11, 44, 50n13, 101, 103, 105, 106, 111, 124, 125, 129, 133n30, 134n36
UNESCO World Heritage Sites, 115, 168
United Nations, 31, 165, 167, 168
Urry, John, 184, 231, 235, 238, 251
Utopia, 6–9, 11, 12, 23n11, 41, 154, 258

V
Vanishing Waves/Aurora, 19, 57, 74
Varadkar, Leo, 121, 257
V for Vendetta, 228, 229
Vint, Sherryl, 210, 212, 215n23
Visegrád Group, 19, 69, 84n20
Von Trier, Lars, 14, 19, 30, 32, 35, 36, 41–45, 47, 48, 50n11, 144, 221
Vuorensola, Timo, 19, 30, 36, 45–47

W
Wachowski Lana, 50n15, 85n27, 198
Wachowski Lily, 50n15, 85n27, 198
Wagner, Richard, 42
Wall: E, 176
War of the Worlds, 109, 118, 122, 209, 243n6
War on Terror, 225, 228, 238
Wells, H.G., vi, 118
Weston, Del, 166
White God/Fehér isten, 67, 68
White Ribbon, The/Das weiße Band, 36, 37, 49n8
Wise, Robert, 116, 128, 169
Withnail and I, 231
Woman is a Woman, A /Une femme est une femme, 14
Womb, 34, 35, 253
World Meteorological Organization, 164
World on a Wire/Welt am Draht, 77, 86n30
Wright, Jon, 112, 115, 117–119

Y
Young, Brigitte, 94, 104–106

Z
Zardoz, 112
Zavattini, Cesare, 15
Zonad, 112, 113, 115–121